Crisis Point

ALSO BY TRENT LOTT

Herding Cats: A Life in Politics

ALSO BY TOM DASCHLE

The U.S. Senate: Fundamentals of American Government
(with Charles Robbins)

*Getting It Done: How Obama and Congress Finally Broke the
Stalemate to Make Way for Health Care Reform*
(with David Nather)

Critical: What We Can Do About the Health-Care Crisis
(with Scott S. Greenberger and Jeanne M. Lambrew)

Like No Other Time: The Two Years That Changed America
(with Michael D'Orso)

CRISIS POINT

WHY WE MUST—AND HOW WE CAN—OVERCOME OUR BROKEN POLITICS IN WASHINGTON AND ACROSS AMERICA

Trent Lott and Tom Daschle

with Jon Sternfeld

BLOOMSBURY PRESS
NEW YORK · LONDON · OXFORD · NEW DELHI · SYDNEY

To Those Who Fought for Our Republic
So We May Work to Keep It

Bloomsbury Press
An imprint of Bloomsbury Publishing Plc

1385 Broadway
New York
NY 10018
USA

50 Bedford Square
London
WC1B 3DP
UK

www.bloomsbury.com

BLOOMSBURY and the Diana logo are trademarks of Bloomsbury Publishing Plc

First published 2016
This paperback edition published 2017

ISBN: HB: 978-1-63286-461-1
        ePub: 978-1-63286-463-5
        PB: 978-1-63286-462-8

LIBRARY OF CONGRESS CATALOGING-IN-PUBLICATION DATA
Names: Lott, Trent, 1941-author. | Daschle, Thomas, author. | Sternfeld, Jon, author.
Title: Crisis point: why we must—and how we can—overcome our broken politics in Washington and across America / Trent Lott and Tom Daschle; with Jon Sternfeld.
Description: New York: Bloomsbury USA, 2016. | Includes bibliographical references and index.
Identifiers: LCCN 2015025162 | ISBN 9781632864611 (hardback) | ISBN 9781632864635 (epub)
Subjects: LCSH: Political culture—United States. | Polarization (Social sciences) | Divided government—United States. | Political leadership—United States. | Right and Left (Political science)—United States. | United States—Politics and government—21st century. | BISAC: POLITICAL SCIENCE / General. | POLITICAL SCIENCE / Government / General.
Classification: LCC JK1726 .L66 2016 | DDC 320.60973—dc23
LC record available at http://lccn.loc.gov/2015025162

2 4 6 8 10 9 7 5 3 1

Typeset by RefineCatch Limited, Bungay, Suffolk
Printed and bound in the U.S.A. by Berryville Graphics Inc., Berryville, Virginia

To find out more about our authors and books visit www.bloomsbury.com. Here you will find extracts, author interviews, details of forthcoming events and the option to sign up for our newsletters.

Bloomsbury books may be purchased for business or promotional use. For information on bulk purchases please contact Macmillan Corporate and Premium Sales Department at specialmarkets@macmillan.com.

Mrs. Powell: "Well, Doctor, what have we got, a republic or a monarchy?"

Benjamin Franklin: "A republic, madam, if you can keep it."

—CONVERSATION OUTSIDE OF THE CONSTITUTIONAL CONVENTION AT INDEPENDENCE HALL, PHILADELPHIA, 1787

Contents

Foreword   xi

Introduction   1

PART I
Conflict

CHAPTER ONE
The 228-Year Argument   9

CHAPTER TWO
The Pulling   17

CHAPTER THREE
The Permanent Campaign   25

CHAPTER FOUR
Down in the Well   35

CHAPTER FIVE
The Media Effect   51

PART II
Chemistry

CHAPTER SIX
A Nation of Men and Women   65

CHAPTER SEVEN
The 50–50 Senate   75

CHAPTER EIGHT
Roadblocks to Chemistry   83

CHAPTER NINE
Experience and Transparency   91

PART III
Leadership

CHAPTER TEN
In Their Own Words   101

CHAPTER ELEVEN
The Leadership Hole   111

CHAPTER TWELVE
Trent and Tom   121

CHAPTER THIRTEEN
The Impeachment of William
Jefferson Clinton   129

CHAPTER FOURTEEN
The World at Large   139

CHAPTER FIFTEEN
Leader of the Free World   147

CHAPTER SIXTEEN
The Center of the Storm   157

CHAPTER SEVENTEEN
9/11 and Its Aftermath   167

CHAPTER EIGHTEEN
The Humility and the Audacity   179

CHAPTER NINETEEN
Courage and Memory in the
United States Senate   193

CHAPTER TWENTY
Fear and Loathing in the U.S. Congress   201

PART IV
Vision

CHAPTER TWENTY-ONE
Writing the Future   207

CHAPTER TWENTY-TWO
A Bipartisan Answer   213

CHAPTER TWENTY-THREE
Electoral and Campaign Reform   217

CHAPTER TWENTY-FOUR
The Money Problem   225

CHAPTER TWENTY-FIVE
Congressional Reform   233

CHAPTER TWENTY-SIX
A Call to Service   243

Conclusion: Duty   257

Acknowledgments   261
Notes   262
Index   276

2016: A Reckoning

"Nearly all men can stand adversity, but if you want to test a man's character, give him power."

—ABRAHAM LINCOLN

"Mad people vote."

—FORMER SENATOR JOHN BREAUX

In the summer of 2016, in the midst of the exhausting presidential campaign—what one journalist memorably called the "hot summer of disequilibrium,"[1]—an actual public health crisis was threatening our country. The deadly Zika virus was spreading in the state of Florida and federal money was desperately needed to stem the tide. As with previous health crises, the country looked to Congress to act. History and common sense tell us this is a relatively basic, nonpartisan issue, where our legislative bodies move the levers of the political process toward the greater good and swiftly provide the needed funds.

But, as with so many other straightforward issues recently, Congress stalled, a victim of its own partisan bickering. Democrats did not like what the Republican leadership had attached to the bill providing Zika funds, and no compromise could be reached. Incredibly, lawmakers left Washington for their August recess without resolving the issue. The optics were awful. The reality was even worse. What is Congress for if not this? Each party of course pointed the finger at the other, but frankly, both were to blame. It was frustrating to the nation, embarrassing to us as former lawmakers, and downright dangerous to those at risk for being infected. "Inexcusable" and "pathetic" were two of the descriptions in the mainstream press. We can think of a few others.

Upon returning for the session after the Labor Day, both parties again failed to come together for the bill and were rightly blasted again by the public and the media, with Ted Barrett at CNN condemning "the raw politics of the standoff." [2] Some members of Congress weren't even pretending it was about the bill at hand anymore. It was a scary revelation: If a health crisis isn't safe from politics, then what is?

After *Crisis Point*'s publication we had the great fortune of traveling around and talking to all types of Americans, continuing the conversation that we began in the book. Many of those we met also share a deep concern for the future of our country. We were able to gauge public reaction to the election as it unfolded, and heard from many vocal Americans regarding their perceptions of Washington. We received more than a few pleasantly surprised reactions to our collaboration; people of different political philosophies writing a book together, traveling to discuss it, and seemingly getting along like old friends in the process.

Right after noting our positive relationship, they would pivot into bemoaning that there wasn't enough of that in Washington; they then would launch into a litany of complaints they had with government and politics. We would nod and then engage with these spirited citizens the best we could. Very often, we agreed with them. It's no wonder that the Pew Research Center found recently that only 19 percent of Americans trust the federal government to do what is right,[3] but even that paltry number feels on the high side.

As the United States' forty-fifth president gets ready to take that solemn oath and a new Congress meets for the 115th session, we are sailing into uncharted territory, a future undoubtedly shaped by the tumultuous campaign of 2016. An election is not just a series of contests to determine the coming players. It is a revealing portrait of where the country is and where it wants to go. A campaign is an amplified version of America presented back to itself, in stereo and Technicolor. The campaign offers the prevailing winds and national mood. The coming cycle will determine what—if anything—our leaders in Washington plan to do with this new knowledge. After all, winning an election is not an ending; it's a beginning.

We first came together two years ago to write *Crisis Point* because we knew too much of Washington was broken, but we didn't know how quickly things would disintegrate. Campaigns are indeed a contest, but the running of the country is not. Government is much more than empty speeches on things that matter, misguided energy toward things that don't, and unnecessary squabbles on ideology that pit America against itself in ways that serve nobody.

When our book was first published in January 2016 we felt the title captured the urgency we attempted to imbue in the pages. The country was about to reach a moment of reckoning and we hoped it would turn out of the skid. But when that reckoning arrived it brought some disconcerting news: our country appeared more fractured than even the most seasoned cynic could have imagined. The vilifying strategies and rhetoric of the 2016 campaign ratcheted up to such levels that the idea of civics as civic entirely melted away. The rupture has wounded this great republic and all Americans—from Washington, to the state houses, and to the individual citizens—need to recognize it is now time for repairing and rebuilding.

The ideas in this book are even more relevant and urgent because they foretold a lot of the ugliest parts of the 2016 campaign. The inertia of the last few years launched a suspicion of government so massive that unqualified people were somehow hailed as saviors. The siloing of the public into their discrete groups gave way to a pronounced and omnipresent villainizing of the other side—from the questions of President Obama's legitimacy to speculations about Donald Trump's sanity to the chants to "lock Hillary up" on the floor of the Republican Convention. Conservative author and commentator Hugh Hewitt summed it up when he called 2016 a "resentment election."[4] Indeed, it was. And deciding a winner doesn't make all that feeling magically go away.

A presidential election year is like all problems with Washington under floodlights. It illuminates issues already lingering under the surface. Just as family issues crawl out from hidden spaces at the Thanksgiving table, any issues with the government are brought front and center in a campaign. Frustration with politics, government, and "business as usual" was so prevalent that even clear symbols of the status quo were taking swings at it.

The reality is that many in our country spend three-plus years tuning out issues of politics. Then for a few months they take a look: they see the combative rhetoric and horse-race news coverage, but very little that has to do with them and improving their lives as citizens. Of course, they're disgusted and how can we blame them? There's a reason why people are loath to engage with the political process.

If we look closely at the political trends emerging in recent years, the 2016 campaign was actually not that surprising. Trump represented the latest iteration in a progression of candidates who have tried to capitalize and maximize the frustration and distrust directed toward the government. His opponent, Hillary Clinton, had to deal with a widely felt credibility gap, dealing with a series of trust issues; even when she was leading in the polls her numbers in these areas were low, which made her opponent's message all the more sticky.

Further, Trump was able to marshal social media to his benefit, enhancing his ability to separate himself from whatever "establishment" he positioned himself against. It was not too long ago that candidates had to rely on getting something printed in the *New York Times* or the *Wall Street Journal* or getting onto the Sunday morning shows. Trump blew up that model, taking a page from celebrities and brands who control their image through social media. With eleven million Twitter followers and an estimated two billion dollars of free media, he destroyed the old model. And it's forever broken.

In *Crisis Point* we actually foreshadowed the arrival of an outsider like Trump. In our discussion about the dying relevance of parties we speculated, "Nowadays if candidates have the money, and access to the media, they are no longer dependent on the party." This is exactly what happened. Not only did Trump not need the Republican Party, he went a step further: he outright went to war with it.

On both sides, the great theme of the election year was the power of the outsider. Both primaries veered from traditional party lines. Bernie Sanders's followers fought Hillary for the soul of the Democratic Party and ended up dragging her to the left. Trump's non-Republican, non-conservative, non-establishment movement stampeded its way to the nomination—an outcome literally nobody expected.

Though they were far apart philosophically, both Sanders and Trump gained a great deal of traction arguing that the system is broken. They were both an outgrowth of public resentment at a government that seems disconnected from the public. Inside Washington, the players are fighting a battle wholly disconnected from what the people care about. The campaign got ugly at times but it was a needed splash of cold water in the faces of establishment Washington. Lawmakers need to be more responsive to the people than to their own internal dynamics and self-interest. There are certainly those on both sides of the aisle who have tried to change the tone and focus in the Capitol, but they are often shouted down for attempting to do so.

One of the positive results of 2016 is the hard-and-fast red and blue, left and right Democrat and Republican distinctions that Washington makes have shown to be less solid than imagined. This is not where the American people are. Both political parties and the media missed what was going on out on the fringes, and being ignored gave those outsiders power, momentum, and a rallying cry. The far left and the far right crashed the middle and everyone acted surprised, but we shouldn't have been. There were a great deal of dissatisfied, disgruntled, and angry people out there for reasons no one fully understood.

In many ways the national debate throughout the campaign wasn't about Democrat or Republican, or even establishment or fringe. It was about whether this country should be open or closed: in trade, in immigration, in a public policy approach. The nationalistic movement took on those who believed that outreach and openness go to the very soul of what America is about, which is where both of us stand.

Trade became framed as an oppositional force against American prosperity and American workers, even though the facts don't bear that out. But the perception is still there, and politically, sometimes that's all that matters. Donald Trump gained a great deal of momentum by hammering home this idea, while Hillary Clinton, who was once outwardly behind TPP, changed her position and came out against it during the primary campaign. We understand the anger and fear about job security is very real, even if the causes are misdiagnosed. Trade statistics show that free trade helps us create jobs by a wide margin, not to mention it reduces the cost of just about everything we buy. The benefit the average American gets from trade is the equivalent of getting a fairly significant raise in their income. But we've seen a decline in real income for most Americans in the last twenty years and it's natural to look for blame. Trade is a ready-made target for that.

Immigration received a similar demonizing, with a great deal of Trump supporters convinced that it was immigrants who were "taking" jobs and endangering their security, neither of which are born out by the realities. We need elected officials that are willing to speak up and explain how trade is to our benefit, and how immigration is an asset to our country. But leadership is in short supply; too many of our leaders do not seem willing to speak up, out of fear that the voters will turn on them. Far too many of our elected officials are leading from behind. They're figuring out what people want to hear and then packaging it back for them. It's literally the opposite of leadership.

The vocal minority is driving so much of the debate, which only highlights the importance of getting involved. Polls show that the country hasn't dramatically changed its position on trade and immigration but the opposition has been much more successful in getting its message out than the proponents have. We live in a world now where anger and loose facts travel faster and easier than truth, especially when it comes from those in power. We are reminded of Thomas Jefferson's line regarding those that prop up falsehoods: "It is error alone which needs the support of government. Truth can stand by itself."

This leads to another troubling trend: a real casualty of the modern era, almost buried by the 2016 campaign, was facts. Conservative radio host Charlie Sykes wearily called it a "post-truth culture" and bemoaned our "postmodern politics where everyone gets to define their own truth."[5] The *New York Times* wrote about the malleability of the concept of a fact in politics, a phrase almost too upsetting to even write. "If you really want to find an expert willing to endorse a fact," William Davies wrote, "and have sufficient money or political clout behind you, you probably can."

Today, truth is an option, and unfortunately, it's not always a politically expedient one. It's not about accuracy; it's about saturation. Once it gets out there, and it's repeated often enough, it becomes fact. With the death of traditional media, the gatekeepers and fact-checkers have been pushed to the side, making them just another voice shouting in the crowd. When no one has to listen anymore to someone they don't agree with, when they don't even have a singular base of truth to work from, how does a country unite for anything?

Our elected officials in Washington need to rise above these trends if they are going to lead. The new president is inheriting a divided country, no matter the margin of victory. The election doesn't wipe out the opposition. Actually, it often strengthens them—they are now aggrieved, an emotion that hardens like concrete. After any election, especially a tumultuous one, there is a substantial wake that follows close behind. It affects the upcoming legislative session, the way both houses of Congress interact with each other, and Congress's dynamic with the new president. We cannot emphasize more strenuously how important it is that the new president sets the tone with Congress, reaching out and working closely with the leadership of both parties in both chambers. Doing it from day one has never been more vital to this nation's progress and future.

All this can lead to a changing of the culture, which is the ultimate hope. For too long it has all been about process and jockeying for position, with very little focus on serving the American people and fulfilling their constitutional function. Bipartisanship continues to be treated as a dirty word, mostly because the threat of being "primaried"—losing to someone from the more extreme wing of the party—looms large. The primary has ceased to be a single period of time; it's a constant threat now, a permanent sickle hanging over the head of a candidate who might dare take a step toward the middle on an issue.

We accept that things are rancorous, but the potential for positive change is actually higher than most would expect after a divisive election. There will be enough new players—and new leadership—to sow the seeds of a new environment if they get planted early. Relationships matter a great deal in Washington; as we argue in the book, the chemistry between lawmakers is one of the great misunderstood forces in Washington. Will the new players just slip into their roles or will they determine them and alter the culture? Only time will tell.

On another positive note, 2017 could be an unusually productive year. Years of failure to address the big issues have created a pent-up demand on issues like energy, tax policy, and especially infrastructure, which should be a bipartisan issue. Our bridges, roads, air, sewers, and airports are crumbling. Infrastructure is not sexy and it rarely gets people excited, but there's a dire need there, and it could be the first step in a series of bipartisan legislation.

It's too early to tell if all the earth-scorching in 2016 produces fruitful result—like the controlled burns of forests done to regenerate new growth. The American people tend to react to crises and challenges. If anything, the harshness of the past campaign could be catalytic in bringing a national reaction that spurs change. We are realistic enough to acknowledge the challenges. However, we are also seasoned enough to recognize there is an opportunity here for rebirth. It's part of the natural cycle of life and since our democracy is a living, breathing thing, it fits that it should too follow that path.

Systems—just like people—rarely change until they have to. Until the pressure is too great, until the old model cannot hold, until the opposition is strong enough to upend it, the status quo remains. We are always living history and how we process the past affects what we do moving forward. We must remember that America is an unfinished idea. And so our work—everyone's work—must continue.

Trent Lott and Tom Daschle
November 2016

Introduction

AMERICA'S strength has always come from its unique diversity—its willingness to not just permit but encourage competing viewpoints in order to strengthen the whole. The adversarial system, embedded by the Founding Fathers into our system of government, was meant to spur debate, challenge complacency, and drive progress. It has sustained our Republic for over 225 years, but we have to face a sad truth: *it has stopped working.* In fact, it has begun to work against us.

Our system of checks and balances was not designed to encourage the kind of inertia plaguing our current leaders in Washington. The quality of our United States Congress—and, by extension, the American government—continues to grow increasingly dysfunctional. As former legislators, Senate leaders, and concerned citizens, we are alarmed.

We have a combined fifty-nine years in Congress, with over sixteen as Senate majority and minority leaders, so we know of what we speak. The center can no longer hold under such mindless and unprecedented partisanship: it is no exaggeration to say that the state of our democracy is as bad as we've ever seen it. The two of us have the experience of leading our parties during extremely partisan and combative times—President Clinton's impeachment, a deadlocked Senate, post-9/11 America—so we are not naïve about how these things actually work. Though we have philosophical differences about the role of government, as well as divergent views on many important issues, we can agree that it is time to sound the alarm.

The United States government is at a crisis point that requires significant changes: in leadership, in action, and most importantly in mind-set. The *New York Times* reported that the most recent Congress was "one of the least productive, most divided in history . . . By traditional measurements, the 113th Congress is now in a race to the bottom with the 112th for the 'do nothing' crown."[1] The dysfunction has created not just antipathy but anger among the public, with a CNN poll finding an 83 percent disapproval rating of Congress.[2] Other polls have approval of Congress regularly in the single digits. Obviously, polls don't tell the whole story—and government should not be at their mercy—but the fact that such a whopping majority of the public has expressed dissatisfaction with Congress is much more than just a canary in the coal mine: it's a whole flock of them.

We've traveled around the world and attended the inauguration of other leaders, and one thing that's remarkable in contrast with ours: almost without exception, foreign leaders take an oath of office to the people. In America, we take an oath of office to support and defend the Constitution. We take an oath not to the masses but to an idea and a set of principles. That's magical.

The Constitution was not written as a precise set of instructions; it was to serve as a blueprint for how the young Republic would sustain itself and grow for the future. Jefferson and Madison's generation had enormous faith in ours—enough to trust our judgment. At the very least, they'd be confused by what has happened. More likely, they'd be devastated. Partisan rancor has overtaken reasoned debate so completely that an entire generation wonders what Congress does all day. And we'd be hard-pressed to answer them.

The two of us entered politics at different times, under different conditions, and from far different perspectives, but our respective stories help tell the larger story of this great nation. Our careers, battles, and accomplishments flow into the larger river of the American story.

Although we don't claim to have a panacea to all the problems, we do understand the key ingredients needed to get us moving forward again. We know that communication within and between the parties—and the relationships that result—creates chemistry, an absolute necessity to the functioning of good government. As we look at the political landscape, we see five things that are desperately needed: chemistry, compromise, leadership, courage, and vision.

During the historic 50–50 Senate of 2001, Congress was numerically deadlocked but not operationally so. As respective leaders of our parties in the Senate, we came together to formulate a historic power sharing agreement, gaining the vitriol of some of our respective caucuses in the process. Trent nearly got a vote of no confidence from the Republican caucus for even negotiating with Tom and the Democrats. But we managed to line up our colleagues behind us—through leadership, compromise, and a good dose of chemistry—and got to work conducting the country's business.

Believing in the necessity for direct communication amid the noise, we installed a phone on each of our desks that rang directly through to the other leader. The phones were practical, but they were also symbolic of an open line of communication we maintained while in our leadership positions. Considering what the country had to go through in those years, it could not have been more necessary.

We also navigated, among other historic and challenging moments, the impeachment of President Clinton, 9/11 and its aftermath, and anthrax in the Capitol. Drawing on these experiences, as well as many others in our long careers as legislators, in this book we will:

- share our insights about how to harness the natural **conflict** that comes from a body of different voices
- explain how to create a culture of **chemistry** that allows for bipartisanship and compromise
- examine the elements of effective **leadership**
- illustrate why **courage** is such a necessary component of that leadership
- present a **vision** for how our government can get moving forward to take on the challenges we face

Bipartisanship is the life force that keeps our government running. It is neither a life raft to be embraced only in crisis nor a naïve idealism to be mocked. Bipartisan negotiation is the pumping blood of democracy, and it has run dry in the current Washington landscape. Without it, government is just voices shouting in a room—with nobody listening. "The best way to persuade," former secretary of state Dean Rusk once said, "is with your ears."[3]

Today's leaders don't practice bipartisanship and the environment of the nation's capital doesn't allow for it. The common ground has been stripped and scorched, allowing no community to grow. The ubiquity of planes and telecommunication have made it feasible to work in Washington without living there.

(In fact, being a Washington resident is regularly used *against* candidates.) True to its name, the media has become a comfortable filter through which both sides can hurl partisan assaults without having to face each other. Meanwhile, primaries have begun to reward the extremes, chasing away moderates and turning off voters through an increasing arms race of outside money and negativity.

But there is hope. And it begins with the strength that already exists within this great nation and its people. It begins with each and every one of us. The future is far from written. During our extensive congressional careers, we each drove hard to push mostly clashing agendas—under presidents from opposing parties—so we speak from pragmatic experience. We have dedicated our lives to serving our country and feel deeply for its future. We sincerely believe that the tide can be turned. Nothing less than the country's future depends on it.

We have decided to join together for a common cause because we know our opposing voices, when joined together, create a force stronger than their individual weight. Our contrasting identities and philosophies also serve as a metaphor for the country itself. Yet we worked together, remain friends, and share a vision for how we can get moving again.

This book is a call to action, a clarion call to our leaders, the voters, the lapsed voters, those in public service, and those considering going into public service. We will show how the country can learn from where it has been, examine how we arrived at the current state of dysfunction, and, hopefully, help to inspire a new dawn of American politics.

Senator Trent Lott and Senator Tom Daschle
July 2015

Part I

Conflict

"For God's sake, my dear Sir, take up your pen, select the most
striking heresies, and cut [Hamilton] to pieces in the face of
the public."

—LETTER FROM THOMAS JEFFERSON TO
JAMES MADISON, JULY 7, 1791

CHAPTER ONE

The 228-Year Argument

THE competitive American spirit is a defining part of our national character. It is what makes our country dynamic, its institutions resilient, and its citizenry vibrant. It gave our Founding Fathers the audacity to defeat one of the greatest empires the world had ever known and the boldness to start their own democratic experiment on a virtually unprecedented scale. Throughout our country's history, that spirit has driven our progress and growth. It has helped to build the United States into the world's last standing superpower and the envy of the rest of the world.

None of this was by accident, nor was it simply good fortune. The framers of the Constitution designed America in a way that rewarded, utilized, and channeled that competitive spirit for the good of the whole. "The Constitution recognized that the great strength of Americans was their drive and ambition," historians Eric Lane and Michael Oreskes write in *The Genius of America: How the Constitution Saved Our Country—and Why It Can Again*: ". . . And it created paths for others to disagree, and resist them, or argue for something different."[1] Although on the Senate and House floors, in the press, and on the campaign trail it seems that inexorable conflict is the problem, we know differently: that fire gives energy and solidity to the work that is done. In fact, our country was built from that tension. The Constitution provided for it because the framers, especially James Madison, knew how valuable that tension was.

But we have lost sight of its value in our current political environment. The system of checks and balances that makes our government work and the party system central to our politics have become dysfunctional. Reasoned debate has devolved into petty bickering. The fighting was built into the system for two reasons. First, it gives voice and platforms to the opposition—long an essential freedom in America. Second, there's a Darwinian result: the ideas strong enough to survive are the ones left standing. Over generations, they are the ideas that endure.

In the twenty-first century hyper-partisanship has blinded us to the inherent value of competing sides. It is neither desirable nor possible for the competing sides to agree on everything, or on most things, but there needs to be opportunity to communicate, an incentive to compromise, and an aisle that is not so wide and barren that even trying to cross it is political suicide.

As students of history, it only made sense for us to start this book at the source: the tension between the two visions of government—and of America—originally expressed by our Founding Fathers. That conflict, which is sometimes simplified as individual freedoms versus involved government, spans our nation's history. American politics has always had this division, from the moment the states first met at the First Continental Congress in 1774.° It continues

---

° Or didn't meet: Georgia didn't even show up because its delegates couldn't agree on a position to take.

today in town halls and at dinner tables, on our cable news shows and websites, and of course, through debate between our political parties.

Certainly, there is much to be dispirited about these days in regard to our federal government. However, we remain eternal optimists because we know our current stalemate is neither inevitable nor permanent. It's in our hands, as it has always been.

At the Constitutional Convention in 1787, four years after the American Revolution officially ended, "the nation's greatest leaders . . . gathered to wrestle its fundamental problems to the ground," in the words of David O. Stewart.[2] They essentially locked themselves in a room for a brutal Philadelphia summer, but they never pinned those problems down.

The debate over America continued and intensified after the Constitution was ratified as it was taken up by Adams, Hamilton, Jefferson, Madison, their parties, and their successors. For the next two centuries that argument has been a constant motivator. It often gets people into politics in the first place, driving their agendas when they get to Washington, and it echoes through the halls, offices, and capitols across the country. Our own political stories are part of that grand old American argument: the argument formed both of our identities, drove our careers, and continues to light our passions.

The party system itself is an extension of the original argument the Founders had at our inception, as historian Joseph J. Ellis writes:

> *The debate was not resolved so much as built into the fabric of our national identity. If that means the United States is founded on a contradiction, then so be it . . . Lincoln once*

said that America was founded on a proposition that was
written by Jefferson in 1776. We are really founded on an
argument about what that proposition means.[3]

The argument gives our Republic its unique vigor and vitality.
Our country's prosperity didn't occur despite this divisiveness but
because of it. We will never solve the argument, and that is the
point: the argument itself is necessary. But it has risen to such a
deafening level that it is drowning out everything else. As a result,
our government is experiencing the kind of paralyzing dysfunction
that it hasn't experienced for a long time, if ever.

The two of us stand on opposite sides of that original argument, but in our time in elected office and as party leaders we
always knew the value in seeking out a middle ground inside of
that argument. We're coming together to sound an alarm about
how that argument has been twisted and turned into nothing
more than a weapon with which to attack the other side. Its essential purpose and value has been lost, drowned out by the noise of
blind and aggressive partisanship.

The man who may have had the greatest influence on early
American political thought was James Madison, author of the Bill
of Rights, coauthor of *The Federalist Papers*, major contributor to
the Constitutional Convention (he took all the notes), and key
architect of the Constitution. His ideas were "to the art of government as brilliant and inventive in its age as Einstein's rethinking
of time and space, and Picasso's reshaping of form and image,
were in theirs," according to Lane and Oreskes. He quite simply
"wrote the blueprint for American democracy."[4]

In the late eighteenth century, representative democracy on
the scale of the original thirteen colonies had been attempted

only once in history: in Cicero's Rome, where it failed. At the time of the Constitutional Convention, "democracy as we now know it barely existed in the world. Indeed, the word *democracy* was essentially an insult, a synonym for *mob rule*."[5]

History sometimes treats Madison as Jefferson's executor, the great pragmatist who served the grand thinker; but this short-changes Madison, who helped lay the groundwork for most of American democracy. Denied a spot in the first cabinet and in the first Senate, Madison would become a driving force in the House of Representatives, where he would steer a great many pieces of early legislation. Considering the animus between the states in those early years, this role was perhaps as essential as any other political office.

In *The Federalist* No. 10 Madison argued—counterintuitively—that the imposing size of the new republic was actually a blessing. The common wisdom had always been that a democracy would require a small and manageable population, one that could be controlled. But Madison believed America's relatively large and growing population to be a virtue because "diversity sustains freedom": the sheer size and inclusiveness would prevent any one side from dominating. "Extend the sphere," Madison explained, "and you take in a greater variety of parties and interests; you make it less probable that a majority of the whole will have a common motive to invade the rights of other citizens . . ."[6]

As Lynne Cheney wrote in her biography *James Madison: A Life Reconsidered*, "This insight—brilliant and prophetic—would transform political thought, taking self-government from an impossible realm . . . and moving it into reality, where interests competed with and checked one another."[7]

There was no way to prevent parties, and even if there had been, it would have been unwise to try. Madison argued that our very freedoms depended on an energized and robust opposition. He wrote:

> Liberty is to faction what air is to fire, an aliment without which it instantly expires. But it could not be less folly to abolish liberty, which is essential to political life, because it nourishes faction, than it would be to wish the annihilation of air, which is essential to animal life, because it imparts to fire its destructive agency.[8]

The diversity was valuable, the interests checked each other, and the Republic was born from that conflict.

Madison and Jefferson's great antagonist was Alexander Hamilton, a Federalist who preached the necessity of a strong central government. He was something of a snob, committed to focusing power in the hands of the elites and the educated. Hamilton warned that it would be suicide to leave the fate of the country in the hands of the masses whom, he argued, "seldom judge or determine right."[9]*

Hamilton and Madison co-wrote *The Federalist Papers* to sell a nation suspicious of having any kind of federal government. The two men's fundamental disagreement on the size and role of that government was not a minor debate—twenty-five thousand

---

* It was an ironic stance, considering that he was the lone Founding Father who came from real poverty, born illegitimate and then orphaned in the British West Indies. As many historians have pointed out, had Hamilton been born in Europe—or anywhere else, for that matter—he would have "languished in obscurity . . . because of his lack of good breeding."[10] In America, however, he rose to become one of the nation's most powerful men and a lasting influence on more than two centuries of political and economic thought.

American lives had been lost so the colonies could rid themselves of King George; there were very real fears that the delegates would simply establish another regime closer to home. It was an intractable dilemma: the new government had to be strong enough to unify thirteen disparate colonies (across a landmass larger than France and Spain combined) but not so powerful that the citizens would feel the need to revolt all over again. The dividing lines over the government's size and reach were drawn. Jefferson's decision in 1793 to leave Washington's cabinet to organize the opposition was something of the Big Bang of the party system. Tensions over the Jay Treaty the next year—which some felt gave too much to Great Britain—pushed the sides even further apart.

The parties naturally began to form on opposing sides of the original argument, but they didn't take center stage until the Adams presidency. President Washington's reputation put him above any faction; his very presence was like a rock that kept the dam from breaking. Once he left office, the fight for the nation's future began in earnest.

In his farewell address Washington warned "against the baneful effects of the Spirit of Party." He feared that the acrimony would plague the new nation, as "it agitates the Community with ill founded Jealousies and false alarms, kindles the animosity of one part against another."[11] Washington, after all, made his life in the army, where conflict within ranks is only destructive.

The president knew a party split was inevitable once he retired to Mount Vernon. It was time for the nation to enter its combative adolescence. As such, the 1790s were, in the words of Joseph J. Ellis, "a decade-long shouting match."[12]

But history has proven something that Washington didn't predict: this was a good thing. Not only did the parties not jeopardize the new nation, they were essential to its growth and development. Washington was indispensable as the first leader, a stable foundation on which the fragile nation could be built. But it was his stepping down, and the influx of party tension and factions that resulted, that helped the country develop and thrive.

"The first test of an aspiring democracy is the acceptance, by the politicians in power, of an organized opposition," Pulitzer Prize-winning historian James MacGregor Burns notes. Burns also argues that "conflict among peoples is not only accepted as inevitable but viewed as essential to the process of change."[13] Far from poisoning the young nation, the parties provided the engine the country needed, allowing the debate to continue on in an organized and productive fashion.

Madison, Jefferson, and the Republicans° became the first organized opposition against John Adams, Hamilton, and the Federalists. Jefferson and Adams were later described as "North and South Poles of the Revolution." That word choice—evoking magnetic pulls on a single entity—was certainly no accident. Adams's ascension to the presidency, Jefferson and Madison believed, "put the entire republican experiment at risk [and] the battle was to the death."[14] At the outset, parties were formed under the highest stakes imaginable. We should not be surprised that they continue with the passion first held by our Founding Fathers. But there has to be purpose to all that fire; it cannot simply serve itself.

°Jefferson's Democratic-Republican Party (called "Republicans") shouldn't be confused with the current Republican Party, which was created around 1854 and elected Abraham Lincoln as its first president.

CHAPTER TWO

The Pulling

HISTORY shows that our government was designed to let the arguments play out. The pulling from both sides is intended to create a strong whole, just as two opposing forces pulling a rope tightens that rope. However, too much tension breaks the rope entirely, an apt metaphor for where we find ourselves.

Our current leaders have become singularly focused on the pulling but ignore its purpose: giving sides a platform, allowing for a competitive forum for ideas, and seeking disparate voices to find the best way forward. It's no coincidence that political language lifts so much from terms of battle, including partisan *warrior*. Trent has frequently been given that label, a version of *good soldier*. The passion that drives political discourse is intense and genuine: both sides feel that nothing less than the country's future is at stake.

The right amount of tension strengthens the whole but there has been so much pulling that the rope is in tatters. Our government has become dysfunctional in the most literal sense of the word. The competitive energy needs to be harnessed properly and channeled toward an environment of chemistry and compromise.

* * *

The Founding Fathers channeled "the explosive energies of the debate in the form of an ongoing argument . . . that was eventually institutionalized and rendered safe by the creation of political parties," Joseph J. Ellis explains.[1] Instead of tearing the nation apart, as President Washington warned it would, the party system gave organization and voice to the opposition so no citizens would have to again pick up their guns. It allowed the argument to continue without tearing the fragile nation apart. By 1861 things had obviously broken down, but the fact that it lasted until the Civil War and has lasted this long after it is a testament to the system's durability.

But in the eighteenth century an opposing party was not automatically accepted as having a right to exist. Opposition against the government in any form looked an awful lot like treason. It fell to James Madison again to shift public assumptions.

In the pages of the Democratic-Republican newspaper, the *National Gazette*, Madison reiterated the value of opposing parties. He argued that factions were the natural next step of the Revolution, that they were there in the argument for independence, in the argument about the Constitution, and that now there was a "third division . . . natural to most political societies," i.e., parties.[2]

Partisanship has become something of a dirty word, and the frustration with both parties has been a constant feature of our political system. Though Jefferson and Hamilton would be shocked by the sophistication of party organization in the twenty-first century, their purpose remains: the parties still serve as the vehicle. Without vehicles there is no effective way to channel the energy, passion, and ideas, nor is there the organizational effort needed to govern. Parties have the infrastructure that gives a constructive forum to the competition of ideas.

Of course, there has been the third-party argument out there for quite some time—but it's wishful thinking that it would work. There's the problem of assumption, as though a third party would just naturally catch everyone who is not a Republican or Democrat. Such a party would be too undefined to serve any purpose.

As a rule, third parties don't work for three main reasons: First, we have built the entire political infrastructure around a two-party system. Laws, regulations, tradition, and the political process are all built with a two-party assumption.

Second, third-party candidates are generally viewed as spoilers rather than contenders. They aren't given the status of a party nominee. Consequently, they are handicapped in meaningful political competition.

Third, largely as a result of the first two factors, third-party candidates can't raise the resources required to be competitive in all fifty states. They generally have to pick and choose because they don't have the budget to compete everywhere.

For these reasons, the most credible candidates don't even seriously consider running a third-party campaign. A serious political figure with a real chance of winning hasn't run as a third-party candidate for quite some time.[*]

Though the organization and sophistication behind parties is indeed stronger than ever, ironically, parties are weaker than they have ever been when it comes to campaigns and elections. The reason is that the money has moved away from parties to 501(c)(3)

---

[*] Teddy Roosevelt—who had been a wildly popular president just four years earlier—received 88 electoral votes as a third-party candidate in 1912.

tax-exempt organizations and super PACs. Candidates used to need the parties because of their organizational effort. There was simply no way to get elected without it.

But nowadays if candidates have the money, and access to the media, they are no longer dependent on the party. Plenty of candidates choose not to run on party labels in certain districts because they don't want to be identified as a party person. Over the last fifty years, the parties have lost ground and consequence. Although they still have significance in organizing the Congress, they have far less relevance in today's political environment.

Much was made of the Republican takeover of the Senate in 2014 and how the country was doomed to be stalled by a Congress of one party and a president of another. But some of the most productive times in the last thirty years have been with a president of one party and the Congress dominated by the other party. President Reagan and Tip O'Neill saved Social Security and delivered our last comprehensive tax reform. President Clinton and the Republicans passed welfare reform and balanced the budget for three consecutive years. There's an inevitable fissure that develops between the two branches and it requires work to overcome it. But it's possible. We have both seen it and have been a part of it.

Some of the tension between the president and Congress results because presidents simply don't like to hear any criticism or even differences of opinion. The president's inner circle tries to shut it out, to insulate the president from those disparate voices. When a congressional leader goes around the president's staff to express that difference, it drives the West Wing staff up the wall.

George W. Bush's inner circle, especially Karl Rove, didn't like Trent going around them to speak to the president, especially to air his disagreements. Closing off a president from different viewpoints might be politically expedient but it is almost always a negative for the country. It seems to be one of the problems President Obama has: walling off Congress or viewing its leadership as a necessary evil—even his own Democratic leaders. Shutting out the critics doesn't necessarily silence them. In fact, it tends to do just the opposite.

The Obama White House has often been too isolated; its leaders could be far more catalytic in bringing together deals between both sides of Congress, but over the past seven years, they have not gotten the traction they need on the Hill. So many times they're virtually a nonfactor in one of the major roles the executive branch can play. There oftentimes has been no convener, somebody capable of pulling people together, which is a necessity. The Senate leaders on both sides—Harry Reid and Mitch McConnell—don't convene because they have such a strained relationship. The only person who is really capable of assembling the highest levels of Congress with regularity is the president of the United States. And if that's not happening, then governing is stalled.

There is a natural tension between the legislative and executive branches, a design feature of the system of checks and balances. Close relationships between presidents and Congress are more the exception than the rule. We both had it with President Clinton, for a time Tom had it with President George W. Bush, and Trent had it for a good deal of Bush's presidency.

In 2005, at a time when the chemistry between President Bush and Congress was sinking, Trent urged the president to have the new majority leader, Harry Reid, over to the White House. He suggested they sit down on the South Portico, look out over the Washington Monument, and have a drink. The sentiment was the right one, but Trent eventually realized his mistake: President Bush was a reformed drinker and Harry Reid was a Mormon.

Recent presidents have done a poor job of reaching out to the congressional leadership, especially before they make public announcements. While he appears to be getting better over the past year, President Obama is guilty of this. It's more notification than consultation, which is a huge mistake. The leadership finds out about the president's decision through the media; they're implicitly expected to go along, creating resentment that builds over time. Congress then has less reason to be cooperative with the White House, which starts the cycle all over again.

What presidents seem to forget—and which still befuddles both of us—is how important it is to reach out to Congress, both for substantive and chemistry reasons. There's no consultation on announcements or strategy and it wreaks havoc on the trust and relationships between the branches. "People respond in direct proportion to the extent you reach out to them,"[3] Vice President Nelson Rockefeller noted, and that couldn't be more accurate when it comes to Congress and the president.

This cycle has been going on during the current administration. Perhaps President Obama sometimes fails to adequately consult Senator Reid because the president fails to see any value in talking to the senators of his party, but every time Reid or a member of his caucus is not consulted, the walls get higher and the job gets harder. That ill will builds over time; those experiences don't create a lot of trust or a desire to be cooperative. It's just human nature.

Tension exists between the parties, between the branches of government, and of course, between the governing and the governed. Patriotism doesn't mean blindly accepting your government's position on all matters. Sometimes it's patriotic to challenge your leaders and to be engaged in—even critical of—what your government is doing in your name. The uniqueness of American patriotism is the absolute right to be a contrarian.

Our founders aimed to create a country that valued the individual and allowed for free expression. Undoubtedly they expected us to challenge our government, our institutions, and pieces of conventional wisdom. At its core, to be patriotic is to hold tight to this belief of what is possible here and why it's possible.

It is an ongoing debate, and sometimes patriotism gets woven into it: a disagreement between those who believe that our country was largely built on the basis of rugged individualism and self-starting entrepreneurs and those who believe that our country was built through collective action. The fact is they're both right.

That debate plays itself out in the proper role of government. In 1835, Alexis de Tocqueville, famous chronicler of early America, wrote of the careful and admirable balance of these two features among the young nation's citizens. Sometimes patriotism is used to defend one or the other side of that argument, which is a false choice.

In *Our Divided Political Heart: The Battle for the American Idea in an Age of Discontent*, E. J. Dionne argues that our country's identity is itself linked to this tension:

> *We ignore this tension within our history and ourselves at our peril. In forgetting who we are, we deny the richness of our national experience and the creative tensions that have always shaped our national character . . . And because we have forgotten that the tension at the heart of our national experiment is a healthy one, we have pretended that we can resolve our problems by becoming all one thing or all another.*[4]

America's greatness lies in the impossibility of such homogeneity. Our country's strength comes from the tension that's inherent in our DNA. We are different, our strength lies in those differences, and we can channel those differences toward productive goals.

The peaks and valleys themselves are a natural part of the cycle. There will always be a role for both parties, for both sides of the argument. Our country only makes sense that way. We have both been around long enough to know that the system is durable, much stronger than the personalities that will temporarily occupy its offices.

CHAPTER THREE

The Permanent Campaign

"One thing our founding fathers could not foresee . . . was a nation governed by professional politicians who had a vested interest in getting reelected. They probably envisioned a fellow serving a couple of hitches and then looking forward to getting back to the farm."

—RONALD REAGAN, 1973[1]

REAGAN'S insight, humorous on the surface, is quite astute. A government designed in the eighteenth-century world has run up against serious issues in the twenty-first, not the least of which is the rise of the professional politician. The observation from the then governor even predates the explosion of the billion-dollar campaign industry of advisors, consultants, and pollsters, which widened the chasm even more.

George Washington was reluctant to be president because he felt an obligation to take care of his homestead at Mount Vernon. Thomas Jefferson famously dedicated most of his life to building (and rebuilding) his home at Monticello. Adams and Madison had similar attachments to their family homes and farms, and a certain romanticism to the time they spent there. Benjamin Franklin dabbled in politics while putting together one of the most impressive résumés in American history, which included author, printer, and inventor. Public service was once seen as an honorable stop on the way to a fuller, more rounded life—not necessarily the central narrative of men's biographies.

George Washington also made it clear throughout his life that he saw himself as a general first. And on his tombstone Thomas Jefferson requested that three accomplishments be carved:

AUTHOR OF THE

DECLARATION

OF

AMERICAN INDEPENDENCE

OF THE

STATUTE OF VIRGINIA

FOR

RELIGIOUS FREEDOM

AND FATHER OF THE

UNIVERSITY OF VIRGINIA

He didn't think his eight years as president were even worth a mention.

Politics is a profession of deep contradictions. Trent is fond of saying that if you really want to be president more than anything in the world, then you probably shouldn't be. The desire to win is essential, but that desire is double-edged: it can cloud the better angels of someone's nature.

Another contradiction that has been magnified in the twenty-first century is that leaders have to be elected to accomplish anything, but ensuring election is a twenty-four-hour job that seems to preclude them from doing anything else. How to reconcile, or at least navigate, these contradictions makes being a member of elected office a tightrope walk.

Politicians worry about the next election—it's in the job description—but we've arrived at a dangerous point where that necessary break between campaigns has vanished. We both can attest that the months preceding an election would always get tough, even mean, but there was the knowledge that it would end. Then two or three months before the next election, everyone would kick into high gear again.

One of the virtues of politics, like a sports match, is that there's a result. After the election there's a winner, and it's cathartic for everyone involved. There's a much-needed cleansing of tensions and of the battlefield itself. Legislation shifts back to the forefront and doesn't have to compete with campaigning. Recently, that basic structure has been upended and the results have been disastrous.

These days there is no off season, no break from the money chase or the partisan warfare. There is no time that's more relaxed, bipartisan, or—dare we say—even nonpartisan. Washington, D.C., has fallen victim to something called the "permanent campaign," a term that dates back to the 1970s but has reemerged to describe today's poisonous environment. Congressmen who need to work together for the government to function are now in constant opposition, always framing themselves as candidates.

The permanent campaign has also led to another unseemly trend: the regularity of congressmen campaigning against their sitting colleagues, something that would never even have occurred to us to do. It has wrecked relationships and poisoned the chemistry that legislation requires. Tom's successor as Senate majority leader, Bill Frist, in an unprecedented move, came to South Dakota to campaign against Tom in 2004. A party leader had never gone and campaigned against the other leader; it just wasn't done. Its implications were troubling—the entire body depends on the two leaders being able to work together.

Part II of this book focuses on the chemistry and willingness to compromise that keep government running; both are being damaged by the permanent campaign. Political theorists Amy Gutmann and Dennis Thompson, in *The Spirit of Compromise: Why Governing Demands It and Campaigning Undermines It*, argue that "though valuable in its place, campaigning is increasingly intruding into governing ... [T]he means of winning an office are subverting the ends of governing once in office."[2]

Much of this is new. Even during particularly heated election cycles, Congress and the White House could still operate outside of the campaign bubble. In the heat of the 1986 midterm campaign, Democrat congressman Dan Rostenkowski and Senator Bill Bradley worked with Republican congressman Jack Kemp, Senator Bob Packwood, and President Reagan on the biggest overhaul of our tax system in forty years. Two days after those midterm elections, Reagan signed the Simpson-Mazzoli Act, which reformed immigration with help from a bipartisan commission.

We can't imagine that type of bipartisanship happening in the heat of today's campaign season; each side would have too much to lose. "Elections have veered into the realm of the tribal," political columnist David Dayen has noted, "somewhat disassociated from policy and more geared toward amping up tribal alliances and denigrating the other side."[3]

"Our political life is becoming so expensive, so mechanized and so dominated by professional politicians and public relations men that the idealist who dreams of independent statesmanship is rudely awakened by the necessities of election and accomplishment,"

young senator John F. Kennedy lamented sixty years ago.[4] Kennedy
had three years in the Senate and six years in the House when he
penned those words, holed up in a hospital bed following surgery
for the back pain that plagued him his whole life. He was quite
familiar with the changing political realities in America; in fact, he
and his family would do much to contribute to them. The Kennedys
would be not in the least surprised at the sophisticated political
machinery of twenty-first-century politics.

The most recent freshman Democratic Senate class was
advised to dedicate a full *four hours a day* to raising money. Both
of us remember trudging over to our respective Senatorial
Committee buildings° to dial up donors, since federal law prohib-
ited us from doing it from our offices. Campaign ads, staffs,
targeted data research—these things all cost significant amounts
of money, but four hours a day is mind-boggling. Simple math
reveals how much time is left over to legislate with such a ludicrous
burden on their time. And it's obvious no one likes doing it; it has
just become a necessity—for the party, for the candidate's
campaign, and for his or her political future.

Congressmen regularly lobby or angle to get on the committees that bring the most fund-raising opportunities. The media
now even covers how much money the candidates have raised.
This gives them another element to the horse race, which they
love covering; but also, those dollars tell a story and can predict
the future. The dollar figures are a clear indication of how serious
a candidate is, how long he or she will last, and whether or not
there's a groundswell of support from the big-ticket donors, an
absolute must in a long and expensive campaign.

° The Democratic one is now dubiously named the Thomas A. Daschle
Building.

Unfortunately, it's an arms-race scenario in which no one can afford to pull back: it'd be political suicide to do so. The only chance would be a situation where both sides are incentivized or forced to lay down their weapons, something we discuss in Part IV of this book.

Last election, *New York Times* columnist David Brooks wrote frustratedly about the fact that no candidate wanted to deal with the near-permanent reality of a closely divided Congress. "The No. 1 political fantasy in America today . . . is the fantasy that the other party will not exist," Brooks wrote. "It is the fantasy that you are about to win a 1932-style victory that will render your opponents powerless," a reference to the FDR-led pulverizing of the Republicans that brought the Democrats to dominance for decades. "We live in a highly polarized, evenly divided nation and the next president is going to have to try to pass laws in that context."[5]

Tom heard a senator compare running for office today to being at a Ping-Pong match in your name—and you don't have a paddle. Outside groups can't technically coordinate with the candidate, but the purpose of that has backfired. The distance makes them more negative, more hard-charging, and more irresponsible in what they say. You're almost like a front-row spectator, watching it all fly back and forth, wondering: *How did I get here?* Advisors flat out instruct candidates: *Go negative, early, and hard. If you don't torch your opponent before he torches you then you're going to lose.* What is more distressing is how well it works.

Negative campaigning has always been part of politics; it goes back to Jefferson versus Adams in 1796, both of whom had newspapers at their disposal that would print just about anything.

We have both experienced it, though neither of us participated in a campaign that went ugly, misleading, or personal. The difference in just the past ten to fifteen years is that now it is negative to the exclusion of everything else. One estimate from a political consultant noted negative ads took up about one-third of the market twenty years ago; today it's close to 90 percent negative.[6] These scorched-earth campaign tactics are by definition both destructive and self-destructive. They don't serve anyone—the winner included. It has become clear that when our political system runs entirely on aggressive and misleading attacks, we all lose.

"Mad people vote," Trent's current business partner, former senator John Breaux, likes to say. And it's true. People tend to be motivated more by anger at the polls than by anything else. People who are simply living and working may have a tight schedule or better things to do on Election Day. The turnout is always very low all over the country, but the mad people always show up. That's where the advisors focus their energy, on stoking the fire: Get them mad and keep them mad.

Voter turnout for national elections throughout most of the nineteenth century was regularly around 75 percent. And this was when voting was a full-day commitment, sometimes a two-day one for travelers who lived far enough away. Nowadays, turnout hovers around 55 percent, which is astonishing. In this celebrated democracy, the envy of the world, about every other eligible voter doesn't vote for president of the United States. Of course, the primaries are even lower and that gap has been growing: 2012 had an embarrassing 17 percent turnout, and the 2014 midterms were the lowest in seventy-two years.[7] The U.S. regularly has one of the lowest turnouts among developed nations.[8]

Voters have become like children torn between two fighting parents. Candidates may win, but the apparent reason for the fighting—the people and their faith in their leaders—is sacrificed in the process. The win-at-all-costs environment destroys everything in its wake and there's still a country that has to be run.

Most of the ads and campaigns lack vision and hope, and fail to communicate an aspiration for where this country should be going. Not that long ago you stayed positive to get your numbers as high as you could, because you knew you were going to lose that strength by going negative in that last month. (Your punches, after all, end up breaking your own hand.) Now it's a straight endurance game: they just hit as hard as they can, as long as they can, with as much money as they can. The debate has been replaced by the slugfest.

The 2014 midterms used *seven times* the amount of anonymous ("dark") contributions than just four years earlier, which itself was not a frugal year by any stretch of the imagination. An astonishing $4 billion was spent on the 2014 midterms, "bigger than the annual economic output of 35 countries," as the *New York Times* put it.[9] It is even more staggering when you think about exactly what all that money buys, close to 1.2 million ads.

It's upsetting to hear candidates say "We have to do this for our base" instead of saying "We have to do this or that *for our country*." Thomas E. Mann and Norman J. Ornstein, in *It's Even Worse Than It Looks: How the American Constitutional System Collided with the New Politics of Extremism*, go so far as to call the behavior of the permanent campaign "pathologies," claiming they "provide incontrovertible evidence of people who have become more loyal to party than to country."[10]

Part of the difficulty is that positivity just isn't as "sticky" of a message. It's hard to come up with a positive message to hang on to and promote throughout a campaign. In fact, nowadays a positive message is vulnerable to being turned into a negative by outside groups or opponents. If a candidate pitched positive messaging, pollsters and advisors would likely try to nix that strategy. In a sad comment on our current system, positivity itself has become too risky.

It has become a vicious cycle—but there's no way around the obvious fact: it starts with the voters. If the data and research showed that positivity brought people out on Election Day, you'd see a shift right quick. As Marc J. Dunkelman argues in *The Vanishing Neighbor: The Transformation of American Community*, "We have to wonder whether the American electorate has disrupted the collaborative spirit in Washington. After all, if there were a political advantage to be had by reaching across the aisle, politicians would likely grab it."[11]

The political climate in our country is so much more polarized than it was just at the end of the last century, an era that had significant partisan issues at the forefront. There's a genuine fear of standing out and taking on positions that you're going to pay heavily for politically; it's best to just stay in the fold and not take risks. It's like those dodge ball games in gym class where everyone is hiding behind someone else or cowering in the corner. The goal is just to stay in the game.

In his book *The Last Great Senate: Courage and Statesmanship in Times of Crisis*, Senate staffer and historian Ira Shapiro laments that the Senate has become just another playing field for politics. Shapiro writes, "Today, the Senate often appears to be just another arena for what has been called the permanent campaign, where the Democrats and Republicans struggle for advantage, more like scorched earth than hallowed ground."[12] When the greatest deliberative body in the world becomes just another battleground for partisan warfare, dysfunction seeps into every corner of the political process.

CHAPTER FOUR

Down in the Well

"Overshadowed by presidents and social movements,
legislators remain ghosts in America's historical imagination."
—JULIAN E. ZELIZER, *THE AMERICAN CONGRESS: THE
BUILDING OF DEMOCRACY*

THERE'S such a rich history to the Senate, from the number you're given when you're sworn in (Tom's is 1,776, which he loves telling people) to the old thick mahogany desks, some of which date back to the early nineteenth century. The election cycles, which are staggered into classes (A, B, C), the inaugural oath—it all ties together the senators, past and present. The continuity and tradition keeps issues of history, duty, and patriotism at the forefront, day in and day out, even as the Senate works to write the future. That continuous line links us all together.

From the very first Senate, a gathering of twenty-two senators in old New York City Hall in 1789, there has been a tradition on the floor itself. Washington's famed Farewell Address from 1796 has been read on the Senate floor every year since its centennial. In the Old Senate Chamber there are notches in the gray marble pillar next to the dais, one for each day they were in session during one particular Congress.

Senators would also carve or write their names on their desk drawers. Trent's Republican leader desk had Bob Dole, Howard

Baker, all the way back to the Republican leader in the early 1950s, William F. Knowland. Tom's leader desk, Desk X, went back to Joe Robinson in the 1930s. All of the Democratic majority leader names are written neatly, with reasonably sized letters, except for the enormous *Johnson-Texas.*

Some of the Senate desks even go back to the original thirteen states. There's something inspiring about looking down and seeing the names of men and women who were there in that exact spot during the great moments or crises in our country's history. Men and women whom most people know just through history books—and there's their handwriting, this was their desk. Under John Kennedy's desk there was a little raised spot where he would prop his feet up because of chronic back pain. The senior senator from New Hampshire always sits at Daniel Webster's desk; the senior senator from Kentucky always has Henry Clay's.

The senior senator from Mississippi has historically occupied Jefferson Davis's desk, which was bayoneted by Union troops during the Civil War. There's even a plug where the desk was patched up. Isaac Bassett, who was the second Senate page to be appointed (by Daniel Webster), wrestled one of the soldiers to the ground, admonishing him, "You were put here to protect, not to destroy."[1] The names only go back so far because Bassett felt the name carving was destroying government property. Every time the Senate would end, he would go through the desks and sand out all the names so they would be perfectly clean for the next session.

The Senate moved to its current chamber in 1859, but the old one is still used from time to time. Trent held a lecture series there and the leadership elections are held there. When Tom was first elected in 1994—he beat Chris Dodd by one vote—we were still literally writing on ballots. Somebody wrote so hard on the paper that it carved Tom's name into the top of the desk. The curator loves pointing that out.

There's a magic that comes from working in a place so uniquely tied to its past. Coming to work at the Capitol and seeing that majestic dome, which is so prominent in the city, or at night, when it's lit up and the flags are flying over the House and Senate chamber—it can't help but affect you. It is "the nearest thing Americans have to a National temple,"[2] David McCullough has said. It's also inspiring that kids from South Dakota and Mississippi, neither with much of a leg up, had the opportunity to work in the United States Capitol.

When they expanded the Capitol in the 1850s, they selected an Italian immigrant named Constantino Brumidi to paint the new murals, a way to honor our country's history through art. Brumidi was a controversial choice because people didn't consider him to be American, but the Capitol job made him one of the most famous artists in the country. His beautiful painting *The Apotheosis of Washington* has an honored place on the inside of the dome. You stand in that rotunda and look up and you see the ascension of George Washington to heaven: our first president is on a cloud, surrounded by angels.

In 1998 two police officers—Officer Jacob Chestnut and Detective John Gibson—were shot defending the Capitol during a break-in. During their memorial service speakers referred to the building as "the citadel of freedom" and "the citadel of democracy," which really rings true. It's the symbol of our country, we would argue, even more than the White House or the Washington Monument. When people think of Washington, they think of that Capitol dome—it's one of the reasons the 9/11 terrorists were likely aiming for it.

Something striking about our Capitol, even with the beautiful Brumidi works, is that it's not nearly as ornate as other capitols around the world. There's a simplicity, a plainness, about those stones in the floor that makes it even more beautiful. It keeps the space grounded, tied to the people. Up until 9/11 the public was free to just come in and wander around. You would walk out of your office and there were your constituents; there was America wandering around the hallways. Every day you were among the people you were representing, in a really wonderful way.

The Senate, with its six-year terms and representatives responsible for entire states, was designed as a tempering device: the "saucer that cools the tea," in George Washington's apocryphal description. Whereas the president will always struggle to represent the whole country and the House has voices looking to stand out in the crowd, the hundred members of the Senate are supposed to be less impulsive, less at the mercy of the winds. The Senate indeed debates, but it also forms a consensus, one that most Americans are comfortable with. It appears that we've gotten away from that. The House historically acts quicker, with passion, in the moment; the Senate is supposed to be the one that hammers out the compromise that, at the end of the day, works for America.

In *The Federalist Papers* Madison explained that the upper house of Congress had two clear purposes: "first to protect the people against their rulers; secondly to protect the people against the transient impressions into which they themselves might be led . . . an anchor against popular fluctuations."[3] In a democracy, Madison argued, there needed to be a mechanism in place to protect the people from themselves.

Ideally the Senate should channel ideas and solutions in an organized way, and allow the best ones to surface. The problem is that these days that power is eroding because of Congress's inaction, its inability to address all the challenges we face. Historically the Senate has been called "the world's greatest deliberative body," but that term is often used mockingly now. Its deliberation isn't substantive anymore but rather procedural: how to jam this bill through, trap this voting bloc, do an end run around this idea. For the most part, it has become pretty backward.

Lyndon Johnson's biographer Robert Caro explains that Madison designed the Constitution "to protect not only the people against their rulers but the people against themselves, [and that] they bolted around it armor so thick they hoped nothing could ever pierce it."[4] What has happened, however, is that this armor is locking a destructive status quo in place. It has begun to ruin and pollute itself from the inside and it's quite difficult to change the environment.

The permanent campaign remains entrenched for a number of reasons, but a key one is the narrow gap between the number of Republicans and Democrats in the Senate. That close differential is also a major contributor to the gridlock stalling the upper house. Since the 1980s the Senate has been in play just about every two years. One election can change the whole ball game; as a result, everyone becomes singularly concerned about keeping power. Current leaders Harry Reid and Mitch McConnell have shown evidence of this, and it trickles down. Senators wake up in the morning, look in the mirror, and know that if they're in the majority, then they're committee chairmen and they have the votes. It affects their behavior enormously—from what they say to how they vote.

The narrow majority also plays itself out on the Senate floor. Leaders need to protect members from difficult or politically radioactive votes that could hurt senators with their party or home state. Senate tactics frequently include adding amendments to bills in order to force members on the other side into a corner with their vote.

Of course, as former majority leaders, we looked out for our members, but the question becomes: To what degree? Certainly not at the expense of everything else. At what point is your duty to your caucus members superseding your ability to legislate? Otherwise, what's the point of being in the majority? Obviously, leading requires a lot more than just playing defense. When so much attention is paid to protecting what you have, priorities get shifted and actual legislation gets ignored.

Every majority leader worries about tough political amendments that the other side offers. During our time in leadership we had to consider our colleagues' positions. Senators in vulnerable states would come to us to say, "Please, I can't vote on this," or "Sorry, I have to vote against you here." We would do our best to persuade them to stay with the caucus but sometimes we had to let a few votes go, depending on how the final tally was going to shake out.

None of this is new; what *is* new is the constancy of it, the ubiquity of this type of mentality. The legislation the leader takes to the floor, what is said, how the caucus is instructed— the majority leader's agenda is to protect and save the majority; the minority's is to take it over. Mitch McConnell even admitted to the *New York Times* that "aggravating the majority" was one of the main jobs of being minority leader. Though we understand the kind of pressures leaders are under, it has become paralyzing. Holding or getting the majority used to be the means—to get things done, to further the party agenda; now it's the end itself.

If the Senate was designed as a cooling influence on legislation from the other chambers, then the moderates in the Senate serve the same purpose for the Senate itself. Not that long ago there was a valuable third group in the Senate that lived in the political middle. It was a small but effective circle that has gradually vanished and the whole body has suffered as a result. Though neither of us camped there, we always valued the moderates' role in tempering our passion on issues like defense, taxes, and executive power.

There are some still in there—a dying breed holding on—but they don't have the freedom to stand out. Circumstances now require the moderates in Congress to toe the line and keep their heads down. They aren't as aggressively engaged in trying to cut deals like John Breaux or Olympia Snowe once did. Becoming a moderate has simply become too high a price to pay.

It's actually extremely difficult to survive as a moderate in Congress. First of all, if you aspire to leadership, you can't afford to be a moderate: your role is to work for and embody the party standard. We each have some moderate positions—Trent on education, Tom on trade—but we never would have climbed the ladder had we spent the majority of our time there. Senate moderates like Ben Nelson and Blanche Lincoln were usually the last people at the table because they were holding out for the centrist position. Tom had to work to get them to join with the Democrats on a great many votes. Among the moderates would be the occasional iconoclast like Zell Miller, a Democrat who was so closely aligned with the Republicans that he was even a speaker at the 2004 Republican National Convention. That's an extreme example, but it still reveals a great deal about the uncomfortable place moderates hold in Congress.

Congress is a representative body, so it reflects the division and partisanship within the American public. Parties have pulled further apart and it has been exacerbated by primaries, which have become the dominant elections. There are far more Republicans in Congress on the far right, far more Democrats on the far left. Congress is continuously being reshaped in sharper, more discrete divisions, and the primaries only encourage this.

Many careers have gone down in flames due to attacks from the more extreme sides of the party—what's now called getting "primaried." For Republicans this has become a regular occurrence. There are a lot of responsible, conservative senators looking over their shoulders, worried about getting attacked by the Club for Growth or the Senate Conservatives Fund and their deep war chests. We hear from our old colleagues all the time about their fear of taking on positions that they're going to pay for heavily. Everyone just wants to stay in the fold and avoid risks. No one wants to get embarrassed, attacked, or ousted.

A strange paradox in Congress is that the large battles—the partisan issues, the "wedge issues"—are in the safety zone. The risky places are in the middle: compromising positions, reaching halfway, making deals with the other side. Instead of going to the issues where common ground can be found, both sides end up going for the big fight. The knock-down, drag-out fights never really lead anywhere in terms of legislation; what they do is shore up party support, raise money, and rally the base. Senators and congressmen get their votes and their money through fighting for their parties' (or states') pet issues. It goes back to the stand-your-ground posture: it's easier to raise money and rally your base as a soldier in the fight than it is as a dealer at the table.

Congressmen should be trying to find something they can do together where both sides have to lead and put votes on the board, like on trade or cybersecurity, and see if the momentum of action carries to other things. Trent calls it finding the pony in all the horse manure. They even managed to turn energy efficiency—which should be bipartisan or even nonpartisan—into a shootout because of all the different constituencies: labor, the environment lobby, the business lobby, oil and gas companies, and international partners.

Today's climate makes it far more difficult than it should be for them to just meet at the table. Their constituencies are so loud or threatening on both sides. It's what happened in the latest immigration battle, which didn't begin as a battle at all. We see it happen over and over again: the pieces are there, the players are there, but somehow the dynamite gets lit by party politics and the whole thing just blows up. It's exhausting to watch.

Sometimes we take visitors up into the gallery of the Capitol and, frankly, it can be a bit dispiriting to watch our government at work below. Nearly 95 percent of the time, if there's not a vote, there are only one or two members speaking and no one listening. Visitors often look at us with a confused expression that says: *What is* this? It's not always so easy to explain. The fact is that our democracy doesn't always work the way we think it should.

The old joke is that in the Senate somebody stands up, nobody listens, and then everybody disagrees. More and more, our leaders in Washington are merely performing the grand argument for public consumption. It's become a predictable type of theater, with a formulaic script and no resolution to the conflict. "The Senate chamber," George Packer wrote, "is an intimate room where men and women go to talk to themselves for the record."[5]

Before the 2014 midterms, a voter told the *New York Times* that all the politicians in Washington were "play acting" and "putting on a show to entertain the rest of us, right next to *People* magazine on the newsstand."[6] It's hard to argue with that perception these days, although as two people who have given a larger part of their lives to government service, it's painful to hear.

John Kennedy noted in *Profiles in Courage* that "mothers may still want their favorite sons to grow up to be President, but according to a famous Gallup poll of some years ago, they do not want them to become politicians in the process."[7]

"In Washington the political debate too often careens between dysfunctional poles," Ron Brownstein writes in *The Second Civil War,* whose title alone reveals the ugliness of the current political situation.

> *[E]ither polarization, when one party imposes its will over the bitter resistance of the other, or immobilization, when the parties fight to stalemate. Either result is a recipe for alienation in large parts of the public . . . By any measure, the costs of hyperpartisanship vastly exceed the benefits.*[8]

What has caused behavior to change? There's a lot more pressure on members to be more partisan, and legislation has taken a permanent backseat to politics. It's important to remember that these are good people and none of them mean harm. What's missing is that vital element of chemistry, which we discuss in Part II. As our good friend Senator Olympia Snowe once wrote: "If we don't work together, or socialize or get acquainted with each other at all, the chances of one hundred relative strangers agreeing on even the smallest of issues are slight."[9]

It's natural for acrimony and distrust to come out of any group of that size with different viewpoints and intense passions.

It takes leadership and adherence to the rules (what's called "regular order") to help lubricate the legislative process, and we don't have much of that right now.

Other tense workplaces can claim that it's just business, but politics is also very personal. People are fighting for their value systems, which you have to honor and respect. Mature individuals find a way to deal with issues without coming to blows. It depends on the leadership, who are sensitive to where those problems are. As leaders in the Senate, we did what we had to do to keep things from getting out of hand.

What helps to cool passions is this: both politics and legislation can be pretty definitive. There's a campaign, then an election, and then it's over (although that time period has been slowly shrinking with each passing year). After the election, you need to move on. We both are hard pressed to remember the names of some of our opponents on elections over the years.

There's a psychological freedom that comes the day after the vote. One day you might be fighting tooth and nail with someone on legislation, and the next day that person is a cosponsor of a bill you need. There's always the possibility that you are going to need that person someday. It's this dynamic that keeps the machinery running—the definitiveness of the vote and the realization that there's going to be another vote.

Trent was fond of reminding his caucus: The most important vote is not the last vote but the next vote. He made it a point with people like Senator John McCain, who could get pretty hot, not to let them leave mad at the end of the day. He always kept his door open so they could come back and work on something else together the next day. You have to have that attitude—particularly in leadership, because it's one big issue after another. It's not one a season; it's every week.

As Republican leader Bob Dole once said about his counterpart Robert C. Byrd: "Today's foe could be tomorrow's ally. You
do not burn your bridges in this place because the very person
you may cut off at the knees is the person that you may want and
you may not be able to find him if you have done that."

The Senate floor itself is a strange mixture of venom and
civility—"a kind of controlled madhouse"[10] in the words of former
senator Gary Hart. You have to speak about members in the third
person and the rules explicitly forbid personal attacks. The intention is that the less personal you make it, the more likely the
debate will stay civil. It's a form of legislative lubrication to call a
colleague "the distinguished senator from Mississippi." In the old
days, there was the other kind of lubrication as well. As a senator,
John Quincy Adams noted that the speeches made by certain
colleagues could be "so wild and so bluntly expressed as to be
explained only by recognizing that the member was inflamed by
drink."[11]

Jefferson's Manual was a collection of the original instructions on parliamentary practice in the Senate compiled by Vice
President Jefferson in 1800. It was particularly focused on "order
and decorum,"[12] advocating for basic civility in such rules as "No
one is to disturb another in his speech by hissing, coughing, spit-
ting, speaking or whispering to another . . ."[13]

Senators, in more ways than one, didn't adhere to Jefferson's
ideal. The third-person references and the civility in tenor is an
outgrowth of what used to be a quite physical period in the Senate.
The early days of Congress were made up of people who lived on
the land, backwoodsmen who tended to take matters into their
own hands. There were a handful of violent incidents on the
Senate floor: in the 1850s Senator Henry S. Foote drew a pistol on

Senator Thomas Hart Benton in the chamber, and Representative Preston Brooks famously took his cane to Charles Sumner, beating the senator to an unconscious pulp.[14]

At one time "political duels were like counter elections," historian Joanne Freeman reminds us.[15] When there was a dispute after the vote, the candidates would sometimes sort it out with guns. Hamilton and Burr's was the most famous duel between political rivals, but it was far from the only one. California senator David C. Broderick became the first sitting senator to die in a duel, killed by the chief justice of his own state.

Doris Kearns Goodwin, in her book about the rise of Teddy Roosevelt, *The Bully Pulpit: Theodore Roosevelt, William Howard Taft, and the Golden Age of Journalism*, noted the corrupt environment that was the norm before TR arrived. After helping elect Roosevelt's predecessor, William McKinley, for president, party boss and RNC chair Marcus "Mark" Hanna decided he wanted to be a senator. "Since the votes were cast by the state legislature in 1898," Goodwin writes, legislators were "bribed and threatened with revolvers; in the end unsurprisingly, Hanna emerged victorious."[16]

Fortunately these practices have been abandoned, but it doesn't mean that passions remain any less hot. We have evolved a great deal down in the well (although there is something to be said about having it out and moving on). There were a handful of times when Trent thought there might be an altercation on the back rail in the House chamber, and another time on the Senate floor. Tom once had to break up two Democratic senators who were nose to nose in the cloakroom. But these are rare incidents; it's usually verbal.

There was a famous incident in 1984 when the enraged Speaker of the House, Tip O'Neill, stood up and insulted Newt

Gingrich, at the time an unknown representative from Georgia. Gingrich had gone into the empty well and—because of the single camera trained only on him—gave the false impression that he was speaking to his colleagues, who wouldn't respond. Tip called Gingrich's antics "the lowest thing that I've ever seen in 32 years in Congress."

When the Speaker finished his tirade, Trent stood up and moved that Tip's words be struck from the record. It was the first time in over a century that this had happened to the Speaker of the House. It was an embarrassing moment for Tip, and Trent assumed the Speaker would retaliate in some way. But it says something about Tip that he went on as though it had never happened; in fact, quite admirably, he never once brought it up.

Of course, Trent was at the center of another storm involving his words in 2002, which ultimately led to him stepping down as Republican leader.

> TRENT: Much was made of what I said in 2002 at Strom
> Thurmond's one hundredth birthday party. I certainly
> made a mistake and carried no ill intentions in my
> comments. Stepping aside as Republican leader was the
> right thing to do for my party, for the president's efforts,
> and for my country. But I was not going to go pout; I just
> went back to work.
>
> I felt the White House, Karl Rove in particular, had
> a hand in my removal. President Bush's inner circle felt
> like I was not compliant enough with their desires, which
> were supposed to be the president's desires, though I
> found out that was not always the case. I had a way of
> going around the staff sometimes to talk to the president,
> which they did not like. By then I'd been leader long

enough that I had a certain amount of orneriness about me. I had been around this city and the Congress a lot longer than they had—including Bush. I felt I had the right to show the temerity to tell the president what I thought he needed to hear—especially at a time when maybe no one else was doing so. I may have been a partisan warrior but I also wanted to keep a good relationship with the Democrats. Among other things, my successor, Bill Frist, went out to South Dakota to campaign against Tom in 2004, which, as I told the press, I never would have done.

I had to fess up to my mistakes and work my way back up the mountain. I worked up to the number two slot again, as whip, which I took as evidence that my colleagues didn't think the attacks against me held water. They knew me; they knew what I stood for.

A lot of people and media outlets noted that nobody had an issue after my speech. It was only after a few days of Internet blogs stirring things up that it became a story. In fact, a few articles called it the first real case of Internet chatter elevating an event into a "news story." "This is just unfair, Trent," a prominent Democrat privately told me. "I've said the same thing about old Strom." Minorities from all over also came up to me and said I got a bum rap. I learned over the years that when you are on top, the press loves to take shots at you. But there's something they love even better than a takedown: a comeback story.

TOM: It was tough losing Trent as my counterpart in the leadership. Our chemistry was unique and, I like to believe, valuable to both sides. Trent and I were students. We started as Senate staff people, then House members, and then U.S. senators. When you go through that progression you develop an appreciation of things that is lost on those new to the process.

The experience of losing the partnership with Trent gave me an even greater understanding of chemistry's role in the process and how necessary it is. Without a healthy dose of it, there is little chance for the two parties to meet on any kind of common ground or reach across the aisle to work together.

CHAPTER FIVE

The Media Effect

POLITICIANS in the twenty-first century also have to navigate, utilize, and cooperate with a massive and incessant media industrial complex. FDR, Kennedy, and even Reagan lived in a much different media environment than today's. The press once protected politicians to an extent, whereas now it's the complete opposite. Former representative Jim Moran spoke recently of a "media which hammers every day normally not for the purpose of informing but for the purpose of inciting."[1] As Tom likes to say, the media has transformed itself from the referee into a participant.

It's true that this country has always had aggressive or biased media. There were newspapers that were over-the-top hyperbolic and not necessarily accurate back in Jefferson's time, but their reach wasn't even close to what it is now. And what goes without saying is how many fewer hours a day people spent with that biased information. They weren't carrying it in their pockets, hearing it in their cars, immersed in it wherever they went.

The modern age makes it harder to be an inspirational leader because so many more of your flaws, or even just your humanness,

come under constant and intense scrutiny. Leaders understandably have trouble rising above all the noise. "An intrusive 24/7
media . . . strips away the distance, detachment, and the aura and
mystique required for great leadership," Aaron David Miller
observes. "And for politicians, too much exposure and familiarity
diminishes the public's willingness to think of the leader as special
or great."[2] Although there are a variety of reasons why we lack
strong leadership these days, the media environment—and its
thirst for more and more nakedness—is certainly part of it. It's
that much harder to look good under all the lights, in front of
all those mirrors.

We've both known the conventional press to be fickle,
mercurial at times. They'll pump you up, boost and protect you,
and then if something happens they'll waste no time tearing you
down. When President Obama arrived on the scene, the mainstream press was tremendously supportive; in his final years in
office, in a mass 180-degree turn, they're almost universally critical. We've each experienced the media's need for a narrative:
your rise, your victory, your fall from grace, your redemption.

Another aspect of the modern media that impacts politics is
that it triggers something that in physics is called "The Observer
Effect"—the act of watching a phenomenon changes it. The press
conference, the talking points, the public apology—there are so
many different weapons in the politician's arsenal that rely on,
and play exclusively to, the media. Some of them are strictly
media events; if a camera weren't there to record it, it wouldn't be
happening at all.

One of the ultimate illustrations of the cameras' impact was
during President Clinton's impeachment trial in the Senate. We
were torn on whether to televise the hearings, and there were
solid arguments made to both of us on each side. We ended up

compromising: during the day we'd televise and after six P.M. the cameras were not allowed. It was an eye-opening experiment, in many ways. The contrast in the quality of discussion and the candor from members was astounding. Senators came up to the podium and poured their hearts out; we all said things that we would never say in front of the cameras. It was much more personal, and so much more edifying.

The Clinton trial was about so much more than just politics. Every senator had to be concerned about how his or her comments could be twisted or used against him or her. Who in public life hasn't been caught saying something stupid? Howard Dean's presidential run in 2004 was sunk not even by what he said but by the way he sounded on television after a victory speech. Trent had one of the more famous gaffes in modern politics with his praise of Strom Thurmond. And it always makes news. It can scare even the bravest public official from honest expression in the face of a camera, even if there is nothing to hide.

The desire to catch slip-ups has led to a new technique that Tom was first introduced to in 2004: campaign trackers. It's someone's job to follow the opponents' campaign with a portable device and capture everything the opponent does and says, hoping there's a sound bite that can be used to attack. It's a new low, in our opinion. Besides the unseemliness of it, it creates an environment where those running for office—who should be inspirational, speak boldly, communicate a vision—are discouraged from doing so. To survive until the election, a candidate's best choice is to play it safe. The practice has evolved extensively since then. In 2015, the Conservative Political Action Committee (CPAC) hosted a seminar called "We're Watching You: How to Video Track 24/7" in order train people in the fine art of campaign tracking. (In a wonderful bit of irony, the seminar itself was being tracked by a tracker from the Left, creating something of a stand-off.)[3] This trend speaks volumes about what winning in politics has come to mean in the twenty-first century.

The ubiquity of the cameras adds another dimension to the political landscape, recording everything from the most casual remarks that could be caught on someone's phone to the most routine congressional hearing being televised on CSPAN. Ernest "Fritz" Hollings, a longtime Senate veteran who lived through decades of change, hated the cameras. "People came to the floor to talk to each other and now they talk to the stupid cameras," he used to say. Hollings may have been from an earlier era, but he was right: cameras have completely changed the tone and the chemistry. Senators no longer talk to each other; it's all about giving speeches, which have become increasingly hyperbolic in order to make news or rally the base. Politicians can get more attention this way, but the effect on intimacy—and trust—has been extremely detrimental to the Senate.

Both of us frequently went on the Sunday talk shows, some-times together; it was part of the job. We never got surly with each other on *Face the Nation* or *Meet the Press*, where we appeared more than on other shows. We didn't do those "gotcha" moments where we could've taken a real potshot that might have been polit-ically advantageous. We enjoyed being on those shows together because we had that camaraderie. We're not sure if the current Senate and House leaders have ever been on together, but we've never seen it. The fact is that the American people want to see the two leaders, even if they disagree, be respectful toward each other. Tim Russert appreciated that. He helped make it informational without giving us questions designed to lead to a heated argument.

One of the problems that Trent had as majority leader was getting Republicans to go on the Sunday talk shows. "We don't like what they're saying, what they're asking, what they're doing," he'd argue. "How are we going to affect that if we don't engage?" The media is there: you have to use them in an honest way to state your position. He noticed how Republicans developed an attitude about the media and avoided communicating with them altogether. "Whether we like it or not," he'd argue, "they are the megaphone."

The conventional press needs to make decisions based on the bottom line, the eyeballs and ears they reach. Their audience only increases with controversy, and that's unlikely to change. "Conflict invariably draws more attention from the traditional press than consensus," Ron Brownstein writes. After all, "cars that collide head-on make more noise than those that merge onto a highway uneventfully."[4]

Modern technology, constant communications, and twenty-four-hour news cycles are the reality. Bemoaning their influence does little to solve the problem. Leaders need to both stand above their noise and begin to use the media more fruitfully. As presidential historian Michael Beschloss has written, the trends in mass communications have risen to such a level of pervasiveness that "a leader without courage and wisdom can be broken by them."[5]

Teddy Roosevelt was a master of this, taking his cause directly to the people and using the media in a way that furthered his agenda. TR understood how valuable the press could be as a gatekeeper to the people. It was his "enterprising use of the 'bully pulpit,'" Doris Kearns Goodwin writes, "a phrase he himself coined to describe the national platform the presidency provides to shape public sentiment and mobilize action."[6] He was a genius at reading public opinion and using journalists to spread his progressive vision. Goodwin continues:

> *In order to aggressively pursue redress for the abuses*
> *and inequity of the industrial age, the president would*
> *need to ride a seismic shift in national consciousness.*
> *[He used investigative journalists as his tool to] not just*
> *explain but vividly illustrate the human and economic*
> *costs of unchecked industrial growth and combination.*
> *The complex and sometimes contentious partnerships*
> *that Roosevelt had forged with investigative journalists*
> *would soon illuminate corruption, as if by heat lightning,*
> *and clarify at last a progressive vision for the entire*
> *nation.*[7]

When Tom was in the Senate, he'd have a "Talk to Tom" night where South Dakotans would call in toll-free to ask him questions. At the time, it was a nearly radical way to stay connected to his district. Nowadays virtually all congressmen use the Internet and social media to stay connected. All have a web page with comment opportunities and ways to get in touch and get involved. This doesn't mean pandering: the people put you there not as a stand-in but as someone with his or her own perspective.

America is not a purely democratic system—we're a republican form of government. The people elect you to go to Washington, to be educated, to learn the facts, and to make decisions on their behalf. We don't govern by referendum. Of course, we don't consciously repudiate what our constituents want, but there's a trust factor involved: they're expecting us to learn the issues and vote on their behalf. Somebody has to take the time to study the issue, make their best judgment. It's part of the culture now: everyone gets to play expert. The comments sections on the Internet reveal this; you have invective, personal attacks, and flat-out lies written right underneath the content. You finish an article online and *boom*, it's right there, implicitly giving it equal weight. It's a false balance and it's problematic.

"We need to get over the childish notion that we don't need a responsible leadership class, that power can be wielded directly by the people," David Brooks argued in a *New York Times* column called "Snap Out of It." He continues:

> *America was governed best when it was governed by a porous, self-conscious and responsible elite—during the American Revolution, for example, or during and after World War II. Karl Marx and Ted Cruz may believe that power can be wielded directly by the masses, but this has almost never happened historically.*[8]

The democratizing of culture has done positive things for this country, but one downside is the armchair-expert culture where people think their opinions should be given equal weight on all things. The media has opened up enormously and given a platform to anyone with an Internet connection. It has been an enormous good for access between leaders and constituents. But a side effect is that it gives a platform to too many outlets for venomous comment. It has created an environment of instantaneous reaction that is neither thoughtful nor useful. Even if you agree with their positions, the tone is enormously troubling.

The new media environment obviously has accelerated and exacerbated some of the problems plaguing Washington. There are so many more venues for hyperbolic exchange today. The discrete channels and audiences are more cordoned off than they have ever been. Whole swaths of the population now stay inside their own bubbles and still feel that they are engaged in a public debate. But it's an illusion. The different groups and demographics in America are like silos: people lock themselves in and only listen to their own kind.

Politicians are responding to a more siloed electorate and the public no longer needs to interact with those who disagree with them. It's an echo chamber on both sides, and it's getting louder and more sealed off by the year. Our computers' browsers now operate with something called a "filter bubble," an algorithm that determines what you already like or are familiar with so it can send it back to you when you search.[9] The filter bubble is an accurate metaphor for how we now live, and it makes for a less informed yet more confident and outraged electorate.

Consequently, our politicians are responding to a more fragmented electorate than in the past—and there's a feedback loop at work. "We have created, and are creating, new institutions distinguished by their isolation and single-mindedness," Bill Bishop wrote in his groundbreaking 2008 book *The Big Sort: Why the Clustering of Like-Minded America is Tearing Us Apart.* "We have replaced a belief in a nation with a trust in ourselves and our carefully chosen surroundings."[10]

This process has been going on in America for a long time, but it has sped up as we've gotten better at it. "What had happened over three decades wasn't a simple increase in political partisanship . . . ," Bishop explains. "Americans were busy creating social resonators, and the hum that filled the air was the reverberated and amplified sound of their own voices and beliefs."[11]

It's one of the things contributing to acrimony and division in America: we don't read the same things; we don't live in the same place; we don't watch the same TV shows. Trent's current business partner (and good friend) John Breaux watches MSNBC for his news, while Trent watches Fox. Add the Internet and social media and it's like we live in two different worlds.

Tom reads the *New York Times*, which Trent reads to know what the enemy is up to. Trent then has to read the *Wall Street Journal* to calm down. Tom does something like the reverse. And all it does is solidify the walls of our silos. Though our institutions were mostly homogenous during the Revolutionary era, the founders recognized the poisonous effect of uniformity. Madison himself knew "the best hedge against extremism was the constant mixture of opposing opinion."[12]

"Mixed company moderates; like-minded company polarizes," Bishop notes. "Heterogeneous communities restrain group excesses; homogenous communities march toward the extremes."[13] This goes for both physical neighborhoods and online communities.

Confirmation bias—looking for that which proves what you already think—seems to be plaguing the public. We have become curators of our own news, our own entertainment—and increasingly our own information. But as Daniel Patrick Moynihan famously said: "Everyone is entitled to their own opinion, but not to their own facts."

The media, especially the technology companies, keep selling the idea that we're closer to each other than we've ever been, but clearly it has never been uglier in the political landscape. Increasing connections has not brought actual closeness, and the two should not be confused. Often they're mutually exclusive. We're not necessarily being connected to all types of America or the world—just more of those we're looking for: those like us.

With the predominance of texting, as well as Twitter, Facebook, and Instagram, there is now a tremendous capacity for instantaneous communication—which has both benefits and drawbacks. Back when you wanted to write a letter, you had to sit down and literally compose it, and it sometimes took you hours to finish. By the time you finished that letter, you might have had cycled through a lot of different thoughts and how you were going to express them. But the instant nature of communications today has made for less thoughtful communications. It's mostly reactive.

We used to walk out of our Senate offices and there'd be ten cameras there with microphones. You couldn't possibly anticipate all their questions, so you'd say things that sometimes you wish you hadn't. Off-the-cuff speakers like Vice President Biden and Harry Reid get into trouble more frequently than they'd like. It has happened to all of us. It happens more now because of the environment of immediacy that the media has created and the public has embraced.

This is an issue in our physical space too. We tend to move into neighborhoods where everybody is like us. About the only place now where we're forced to identify, communicate, and inter-act with people with other views and backgrounds is in the work-place, maybe at the universities. It contributes to our restrictive views. Most people are not exposed to what others might think.

In his book *The Vanishing Neighbor*, Marc Dunkelman discussed "our search for affirmation" and how it "has compelled us to avoid relationships that expanded our intellectual horizons or drove conflict . . . [W]e no longer have to maintain a close friendship with the woman who wants to haggle over politics." We are increasingly living in a world of our own making, both physic-ally and virtually, and the results reaffirm and codify what we already think or want to believe. There's something antidemo-cratic about the rigidity of that model.

Yet, it's important to remember that it's still very early in the lifetime of this new media. The Internet itself is about twenty years old—a blip in the long arc of history. Social media is less than half that old. We're still learning to cope with and adapt to all the new media forms and outlets that have sprung up since the turn of the century—in our politics and in our lives. When you're inside of it, it's hard to recognize that long arc. We're reminded of Patrick Henry. He said nostalgically, "When the American spirit was in its youth, the language of America was different: liberty, sir, was then the primary object."[14] Henry was bemoaning the loss of things essential to the heart of the American Revolution, a time he believed had passed.

That was in 1788.

Part II

Chemistry

"I don't like [Henry] Clay. He is a bad man, an imposter, a creator of wicked schemes. I wouldn't speak to him, but, by God, I love him!"

—JOHN C. CALHOUN

CHAPTER SIX

A Nation of Men and Women

"The two-party system remains not because both are rigid but because both are flexible."

—JOHN F. KENNEDY, *PROFILES IN COURAGE*

"POLITICS is chemical," our colleague Ted Kennedy liked to say, and few understood the dynamics of the Senate as well as Teddy did. A member of the U.S. Senate for forty-seven years, he managed to straddle that tricky line between fighting for his party's agenda (he was known as "the Liberal Lion") and reaching across the aisle—on issues from education to immigration to his lifelong cause, health care. Kennedy understood the enormous value of chemistry in any group thrown together to do shared work, from the smallest office to the United States Senate.

Chemistry can exist only under the right conditions, especially among entrenched opposition. Natural allies will usually find each other, but others require the right environment—one characterized by trust and open communication. In politics, chemistry is that X factor that turns a body of disparate voices into a community. It doesn't mean a *homogeneous* community but rather one where opposing voices are free to speak openly and productively. When Congress, especially its leaders, has the kind of poisonous chemistry it currently possesses, it ceases functioning like a community. Opposition digs in and things shut down, both figuratively and literally. If there's no chemistry, then there's little chance of compromise—and, by design, Congress can't function without compromise on some level.

First of all, procedurally, one side rarely has the numbers to ram things through and overturn a Senate filibuster (which requires 60 votes). Secondly, legislation is complicated, and there are far too many conflicting forces at work for things to get done without men and women making the conscious choice to work together. Sacrifice, trading, and deal making will not and cannot happen any other way.

Senate giant Henry Clay, who single-handedly kept the Union together in the decade before the Civil War, was praised as "the Great Compromiser." Today that nickname might be considered an insult, a knock against the sturdiness of his principles. That's a false understanding of the concept of compromise, and of personal integrity as well. It is not another word for giving in or selling out. Longtime Senate aide Mike Lofgren writes that "Ronald Reagan himself, the icon . . . of present-day Republicans, had little reluctance to negotiate over issues of taxing and spending, declare the resulting compromise a victory, and move on."[1] Men and women shouldn't sacrifice their beliefs or their values, but a functioning government requires compromise. Indeed, a functioning society depends on it as well.

The Founders knew that their democratic experiment couldn't work without compromise in various forms. We cannot afford to forget how crucial compromise was in those early years of our Republic. Our Founding Fathers' willingness to do so is not a reflection of how close the different positions were or how weakly they defended them. We should not assume that because they were willing to come together, it was easy for them to do so.

James Madison, the chief architect of the Constitution, knew that the "new political structure"—the one that has lasted all this time; the one we still operate under—"only worked if its participants were willing to compromise," according to Eric Lane and Michael Oreskes in *The Genius of America*.[2] Benjamin Franklin's use and championing of compromise at the Constitutional Convention is likely the only reason the document ever made its way out of that room in Philadelphia to be ratified by the states.

Furthermore, Adams and Jefferson may have been political rivals, but without their compromising through America's first decade, there might not have been a second. "There are several crucial moments when critical compromises were brokered because personal trust made it possible," historian Joseph J. Ellis tells us. "Though the American republic became a nation of laws, during the initial phase it also had to be a nation of men."[3] That phrase, *a nation of men*, is so crucial. It reminds us that the system is made up of people (men and women) and it is only as strong as those currently responsible for it.

Compromise is, in the words of President Kennedy, "the sense of things possible." When the budget agreement between Clinton and the Republicans passed in the 1990s, which led to a balanced budget and a surplus, the hurdles were extensive and it wasn't all pretty. It was not easy for Tom and the Democrats to accept, but there was one thing we did have: President Clinton was willing to compromise and make a deal—and he pushed it to the very last day.

"Compromises are by definition imperfect to the people involved," Oreskes and Lane wrote. ". . . The more the issue has a moral dimension, the more potentially awful the compromise can look. One of the reasons our politics has become so brittle is that we seem to be seeing so many issues through a moral lens and therefore find it hard to find common ground for compromise."[4]

Far too much of politics gets positioned as us-versus-them or as stand-your-ground issues; it's destructive and it misses the point. It's smoke and mirrors, really. True, the battles happen, but very often they are invented by those who benefit from the appearance of fighting. It's no wonder we're at such an impasse.

John Kennedy wrote in *Profiles in Courage* that "we can compromise our political positions, but not ourselves. We can resolve the clash of interests without conceding our ideals . . . Compromise need not mean cowardice."[5]

As Senate leaders between 1996 and 2002, each of us kept a phone at his desk in the Capitol that linked directly to the other. We don't remember where the idea came from, although it was likely inspired by the famous hotline that links the Pentagon to the Kremlin, set up after the Cuban missile crisis. (Now it's a computer link.)

The elaborate hoops that are involved when the two leaders want to talk—staff, media leaks, witnesses—are considerable. We both recognized that those hoops are sometimes part of the problem. Like in an old game of telephone, the message often gets distorted by the time it reaches the other side. Our phone was a way to cut through that, protect our relationship, and build trust. It was simple: when one of us picked it up, it would ring at the other's desk. It gave us a chance to talk directly and to get around our staff, who sometimes didn't want us negotiating as much as we did. The phone was an extension of the open line of communication we tried to have during those years, which were tumultuous ones on many levels for the country.

There were also times when one of us would walk over to the other's Capitol office for a face-to-face private moment. It's probably fifty yards from office to office, but it's one of the longest walks you'll ever take. Of course, any time we did it, the media immediately wanted to know what was going on. Often in politics you don't want this kind of interaction to be made public: if it involved a deal, it might be too early for that. We could avoid media inquiries just by picking up that phone and not generating the spectacle of walking to the other's office. Or Trent would just slip through the back door of Tom's office, or vice versa. Sometimes these talks were to sort out a problem; perhaps one of us had been unfair in our machinations. Politics gets personal, sometimes messy, but we tried to keep a barometer on each other. We were sensitive to each other's feelings and the challenges we faced. It made a huge difference.

The more we talked one-on-one, the more it became natural: just two men sorting things out. It is often the little things that matter far more than the big ones. You can't pass a rule requiring those little things that build confidence; it's simply a function of civility and leadership. All you can do is create and promote that environment. The day in 1996 that Trent began as majority leader, he brought his leadership team to Tom's office to offer an introduction and asked Connie Mack to give a prayer. It was a small thing, but it was not pro forma. Those little things add up over time and help build trust along the way. It's not just congeniality for its own sake; there's a pragmatic reason for it.

We do a good number of joint appearances these days, and there are usually audience members who look perplexed at seeing the two of us together; they often ask, "You guys are friends?" We get this a lot because our positions are so far apart and we occupied such contrasting roles in the political landscape. But people seem to appreciate that even though we disagree philosophically, we are able to talk candidly. More importantly, when it mattered for our country's sake, we were able to work through our differences. We're not in any way claiming that our relationship is superior; it's just an example of how sides can meet in the middle if there's respect and open communication.

Audiences often follow up with some version of "Well, why don't we have that now?" The public can tell; chemistry is visible like that. Our country is understandably frustrated by a lack of communication between the parties—the party leaders specifically. Our government can't function if the leaders don't trust each other and don't communicate. One doesn't need to understand politics and government to grasp that it's a basic need.

Frankly, we also enjoyed each other's company. Sometimes we knew the other was the only other person in Washington who had the same kinds of headaches, responsibilities, weights to carry, people to answer to, people to chew out, calls to return, etc. It created something of a bond between us that has gotten stronger through the years.

One of our fondest memories was in '96 during what we call "wrap-up." The senators all went home for the end of the session because there were no more votes, but it was late afternoon and we had a lot of bills left out. In the next three hours the two of us moved something like forty-seven bills. We were the only senators in the building, but we had to go through the process to get them cleared. We called it a hotline: senators could object from their office, and a single objection could hold a bill up; they didn't even have to come out on the floor. We hotlined those bills but we didn't give them a lot of time to say no. We'd say to the empty room, "Anybody object?" Then we'd look at each other. "Well, looks like no one objects, so let's do it."

An example of how effective political and personal chemistry can be—one that the country substantially benefited from—was the relationship between President Reagan and the Democratic Speaker of the House, Tip O'Neill. Philosophically they were at different ends of the spectrum, but, according to former O'Neill aide (and current cable news anchor) Chris Matthews, "even though the rivalry was so often ferocious . . . [t]here was a sense, on a certain level, of working together in service of the country."[6]

When Reagan came into office with his tax plan, he zeroed in on O'Neill as the most important person he needed to win over and worked to get him. Tip had been unhappy with the way the Carter administration had kept him out of the loop. Reagan's chief of staff, James Baker, knew this and briefed Reagan on how best to endear himself to the Democratic Speaker. So began a courtship.

The unique thing is that President Reagan never persuaded Tip on an issue, but he did get an agreement that the Speaker would bring it to the floor and allow it to be voted on, which was critical. Tip could have used his position to block it from ever getting to a floor vote. He felt that the president deserved an opportunity to make his case and have it voted on. Things like that build respect and over time, a relationship. Nowadays too many lawmakers think only short-term, how to win in the moment, without thinking about the repercussions down the line.

Reagan persuaded Tip to work with him on a procedural level. Persuasion is like an onion, with layers that you can peel back. The president never could have persuaded Tip to take his position. The two most powerful men in the country went back and forth and found common ground by peeling back each one of these things, substantive and procedural. Layer by layer, they put a deal together.

This is the beauty of good legislating: it's complicated and extremely intricate. Looking at it just one-dimensionally or even two-dimensionally would be to miss the whole thing. It's essential to see and appreciate the nuances. Both Tip and President Reagan really understood that. The two old-school Irishmen had remarkable chemistry, which allowed them to work together through those layers. Tip told Matthews that "despite our various disagreements in the House, we were always friends after six o'clock and on weekends.

"[Reagan] seemed to like that formulation, and over the next six years he would often begin our telephone discussions by saying, 'Hello, Tip, is it after six o'clock?'

"'Absolutely, Mr. President,' I would respond."[7]

Their chemistry and mutual respect was such that when the tax cuts needed to be rolled back and Republican House members pulled away from Reagan, Tip admonished them about their "debt and duty" to their leader. Politically, the Speaker could have let Reagan fall on his own sword, but Tip didn't let that happen. We can't imagine a Republican Speaker today chewing out Democrats for not standing with their president. It's mind-boggling how much things have changed.

There's a long tradition to this kind of camaraderie that keeps government up and running. The Founding Fathers "knew one another personally," Joseph J. Ellis writes, "meaning that they broke bread together, sat together at countless meetings, corresponded with one another about private as well as public matters." Reminding us that we have always been a nation of men and women, he continues:

Politics, even at the highest level in the early republic, remained a face-to-face affair in which the contestants, even those who were locked in political battles to the death, were forced to negotiate the emotional affinities and shared intimacies produced by frequent personal interaction.[8]

Legislative leadership is about relationships as much as it is about politics. In fact, they're often one and the same thing. It usually just starts with two people and a conversation—and from there everything and everyone pours in, and sometimes it becomes law of the land. But without that original catalyst—sparked by good chemistry—it never has a chance to get off the ground.

CHAPTER SEVEN

The 50–50 Senate

AFTER the 2000 election, while the lawyers invaded Florida and the country tried to sort out who would be the forty-third president of the United States, we had our own crisis up on Capitol Hill. The Senate was tied, dead even, 50–50—unprecedented in the history of our nation.

It had been tied 37–37 once before, during the Great Senate Deadlock of 1881. The special session back then, just to nominate cabinet members and federal appointees—which should have taken a few days—ended up lasting eleven weeks. With a disputed election and Clinton's impeachment ordeal still fresh in everyone's mind, we just couldn't afford another constitutional crisis on our hands. There was no way the American people would stomach it.

On December 12 the Supreme Court ruled in favor of Bush-Cheney, giving the Republicans the White House and a de facto majority in the Senate. (Constitutionally, the vice president is the Senate's tiebreaking vote.) However, the Court's decision didn't make it any easier for us to figure out how to divvy up the money, the committees, the chairmanships—all the workings of the Senate that often operate based on a single principle: who's in the majority and who's in the minority. As Senate leaders, we had to come up with a new agreement, mostly from scratch, in the face of mounting pressure, minimal guidance, and some irate caucus members on each side.

TRENT: Looking back on it, it was all a little audacious on our parts. Tom and I agreed to split the money and committees evenly, with the Republicans getting the chairmanships because we had the tiebreaking vote. The power-sharing agreement we devised gave equal numbers of members on the committee and we split the budget equally, except the Republican chairman would have a little kicker for office expenses and a small staff.

It all came down primarily to the committees and how to organize them; that's where all the money goes, so that's where all the power is. It wasn't each committee deciding for itself; *we* were deciding for them, essentially telling them how to organize, which was obviously a controversial thing to do.

The Republican caucus met in the Old Senate Chamber of the Capitol, where I presented the deal to my colleagues, assuming that they understood the facts of the situation as I did. It seems that I misjudged them. In fact, just about all hell broke loose. Some of my best friends, including Phil Gramm, and even my whip, Don Nickles, were just enraged, arguing that Tom had taken me to the cleaners. Passions were high and things got quite intense. Mainly, some of the caucus revolted because they didn't want to split the money evenly—an indefensible position, in my view.

I made a deal with Tom that I thought was fair and reflected the reality of the situation. I sat there listening to the Republicans debate—I was just about wiped out by that point—thinking that if the conference didn't accept the deal, there was going to be a vote of no confidence and I would have to step aside as leader.

The turning point was when Pat Roberts of Kansas—not someone who was always my ally or much of an aisle crosser—stood up amid the rancor and shut it down. "Guys, guys!" he yelled. "What are you talking about? It's *fifty–fifty*. It may not be perfect, but Trent did the best he could. Now let's get to work." It just changed the atmosphere on a dime. Others got up and spoke in support of me and the deal, putting the genie back in the bottle. Roberts just stopped the train on its tracks and the Republicans finally came around.

I saw Harry Reid on the floor the next day. Harry has always been a perceptive guy, and he took a look at me and said, "Jeez, this must've have been hard for you. You don't look good." I'm sure I didn't, and I hadn't been sleeping too well. Part of it was the atmosphere. It was a trying eighteen months: the impeachment trial, the contested election, then the deadlock. I think my face probably reflected not just how I felt but how the country was feeling at the time.

Strange as it sounds, I had a premonition at the time that the Republicans weren't going to be in the majority a long time. I sensed we had a short window, and if we didn't find a way to come to an agreement, then we were going to be tangled up for three or four months. The major window of opportunity in every Congress,

especially with a new president, is that first six months.
The Republicans were in the White House, so I knew we
were going to get the tax cuts and pass No Child Left
Behind. I wanted to get the Senate agreement out of the
way and get going because I felt like time was short. As it
turned out, I was right. In fact, we kept the majority all
of five months.

TOM: We were each accused of making a deal under
    everyone's noses. I had to fend off Democrats who didn't
    think I was partisan enough. I was criticized for making
    agreements with Trent before my caucus felt like they
    had adequately vetted the terms. There was a lot of "We
    should've been told more about this" and "Why weren't
    we consulted on this?" The best way to explain it is that
    Trent got criticized for the deal he made, while I got
    criticized for making a deal at all.

    Another thing that contributed to the environment
    and the urgency: we had just had a tumultuous
    presidential contest that took thirty-six days to resolve
    and even then not to the satisfaction of half the country.
    It was also not that long after the impeachment trial, and
    the country was just exhausted.

    A lot of the Democrats felt the longer they held out,
    the better the deal we were going to get. Some of them
    resented how quickly Trent and I moved—though,
    considering the new session was approaching, it wasn't
    really that quick at all. Trent and I would talk openly
    about how we were going to take heat, but the well of
    the Senate was a poisonous place and we had to get on
    with running the country. The pushback comes with the

territory. Somebody has a question, somebody has a complaint, and of course, somebody would always like to have your job.

Leaders needed to step in, and I think our colleagues recognized that even though this is not how they would cut the deal, we needed to get the job done. In every situation where we had to cut deals or make arrangements, somebody was going to be unhappy. Too often, people want to make the perfect the enemy of the good.

It had been a mean election in 2000, with several really close, acrimonious races and a few recounts. We just went through one crucible, and a huge crucible lay ten months ahead. We look back and we minimize some of this in the face of what happened the next year and in the coming decade, but at the time it was tough. Trent and I both muscled through and endured; we came out of it with the support of our conferences, as well as a stronger bond with each other.

In May 2001, Republican senator Jim Jeffords of Vermont turned the Senate upside down by switching parties. He registered as an Independent but would caucus with the Democrats. The move flipped the Senate, made Tom majority leader, and gave the Democrats chairmanships and majorities on all the committees. It's one thing to lose in an election, but to lose when someone walks across the aisle—that's much harder to swallow.

In the Senate, the majority is the whole ball game. Luring someone to switch parties involves quite a few carrots, and we each worked Jeffords—and his family—for weeks. After all the 50–50 haggling, Jeffords inverted the Senate in one swoop. To the rest of the political world it was a shock, but we both were involved with the machinations of it for some time. It was a big deal when it finally happened, but neither of us was surprised.

TOM: Trent and I had each worked Jeffords for weeks before his decision. We offered Jim a chairmanship—the Committee on Environment and Public Works—which Harry Reid voluntarily relinquished. Jim told me that one of the factors influencing his switch concerned President Bush. He criticized Bush quite a bit on education, which the president did not like. Perhaps as retaliation, the president didn't invite Jim to an important teacher event at the White House, one that included many teachers from his state. Jim felt considerably insulted by the snub. But luring him over did take some cajoling.

TRENT: Tom and Harry Reid worked him for weeks. At some point I picked up what was going on and did everything I could to talk him out of it, including frequently talking to his wife and children. Jeffords, John Ashcroft, Larry Craig, and I had formed a barbershop quartet, the Singing Senators—partly in order to keep Jim in the fold. Though we weren't ideologically aligned, Jim and I had a good relationship. We entered the Senate together in 1989 from the House and sat in the back row—along with other "not-ready-for-prime-time" senators. But he was from Vermont, not a conservative bulwark, and didn't share a lot of the Republican base positions.

Jeffords's wife was a real liberal Democrat—socialist, even. But because of that quartet and spending some time together, she shifted. There was a trip that she really thought was going to be miserable—traveling with three right-wing Republicans and their wives—but she just thoroughly enjoyed it. The wives adopted her, took her under their wing. The Jeffords family did not want him to switch and I tried to utilize them as much as I could.

Another thing is that during the No Child Left Behind debate, before we brought it to the floor, Ted Kennedy was just turning Jeffords into a pretzel in my office. When we started moving it to the floor, I nudged Jim aside, who was the chairman, and had Judd Gregg manage it on the floor. Jim was the chairman of the committee and it was his pet issue, so that likely angered him as well.

But the Democrats gave him a sweet deal, they gave him the kitchen sink: money, earmarks, a chairmanship. Mostly, the Republicans took it with grace, because what choice did we have? But it was monumental.

It was also disorienting for me for a short time. I had been majority leader for six and a half years at that point; some things were just second nature to me. Soon after the switch, I found out what the schedule was going to be, so I talked to the president about it. Noticing that I did that, Tom came over to gently remind me that he was majority leader, so that would be his job from now on.

CHAPTER EIGHT

Roadblocks to Chemistry

HISTORIAN Joseph J. Ellis describes how John Adams, in discussing those early years of the first Continental Congress later in his life, insisted that "no true history of that fateful time would ever be written . . . because the most important conversations occurred 'out of doors' in local taverns and coffee-houses."[1] Both that Second Continental Congress and the Constitutional Convention a few years later would have been enormously different if the members were heading home every weekend. (Of course, distance and transportation made that impossible.)

History shows that as much got done outside of that room in Independence Hall as inside of it. The men were stuck there with few distractions and a single imperative: Create a country from scratch. They did it during business hours and leisure hours, and formed relationships that did as much to form the nation as the work itself did.

Times have changed enormously, but the fact remains: the U.S. government is made up of people, and the chemistry among them and the relationships between them are absolutely critical parts of the institution. Those interactions are part and parcel of politics, and we undervalue them at our peril. The ability of people to feel comfortable with each other is an indispensable part of all workplaces, especially a place like Congress where each member's objectives are different, often clashing. A handful of key forces have hurt the chemistry in modern-day Washington and prevented relationships from forming—and the first has to do with the capital city itself.

Tom likes to emphasize that the thing that has had the most negative impact on chemistry in Washington is the airplane. This is not confined to D.C., of course: there has been a 900 percent increase in airplane flights over the past fifty years.[2] Flying in and out of town has become regular practice in a society accustomed to the convenience. Airplanes have stepped up the speed of business, shrunken the world, and allowed for greater flexibility in work and leisure. But it has been an absolutely toxic influence on Washington. The ubiquity of the airplane has turned the capital into a transient city, its comings and goings more reminiscent of a convention center than the seat of the nation's government.

Legislators nowadays spend very little time in Washington, but even worse in some ways is the fact that this has become a peculiar badge of honor. The current House majority leader and Tom's own congresswoman from South Dakota are just two members of Congress who brag that they sleep on the sofas in their offices. Bizarrely, this has become a common point of pride. We assume it's a way to show how un-Washington they are, unsullied by Beltway culture. Besides being empty posturing, it's detrimental to the work that needs to be done. It also doesn't really make any sense. Would Wall Street brokers argue they were untainted away from New York? Would tech experts claim they were purer for living outside Silicon Valley? It's preposterous, frankly.

Today there is an almost visceral antipathy toward Washington among the average American, and politicians play to that. It starts with an either/or mentality: being part of Washington means you're part of the problem. During the 2004 Senate campaign, John Thune produced attack ads on Tom that used audio of Tom saying "I'm a D.C. resident" twice in a thirty-second ad. It was an effort to separate Tom from his fellow South Dakotans and it was effective: Tom lost his Senate seat on the strength of those attacks. He and his wife had just purchased a new home, and Thune made that an issue. Washington real estate is costly, and the house was much more expensive than a typical South Dakotan would have been able to afford. A big house in Washington—whether you want it to or not—can be turned into a symbol of what your preferences are, where your heart is, and where your head is.

Residency has become an increasingly common attack point, a vulnerable spot for any representative living in D.C. Senators Mary Landrieu and Pat Roberts most recently had to fend off similar attacks in the last election. Whether it's fair or not seems to be beside the point. Once you're painted with that economic and cultural brush, it's tough to shake it off. It's unfortunate, because so much can be gained by legislators living in and around the D.C. area. But it has become politically dangerous to do so.

We have reached a point where, misguidedly, Washington, D.C., itself gets framed as the enemy. You see it all the time: someone's accused of having "gone Washington" or something else is knocked as being "inside the Beltway." Perpetual candidates try to demonstrate that they're not part of the problem by having as little to do with Washington as possible. It's as though there were a virus in the air or the culture of "insiders" might rub off on you like in a zombie movie.

It has become a sticky message for a reason: people believe it. The familiar refrain is that our problems in government are due to the insiders; we need new people, untainted outsiders, to get in there and clear the place out. But of course you need insiders; they're the ones who know how things work because they have been down these roads before.

Far too many lawmakers never move their families here because then they can campaign on how they've somehow remained real or untainted. But here's the problem: Congress was in session 112 days in 2014—about 9 days a month. (It's actually less, because they're flying in on day one and out on day nine.) That means 21 days they're somewhere else; it has become impractical for members to have their families here.

So it's not just an aversion to Washington; it comes down to the hard fact of where lawmakers spend most of their time. If they're home from Thursday to Monday night, then they can be in their states or districts with their families and their constituents at least four days a week. But the job is getting short shrift.

The impractical way Congress is scheduled—crunching everything into a Tuesday-to-Thursday window—exacerbates the problem and feeds into it. It's a three-day workweek where every vote and meeting is jammed into the middle of the week. As Tom likes to say, we can't govern only on Wednesdays; there's no time to work on complex legislation and to build relationships. Congressmen are focused on when they can leave on Thursday and jump on a plane. Everyone is heading to the airport, kids and wives don't know each other, and as we have learned in the age of the Internet, it's much easier to attack someone you don't know or don't have to face.

Additionally, all bills need to pass through both houses, but the Senate and the House aren't even there at the same time:

each is in and out over different two-week periods. When Trent was Senate majority leader, he used to say to House leader Dick Armey, "Our bills are passing like ships in the night." And it has gotten worse.

The transience of the lawmakers themselves, which the airplane has made all too easy, has created a corrosive new normal. D.C. is regarded as a poisonous environment, which has *made* it a poisonous environment. The chemistry among our lawmakers is toxic due in large part to the fact that nobody knows each other. As former senator John Breaux, Trent's business partner, has said, "It's difficult to stab someone in the back in the morning when you had dinner with them the night before."[3] Worse, there's no time for legislators to even try to get to know each other. They know the cable news versions of each other or what they hear through partisan sources.

Even the private Senate dining room has been phased out. It was a small room across the hall where only senators could dine; a place for informal, open, and honest conservation. Trent ate lunch there just about every day with fellow senators, everyone from Pat Moynihan to Jesse Helms. In that private dining room everybody sat family-style, at two tables, Republicans and Democrats together to an extent. It would be opened up for a couple of hours in the afternoons, and it had a practical impact: most senators aren't going to take an hour off just to meet somewhere and have a glass of wine, but the Senate dining room was right there: you couldn't get any more convenient than that.

It was a small thing, but those environmental features help build chemistry. When Apple CEO Steve Jobs was designing the new Pixar building, he insisted that all the bathrooms be located in one part of the complex: it would force those from different departments to interact, if only briefly.[4] Jobs understood that those interactions were incredibly productive, creative, and useful.

It seems like nowadays, when senators are in Washington only three and a half days, the private dining room would be that much more important. When else are they going to even see each other? Where are they going on days when they're in town but not in session?

We both understand the need to go back home. Tom and his wife kept an apartment in Sioux Falls before taking over his childhood home in Aberdeen. Trent knew he had to maintain a home in Pascagoula or his neighbors and high school classmates would say, *Oh, he's gone Washington; he's not with us anymore.* It was a place he went to recharge his batteries, sit in his wooden rocker, and listen to the wave action on the Gulf; it was all very rejuvenating. But neither of us forgot where our job was.

We understand why constituents want their representatives to stay connected to their district or state. But if they don't spend most of their time in D.C.—except for extended recesses like in August—they're not legislating. It's appearance versus reality, perception versus productivity. We'd often spend most of Monday getting ready for the week, including part of Friday. There are hundreds of pages of reading, research, and preparation involved in being an engaged legislator. If you're showing up on Tuesday, then you're not prepared. It's that simple.

"America is a full-time nation," Representative Bob Livingston has said, "and it demands a full-time Congress." Considering their extensive and central role in running the country, it's amazing how rarely Congress meets. For most of our country's history, you lived here because you worked here and the bulk of your time was spent here. But that has become an outdated notion.

The transient culture has led to the death of community among lawmakers in Washington. In the early nineties, in Annandale, Virginia, Trent lived on the same street as Representatives Jerry Huckaby, Billy Tauzin, John Breaux—all Louisiana Democrats— and Mike DeWine, a Republican senator from Ohio; they and the Lotts all lived within two blocks of each other. Their spouses were friends; their kids went to the same schools and played together in the neighborhood. Families all over America naturally bond under these circumstances, and members of Congress are no different. That just does not happen today: the airplane, the schedule, and the "Beltway bogeyman" have made it impossible.

The two of us now have infinitely better chemistry than we had twenty years ago, when we hardly knew each other. Over time, we developed an affection and friendship that started to have *business* repercussions. It's not just congeniality; it's business. Some may argue that we're out of government—out of the "fire," as it were—but if you go back and watch those old Sunday shows like *Meet the Press*, our dynamic hasn't really changed.

The three-day workweek, the ease of travel, the media slug-fest: all of these have a corrosive effect on working relationships. They strip away the fellowship that existed in the old days when lawmakers played poker and drank whiskey and their spouses knew each other. That fellowship created an abundance of chem-istry that affected their work in a positive way. Unfortunately, today's fast-tracked, extraordinarily intense world isn't conducive to creating that kind of chemistry. But we have to figure out how to restore it. We agree that it's undoubtedly the biggest problem facing the Senate today.

CHAPTER NINE

Experience and Transparency

"Five years is a long time to carry a grudge, Seab."

"Maybe for a young fellow like you. In my table of time, it happened just like yesterday."

—ADVISE AND CONSENT (1962)

A FTER a speech recently, during the Q&A, an audience member asked Trent, "Shouldn't we just throw these bums out and get completely different people?" It's a common sentiment, one we've both heard before. "Not at all," Trent replied. "It's actually the opposite. We've got a lot more people in Congress now that have never been there. The ones really causing problems are the *newer* members."

It's not as punchy as "Throw the bums out!" but it's true. No continuity means no relationships, no understanding of history, and no recognition that you will be on the other side at some point. When the turnover in Congress is so high, the memories stay short and the big picture gets lost.

"It's not just that the extreme wings of both parties are emboldened," CNN's Dana Bash recently argued. "It is also about experience—or lack thereof, in that art of legislating— knowing what it means to give a little to get a little."[1] The throw-the-bums-out mentality clouds a lot of that common sense.

Representatives are now sent to Washington and told to "stand their ground." This digging in of heels has hobbled the legislative body; men and women told not to give an inch have paralyzed government. You have to approach legislating with two things in mind: there are times when you stand your ground and times when you find common ground. The fact is that governing is not the same as campaigning. To govern, you have to get beyond empty rhetoric and speeches. You have to find common ground to move the country forward. As Walter Isaacson notes in the introduction to his book *Profiles in Leadership: Historians on the Elusive Quality of Greatness*, "the greatest challenge of leadership is to know when to be flexible and pragmatic, on the one hand, and when it is, instead, a moment to stand firm on principle and clarity of vision."[2] That balance is so crucial, and our best leaders have exemplified it.

Standing your ground does very little for the whole. In most instances it looks an awful lot like obstruction. You might have been elected by half the people, but you're there to serve all of them. "There's a lot more of the view that compromise is a sign of weakness," former Senate majority leader George Mitchell, one of Tom's mentors, has observed, "and that sticking to your position is a sign of strength and conviction, and I think that loses sight of what real strength is, what real conviction is, and what a real desire to get things done is."[3]

And it's rarely sexy, nor does it make for good copy (or a good political ad) for legislators to compromise. Isaacson memorably wrote, Henry Clay notwithstanding, "Compromisers may not make great heroes, but they do make great democracies."[4] Unfortunately, compromising has been getting used *against* legislators in primaries lately—evidence of them "selling out" the party. So the feedback loop continues and the sides grow further apart.

"The change, then, isn't that Americans today are necessarily more polarized, or are less inclined [to] compromise," Marc

Dunkelman argues in *The Vanishing Neighbor*. "It's that those on the other side of any given issue now are not only wrong, they're almost alien."⁵ This is at the heart of the constant political battle—this demonizing of the other side. Once the opposing party is framed as an enemy, the goalposts get moved. It's not about getting things done, even things that serve your party's agenda. It's about how that happens. Now compromise or trading makes you look bad—and politically vulnerable.

As much as compromise has become a dying art, the senators who do reach across the aisle to work together don't want it known; mere communication with the other side has become bad politics. We used our hotline and back doors for a reason, but there's a level to the secrecy now that is almost absurd.

A Democratic senator recently called Tom to say he had been working with a Republican senator on changes to the Affordable Care Act. The Republican senator was deathly afraid that even the fact that they were speaking would get leaked and he'd get killed for it. He asked for Tom's advice but he kept emphasizing, "Please, keep this all confidential."

It's encouraging that that kind of conversation is taking place, and Tom was flattered to be consulted, but it's mind-boggling that lawmakers have to meet privately about a beneficial goal like that. Everybody recognizes there are changes to the ACA that have to be made. Whether it's technical or substantive, there ought to at the very least be a conversation about it. But right now there is a significant fear. Not to criticize the Republican senator for going about it this way—it's impressive that he's willing to do it at all—but it's reflective of the environment he is working in. There's a level to the secrecy that is downright destructive. Conversation itself is now dangerous. How did this happen? How do we fix such a narrow-minded outlook?

* * *

Transparency is not an all-or-nothing proposition: for it to be effective, it needs to strike a balance. The public has a right to know—honesty and candor are necessary—but the government cannot function under blinding lights. Most people understand why there are no cameras in the Pentagon, the CIA, or even the Supreme Court. When we kicked the cameras out in the evenings of President Clinton's impeachment trial, it made such a huge difference. We're convinced those evenings created a release valve that kept things decorous—and on the rails.

The reality is that most of the great debates—with the exception of *the* Great Debates—do not take place on the floor. They take place in offices and conference rooms. No Child Left Behind got passed because of meetings in the Senate library with Trent, Ted Kennedy, and a few other senators. But it's difficult to explain to those who elected you that you don't want them to see what you're up to.

The constant coverage has a real impact on how or whether senators make deals. Lawmakers are so concerned about being misquoted or being accused of "selling out" that they're reticent about making genuine offers to the media, who can twist it any way they like. It's not until the cameras are turned off that the nuts and bolts of real legislating happens. Even the most unobtrusive media, like CSPAN, has a profound impact on the way legislation has played out over the last thirty years; some of it has been positive, but there's a price to pay for that transparency. We believe it is too high a price, a situation where the operation may have been a success but the patient ended up dead.

The pushback question on less transparency is obvious: "What do you mean? You're going to say something different in the back of the cloakroom that you wouldn't say on the floor of the Senate."

Or: "You don't want your constituents to know that you're caving on a budget issue." And the answer may be yes. Blanket transparency does make it a lot harder. It's impossible to work out the details of complicated legislation on the floor of the Senate or the floor of the House. A lot of people lay the source of the tension at President Nixon's feet with Watergate, but it's more complicated than that. There are groups now whose sole purpose is to fight for more transparency, not less. They're well intended, but they seem to be missing the larger picture.

Starting in the 1980s into the 1990s there was a real push for so-called sunshine laws which let the public in on every nook and cranny of what the government is doing. We support the idea in principle; in fact, as a member of the Rules Committee, Trent pushed through a resolution in the House to televise the House floor proceedings before the Senate did it. But it affects the quality and the honesty of the debate. There's an impression that anything behind the scenes in Congress is unseemly, but it's a false proposition. The constant coverage has a real impact on how, or whether, senators make deals.

Some have managed to do it despite the pressures, and they should be commended. Republican Lamar Alexander and Democrat Charles Schumer—the number one and number two on the Rules Committee—had quiet meetings on lowering the number of nominations that the Senate has to confirm by a third. The traditional process had atrophied, so they met in private and got a deal done. It's an example of what is possible. They worked with the knowledge and the approval of their leaders—Reid and McConnell—and came up with a product. Those things snowball, and Schumer and Alexander continue to whisper back and forth to each other.

Another recent example: Democrat Barbara Boxer, a committed California liberal, has shown leadership getting a highway bill with Republican Jim Inhofe in 2013 and a water resources bill with Republican David Vitter in 2014. They set a template of what could be done. Neither one of those bills has historically been partisan, but that's the point. Why not work on these areas where they agree, just to get the ball rolling?

Through the National Democratic Institute, Tom was recently speaking abroad to a group of six to eight legislators from different parties in the Republic of Georgia and he emphasized this exact point: You need to do some small things before you get to the big things. Look for some small possibilities that could really offer some opportunities to demonstrate that all bipartisanship isn't lost. Infrastructure shouldn't be a partisan issue: everyone's for it. It's just the paying for it that causes debate. There really has to be a time where they shut the cameras off and the media doesn't become such a major factor. There's a balance that needs to be struck, and the challenge is making those calls and doing it in a way that is institutionalized.

"Strong evidence . . . suggests that people will often follow their political party even if their own independent view suggests that their party is wrong," Cass Sunstein writes.[6] This happens at the highest levels of leadership too. ". . . Any president knows that if he supports a particular policy, a lot of people will oppose it immediately, and that if the administration maintains a discreet silence, some of its preferred policies, might, ironically, get enacted."

The partisan rivalry and tension is entrenched. Some of it goes back to the first days of the Republic. After Adams won the election in 1796, Jefferson agreed to help his rival in securing a treaty with France. But rather than sending a letter, Jefferson leaked it through Madison and Benjamin Rush. Jefferson was the leader of a Republican party that didn't want him working with the administration on a treaty with France. And he was about to be Adams's vice president!

This was quite early, before parties really solidified and when "nothing like the full-blooded machinery of a modern political party system existed," writes Joseph J. Ellis.[7] Jefferson's ally James Madison understood that "Jefferson must not permit himself to be drawn in to the policy-making process of the Adams administration, lest it compromise his role as leader of the Republican opposition."[8]

We are realists about how parties will always, on a certain level, be at odds. Their identities are defined in opposition to each other, after all. Part I focused on the necessity and usefulness of that tension. Part II examined the importance of chemistry and compromise in the process. Part III will put forward the best way to ensure for all of it: leadership.

Part III

Leadership

"Public business, my son, must always be done by somebody or other. If wise men decline it, others will not; if honest men refuse it, others will not."

—JOHN ADAMS

CHAPTER TEN

In Their Own Words

ALL leaders have unique strengths that work in concert with what the people need and what the times demand. Ronald Reagan instinctively knew how to inspire the masses. At a time of low morale in the country, he tapped into something in the American psyche that no other leader was speaking to. Speaker of the House Tip O'Neill acted as a conductor of sorts, letting all his colleagues feel that they'd been heard before making his decisions. According to former aide Chris Matthews, the Speaker gave the toughest grilling to the one he knew he was going to side with, just so the loser felt he'd been heard. It was a way to pay respect to—and win respect from—those he'd beaten or overruled. Tip understood that each day brought a new battle with new allies, so he was careful about burning bridges.

As Senate majority leader and as president, Lyndon Johnson led through the force of his personality. There is a famous photograph of him invading the space of Senator Theodore F. Green, giving him the famous "Johnson Treatment." LBJ was a virtual athlete of persuasion—cajoling, carousing, threatening, whatever it took; he had a "feral magnetism," as one writer memorably put it, that allowed him to get away with it.[1] Johnson was never afraid of running roughshod over both Democrats and Republicans in order to get something done. Though his style has fallen out of favor, Johnson was one of the most valuable leaders of the twentieth century: we wouldn't have had Medicare, Medicaid, the Voting Rights and Civil Rights Acts, or many other pieces of critical social legislation were it not for him.

His successor as Senate majority leader, Mike Mansfield, was quite the opposite, leading coolly through logic and reason. He gave his colleagues freedom and opportunity—and they responded. Mansfield was also credited with bringing a "moral authority [to] Capitol Hill,"[2] something in short supply these days.

In the late 1990s Trent's former executive assistant, Susan Wells, and the secretary of the Senate, Gary Sisco, came to him with an idea. They felt that the modern history of the Senate was not getting recorded properly and they were in a position to correct that. The germ of Susan and Gary's idea evolved into the Leader's Lecture Series, in which former majority leaders and minority leaders (as well as some vice presidents and presidents) came in to the Old Senate Chamber with a simple guideline: Tell the Senate whatever they thought we needed to hear.

The Old Senate Chamber is a majestic place that breathes so much history. Entering that room is as much like going back in time as anyplace we've ever been: the red and gold canopies, the velvet valances, the smell of old mahogany. There are no windows—they wanted to keep out the noise—but there is a round skylight that beams light from above; it's almost spiritual. The amphitheater seating is like something out of ancient Rome. There, underneath that ornate coffered ceiling and those marble columns, "our predecessors wrote the laws before the Civil War," our colleague and resident historian Robert C. Byrd said. "Daniel Webster orated, Henry Clay forged compromises, and John C. Calhoun stood on principle."

The Leader's Lecture Series ended up doing two things that strong leaders naturally do: it unified and it motivated. The location itself was a testament to the past and even to nonpartisanship; the old chamber doesn't have a Republican and Democratic side, so we all just sat together.

Trent's goal was partly to just get us all in a room together, enjoy each other's companionship, and see if we could draw inspiration from previous leaders: George Mitchell, Bob Dole, Howard Baker, Gerald Ford, Robert Byrd. Each had a wealth of experience and wisdom that was both helpful and inspiring.

LEADER AS FACILITATOR: MIKE MANSFIELD

Trent invited Mike Mansfield, one of his and Tom's greatest influences, to inaugurate the Leader's Lecture Series in 1998. Mansfield took over the Senate in 1961, at a time when a whole new generation of senators—like Frank Church, George McGovern, and Birch Bayh—were demanding more of a voice. The rising generation wanted more power and would not let LBJ continue to be the dominant force he had been.

Lyndon Johnson had been the most effective Senate leader in history. But when the Democratic caucus found out Johnson thought he was going to continue to run the Senate as vice president, the senators revolted. (To quiet tempers, Mansfield took the blame.) The overwhelmingly negative reaction so infuriated and humiliated Johnson that he didn't return to the Senate chamber for six months.[3] The evolution that occurred within the Democratic caucus at that time was actually a type of revolution, and Mansfield was the ideal leader for it.

Johnson was the last of his breed, in large part because circumstances would not allow for another. Mansfield understood the changes that were sweeping through the Senate and the country. But it was also his nature to lead in a vastly different way. Leaders ever since have been more in the Mansfield tradition mostly because the senators have demanded it. It's unlikely that he twisted one arm in his sixteen years in charge, the longest tenure in the Senate's history.

Mansfield let the Senate have its own head and led by making others feel empowered. He was also a courageous man who stood by principle whether or not it was politically beneficial to do so. Early on he spoke out against President Johnson's plan to bomb North Vietnam and later helped force Nixon's hand on withdrawing troops from Southeast Asia. In order to remind him of the reality of their responsibilities in Washington, Mansfield kept a card in his breast pocket with updated numbers of the U.S. dead and wounded in Vietnam.

Mansfield had the rare ability to face a room of ninety-nine others as equals, grant them the respect that their office demanded, and find a way to harness that into action. He was wise enough to lead through quiet persuasion and inclusion, which sometimes meant letting others lead. He showed respect to Republicans like Everett Dirksen by allowing them to take center stage when the occasion arose, as it did during the debates over civil rights legislation.

For the first Leader's Lecture, on March 24, 1998, Mansfield gave the speech he was planning to give on the day President Kennedy was assassinated in 1963. He ended up never giving it because of what happened in Dallas; he just quietly inserted it into the *Congressional Record.*

The speech was a call to action of sorts—to both President Kennedy and to his Senate colleagues. Before he read his speech that day to us, he quoted Laozi: "A leader is best when people barely knows he exists . . . When his work is done, his aim fulfilled, they will say: 'We did this ourselves.'"[4] It is a perfect distillation of the way a leader not only encourages and inspires but is also embodied—and lives on—within his followers.

Mansfield's speech addressed what he perceived as the ongoing gaps—both between senators and their constituents, as well as among the senators themselves, and how these holes could be mended. He said:

> *The remedy lies not in the seeking of shortcuts, not in the cracking of nonexistent whips, not in wheeling and dealing, but in an honest facing of the situation and a resolution by the Senate itself, by accommodation, by respect for one another, by mutual restraint and, as necessary, adjustments in the procedures of this body.*

One of things brought home to us that evening was the resonance of his words thirty-five years after they had been written. Now, another eighteen years after hearing them, we think they could have been written yesterday. His speech was really a call to each lawmaker, on his or her own, to create a climate that is conducive to action:

> *The constitutional authority and responsibility does not lie with the leadership. It lies with all of us individually, collectively and equally . . . [T]hat principle cannot be made to*

*prevail by the rules. It can prevail only when there is a high
degree of accommodation, mutual restraint and a measure
of courage—in spite of our weaknesses—in all of us.*[5]

Those words speak directly to his humanity. Manfield carried a modest air that seemed to betray his true stature. He was a giant who didn't act like one, nor did he need to. Biographer Don Oberdorfer wrote that Mansfield "was a man of genuine humility who rejected all pretension and claims to greatness—which, in the view of all who knew him, made him all the greater."[6]

The Senate was a much more democratic place with Mike Mansfield at its helm. At Mansfield's memorial service in 2001, Tom said that Mansfield "understood that in this body of loquaciousness there is an eloquence to simplicity, that in this place of debate there is always an opportunity for decency." Our predecessor continues to point the way forward. Mansfield often claimed that when he was gone he wanted to be forgotten. But Tom told the audience that that was unlikely. "With all due respect to my dear friend and teacher," he said, "he will never be forgotten."

LEADER AS CONCILIATOR: HOWARD BAKER

Widely admired on both sides of the aisle, former Majority Leader Howard Baker was one of the first live Republicans Trent ever met. "What really makes the Senate work—as our heroes knew profoundly—is an understanding of human nature, an appreciation of the hearts as well as the minds, the frailties as well as the strengths, of one's colleagues and one's constituents," he told us in his Leader's Lecture on July 14, 1998. It's an empathetic view and it reflects how Baker led during his time in the Senate.

As Trent said in his introduction to Baker's speech that evening, public service was in Baker's blood. Both of his parents served in the House of Representatives and he visited the Senate as a thirteen-year-old in 1939. He told us that the same ventilation system whose installation Jefferson Davis supervised in 1859, the new chamber's first year, was in use that day. We claim that the Capitol physically connects you to the past, and that's as much of an illustration of that bond as either of us can think of.

Baker was a realist and spoke eloquently to us about how the Senate is made of dedicated but in fact regular men and women. "The founders didn't require a nation of supermen to make this government and this country work, but only honorable men and women laboring honestly and diligently and creatively in their public and private capacities,"[7] he said.

Baker simply wasn't afraid of speaking his mind. He had the courage of his convictions and the courage of his platform. Even from day one. After Baker's very first speech in the Senate, his father-in-law, Republican leader Everett Dirksen, said: "Howard, perhaps in the future you should guard against speaking more clearly than you think."[8]

But Baker continued to show strength, especially against his own caucus, on issues from the Panama Canal Treaty to the AWACS sale to Saudi Arabia—issues that put him in the minority among his party. But when it was needed, he was inclusive, operating as a true consensus builder. He spent a great deal of time listening and talking with members, especially Democrats, and remaining accessible. Our current leaders could learn a great deal from the way Howard Baker made himself a channel, letting both sides work through him. "Friendly and unfailingly courteous," the *New York Times* wrote, "he was popular with lawmakers in both parties, a kind of figure almost unrecognizable on Capitol Hill today."[9] But he was no softie: Baker was known to lock competing sides in an office or conference room and refuse to release them until a compromise was reached.[10]

One focus of his Leader's Lecture was how the Senate had become more of a collection of independent parts, each with its own sophisticated operations, and less of a unit. "I herded cats," Baker told us that evening. "Trent Lott and Tom Daschle have to tame tigers." He also focused on the way politicians of the past could separate their business from their personal grievance, most famously embodied in the rivalry between John C. Calhoun and Henry Clay:

> *[Calhoun] loved Clay because Clay was like him, an accomplished politician, a man in the arena, a master of his trade, serving his convictions and his constituency just as Calhoun was doing.*
>
> *Calhoun and Clay worked together because they knew they had to. The business of their young nation was too important—and their roles in that business was too central—to allow them the luxury of petulance.*

The luxury of petulance—a great phrase. Baker understood that the battles have an endpoint. "I found myself engaged in fire-breathing, passionate debate," he admitted. "But no sooner had the final word been spoken and the last vote taken than I would usually walk to the desk of my most recent antagonist, extend a hand of friendship, and solicit his report on the next issue for the following day."

Addressing this ability to shed the battle armor and move on, Baker told us:

People may think we're crazy when we do that. Or perhaps
they think our debates are fraudulent to begin with, if we
can put our passion aside so quickly and embrace our
adversaries so readily. But we aren't crazy and we aren't
frauds. This ritual is as natural as breathing here in the
Senate, and it is as important as anything that happens in
Washington or in the country we serve, for that matter.

He had the wisdom to recognize that neither side is served
through partisan grudges, political pandering, or unwieldy attacks.
He continued:

It is what makes us America and not Bosnia. It is what
makes us the most stable government on earth, and not
another civil war waiting to happen.
    We are doing the business of the American people. We
do it every day. We have to do it with the same people
every day. And if we cannot be civil to one another, and if
we stop dealing with those with whom we disagree, or that
we don't like, we would soon stop functioning altogether.

And he lived by those words. When Tom got elected Democratic
leader in 1994, Baker reached out the very next day and asked to
come by his office. "I just want you to know that I'd like to be a
resource to you," he told Tom. "Anytime you want me to help in
some way, I want to be able to do that." To offer that to the leader
of the other party, after he had left Congress, was just the most
generous and classy thing. Baker had a very laid-back Southern
style. Even the way he dressed was uncharacteristic for a majority
leader. His easy demeanor had a way of relaxing you and making
you comfortable.

After his tenure as Republican leader, Baker would go on to serve as President Reagan's chief of staff and as U.S. ambassador to Japan. The differing skill sets involved in those three jobs reveals what an accomplished figure he was. One of his obituaries noted that perhaps no one else was ever as qualified to be president who never got to be one. James Baker said that when Howard moved on to the White House, he was "the ballast of sound ethics" during Iran-Contra and "the quintessential mediator, negotiator, and moderator."

Ironically, or perhaps notably, his political rise may have been hampered by his ability to bring sides together. One journalist noted his "talent for compromise that propelled him to the leadership of the Senate was the undoing of his ultimate ambition."[11] We think Howard understood what he was sacrificing and was fine with the choice. The Senate—and our nation—is the stronger because of it.

CHAPTER ELEVEN

The Leadership Hole

"When the leader arrives, people are full of panic, uncertain what to do and defeatist about the future. When the authentic leader has spoken, they have been given back their courage."

—WILLIAM REES-MOGG,
BRITISH JOURNALIST AND POLITICIAN

BECAUSE U.S. history has a set narrative that is repeated, taught, and studied, there is the danger of assuming that certain events were all a fait accompli, a done deal. But history, by definition, is written after the fact, once perspectives have coalesced and the big picture has become clear. In the moments themselves things are much murkier, scarier, and decidedly unknown.

The United States has needed strong leaders at crisis points in our history when the outcome was in no way assured; remarkably, we've been fortunate enough to have them. There are few things that inspire me more about public life than hearing these stories about what people did to rise to the occasion. Without the right leadership—Washington, Lincoln, both Roosevelts—our country's history would be decidedly different. Perhaps there'd be no country here at all. We rightly venerate the Declaration of Independence, but it was not a ceremonial document: it was "the most radical summons to leadership in American political history," scholar James MacGregor Burns writes.[1]

There is no way of knowing even how the *world* would be different if the right leaders hadn't stepped forward at key times.

Decisions made in the final years of World War II by a handful of men set the course for world events for the rest of the twentieth century; in many ways, they continue to shape things in the twenty-first.

"Leadership is getting people to a place that they wouldn't have gotten to already," says author and technology officer Nathan Myhrvold. "If you see a parade going down the street and you run up in front of it, they're not actually following you."[2] One purpose of leadership is to provide the kind of decision-making capacity that is imperative in times of crisis. The American way itself was saved by our leaders' ability to take charge when it mattered most.

Aaron David Miller, whose book *The End of Greatness: Why America Can't Have (and Doesn't Want) Another Great President* attempts to evaluate each U.S. president on an objective scale, believes "the greatest moments in the presidency are driven above all by crisis, and not just by your garden variety emergency. They result from calamities that are hot, combustible, and inescapable."[3] Crises do tend to bring out leaders, but this points to something difficult about our current dysfunction in Washington: it is also a crisis of leadership. It has been consistent and slow boiling enough that we may not always notice it—like the lobster that doesn't know it's being cooked.

The second purpose of leadership—to provide inspiration— is less quantifiable. Since inspiration is often measured by impact, result, and reaction, the force is usually invisible. It is tough to define, so we often look beyond words to convey it. The stone and marble tributes that fill Washington, D.C., are not just there for aesthetic reasons or as tourist attractions. They have a genuine and profound purpose: to honor our heroes and carry their inspiration to future generations. That inspiration doesn't always translate through the dates and facts of our history books, so we built the

Jefferson Memorial, the Lincoln Memorial, and the Washington Monument. "Great men have two lives," diplomat Adolf Berle said a few weeks after FDR's death, "one which occurs while they work on this earth; a second which begins at the day of their death and continues as long as their ideas and conceptions remain powerful."[4]

That inspirational element of leadership is critical, and unfortunately we've lacked it for a number of years. The country clearly yearns for it. "The need to search for the great leader to guide or even rescue us is an ancient—even primordial—impulse," Miller argues.[5] Part of strong leadership is the ability to tap into this impulse that people have. In 1980, Ronald Reagan was able to do it for an American public that had been going through a crisis of confidence; he got elected because he provided the people with an alternative view of themselves, one that inspired them.

Barack Obama's historic 2008 campaign also tapped into this impulse quite palpably, mobilizing a committed and impassioned group of voters and activists, some for the first time in their lives. Miller's book concludes that the transformative leaders have gone extinct. We don't necessarily agree, although we do think they have been endangered for quite some time. The current culture in Washington is not motivating or creating them—which, of course, makes them all the more necessary.

James MacGregor Burns, who won a Pulitzer Prize for his study of leadership, claimed it is "one of the most observed and least understood phenomena on earth."[6] The concept is often referenced but frequently misunderstood and misapplied. It is bandied about from podiums and into microphones by men and women who are savvy enough to know they *should* be talking about it. But it's merely a tool for them, not the genuine article. Many politicians tend to pay lip service to leadership without understanding or exercising it. It has become an empty buzzword; its actual embodiment has been glaringly absent.

A poisonous environment does not simply change without a powerful and undeniable catalyst, which is almost always triggered by leadership. What we know well from our times in the Congress is that culture is dictated from the top down. Ask the manager of any business, the coach of any team, or the leader of any organization: culture, both positive and negative, comes from the top.

There are simply too many separate agendas and personalities for the environment to change any other way. In addition, there are powerful crosscurrents from well-funded outside groups that have dramatically influenced Washington's political culture. It has become virtually impossible to create the chemistry necessary for effective government. Leaders are left with few of the levers of power that their predecessors depended on and used. And thus we are adrift.

We will not see any change in the current environment in the Congress until relations among our legislative leaders improve. With due respect—and much sympathy for how hard their jobs are—the chemistry among the members of the House and Senate is tied directly to the chemistry among their leaders. And right now there appears to be very little. The result is that vitriol has filled the vacuum.

When you combine the lack of relationship between the leaders in both parties and both houses with the lack of communication from the current White House, it's not surprising that our government is stalled. This isn't the sole reason why we have such dysfunction in Washington, but it's a big part of it.

Legislation can get complicated but the complexity isn't the problem; it's the simple things that matter: communication, trust, and relationships. We're not sure if there's one dynamic personality out there who can cut the Gordian knot, but we would love to see somebody try. Even the trying would get the country moving in the right direction.

We recognize that the times are different and we want to refrain from becoming "armchair leaders." Yet there are lessons to be learned and best practices that could be applied. The strong chemistry the two of us had in the Senate set the tone among the members of our respective caucuses even when things got heated, as it did during President Clinton's impeachment trial, after the election of 2000, in the aftermath of 9/11, and during the War on Terror. Leaders need a working relationship that is based on trust and a level of confidence in each other, which is nearly impossible to have if things are too political.

Of course, it didn't always work. We partook in a great many partisan debates, had to supervise some knock-down, drag-out fights, and negotiated numerous personality and philosophical conflicts among our caucuses. We had issues we didn't immediately resolve and some that didn't get resolved at all. But the chemistry was strong, the lines were open, and the system worked. And as always with these types of issues, the good chemistry started at the top.

Public faith in government has been sinking for quite some time. It seems to have reached its nadir—or at least we should all hope it has. One of many polls conducted before the midterm elections in 2014 found that just 5 percent of voters said most members of Congress deserved reelection.[7] Congress's approval a few weeks into the new session was a dismal 15 percent. A CNN poll showed that 68 percent of Americans were either "angry" or "very angry" about the direction our country was moving in. Public opinion has traversed past apathy and has been trending into anger.

We did a panel discussion last year with a few other veteran lawmakers for *Esquire* magazine regarding ways to fix Congress. Barney Frank, never afraid to speak his mind, said something interesting: he was reading a poll regarding various institutions and the public's approval of them. What he noticed was that "the institution that got the lowest rating from the people was the one that people have the most influence in shaping. So maybe the American people ought to do a little looking in the mirror."[8]

Frank's point is an astute one. In a democracy, where the public selects its leaders, there's a self-directed quality to our disappointment. We'd like our leaders to be our torchbearers, but they're also our mirrors. "We enjoy bashing Congress because they are us," says James MacGregor Burns, "they represent the good and the bad in us . . . [Congress] is supposed to rise above us and so often fails to rise above us."[9]

As they should, the low approval numbers reflect back on all of us. The fact is that Congress's approval numbers hover close to single digits, but *96.4 percent* of incumbents were reelected in 2014.[10] That should set some alarm bells off: What else with such a low approval rate would get renewed by such an overwhelming majority? The public has to take some responsibility for such a drastic discrepancy between what they say they want and what they choose to get. In Part IV we discuss the system that selects the nominees and the ways in which it is skewed, but some of the blame still falls on the average citizen.

Nevertheless, the poll numbers are enormously dispiriting. The American people perceive Congress to be ignoring areas that matter to the average citizen, whether it's social issues, infrastructure, the economy, or immigration. The view that nothing's getting done is at the heart of their antipathy and frustration with Congress. But it's also *personal*. Americans aren't better off and they want to know why.

During the 2014 midterms, when we began this book, the air in our capital was filled with as much acrimony and politicization as we've ever seen. But here's the thing: it didn't decelerate afterward. There was the predictable biennial talk of change and cooperation, but it lasted about a week. The fact is that there's just not enough incentive for elections to actually change things. It may change who is on top and who is on the bottom, but the essentials stay the same; consequently, so does the atmosphere. Despite the claims in their speeches, neither party's leadership is looking to encourage or effect actual change. They have no incentive to do so, especially since a change threatens to take their power away.

It would be unfair to paint the whole body with that brush, but it's a reality. The status quo isn't just about inertia; it's about embedded interests. Perhaps an election in the near future will produce a pivotal moment, bringing in enough new congressmen and women who say, *I got elected because the people told me we have to work together.* But until that incentive is there, they'll continue to run in circles, or, more accurately, stall in place.

It's strange that elections seem to have the opposite effect of their intention. Their purpose should be to create leaders, but we think there has been a paradigm shift. Now the campaign season serves nothing but itself; winning has gone from being the means to being the end. The American people are the victims of the self-feeding power structure, which has left them almost entirely out of the equation.

The prime focus of Senate and House leaders is political defense: protecting the caucus from taking tough votes that can be turned into thirty-second campaigns. Their concern is the endangered members of their party rather than the fate of our country. This habitual tactic is actually the opposite of leadership, since it is based on fear and selfishness rather than courage and sacrifice. And it is has brought our legislative bodies to a standstill.

The perpetual campaign—the fact that congressmen and senators are running for office year-round, always raising money, always defending (or preparing to defend) themselves from inter- or intraparty attacks—is also to blame for the lack of leaders. It has paralyzed both the development of leadership and the ability of leaders to set an agenda and move things forward. "Every day . . . is Election Day in Washington," Obama advisor David Axelrod has said.[11]

James MacGregor Burns discusses the difference between leaders and "mere power holders" and that captures the gap between what we have right now and what we need. Washington has run amok with power holders when what we need are true leaders. Burns spent his life studying leadership, and he argues it's a fundamentally moral concept because "we don't call for *good* leadership—we expect, or at least hope, that it will be good. 'Bad' leadership implies *no* leadership . . . [T]here is nothing neutral about leadership; it is valued as a moral necessity."[12]

It's not just that we're rudderless without leaders, flailing about without a plan; it's that the moral compass is missing as well. Not only are we heading in the wrong direction, we don't even have the mechanism in place to point us the right way.

Leadership requires the right mix of optimism and pragmatism. Optimism is the engine that drives progress, as well as the magnet that draws people in. But pragmatism is necessary as well: we need leaders who understand what is movable and what is not, what is changeable and what is not, what is the American way of being headstrong and what is just institutionalized madness. Then they need the initiative to do something about it. A group of men and women need to decide that they are going to provide the leadership to change things. *New York Times* columnist David Brooks recently argued, "We don't suffer from an abuse of power as much as a *nonuse* of power." Or we would argue, more accurately, power is deliberately and routinely being used for all the wrong things.

If you come to Washington without a philosophy and a set of ethics, you're certainly not going to grow them here. There's pressure, diversions, party loyalty, tensions between your district's needs and the rest of the country's. Forces press in from all sides. The leaders who succeed are those who have principles they stand for and a vision they communicate.

But beyond that, to get something done, you have to be prepared to seek consensus. It requires both inclusion and inspiration—understanding your group's needs and giving it a vision that excites, organizes, and ignites its members. That's what the U.S. Senate teaches you to do.

The Senate runs on unanimous consent: anyone can stop anything for just about any reason. Its rules and dynamics force each senator to seek consensus and compromise. Some iconoclasts in Congress these days are strong on principles but weak on articulating a vision. Being a lone wolf may play well at the polls and produce press coverage, but it does nothing for the American people.

We've seen people get into leadership positions and, all of a sudden, rise to the occasion. And the reverse is true: great leaders sometimes get ramrodded into emergencies or forced to make the big decisions, which can be a very humbling experience. That is one element of leadership, especially presidential leadership, that is uncontrollable: the times. In *Team of Rivals: The Political Genius of Abraham Lincoln*, Doris Kearns Goodwin notes that, as a young congressman from Illinois, Lincoln worried that there was no great purpose or cause by which to define himself. This is hard to fathom in hindsight, because it separates Lincoln from the defining cause of his presidency, his life, and the nineteenth century. But he just hadn't reached his "times" yet.

"More often than not," Aaron David Miller notes, "effective leaders intuit what the times make possible and then, if truly skillful, exploit and enlarge that opportunity and help shape the politics that sustain it."[13] The times create the leaders, but it goes both ways: the truly historic leaders influence the times. It is often the interaction between the two that shapes events. Could we think of Lincoln the same way had it not been for the Civil War, FDR if not for the Great Depression, George W. Bush without 9/11? Those events didn't just define their presidencies; they ended up defining the nation and the men themselves.

CHAPTER TWELVE

Trent and Tom

TRENT: I grew up a traditional Southerner. My dad was a
shipyard worker and my mother was an elementary
school teacher. I have joked with Tom that the same
people that motivated him to get into politics—Walter
Mondale, George McGovern—are the ones who helped
make me a Republican. But the fact is that I always was a
Republican, I just didn't realize it when I was younger.
People forget how Democratic the Deep South was back
in the sixties and early seventies. I hadn't even met a live
Republican until I was twenty-one years old. A guy on
the Ole Miss campus came up to me to ask if I wanted to
join the college Republicans. I was suspicious; I thought
it was some kind of subversive group.

I was always a talker, something of a performer.
Early on, my mom said I would talk to a post. And
politics, which is a type of performance, was in my blood:
I was clearly influenced by both of my grandfathers
and my uncle, whether consciously or not. I remember
attending political rallies for my uncle and handing out

push cards as a young boy. My mother's father was a justice of the peace who rode the circuit on a horse and carried a .38 shoulder holster pistol.

After I graduated Ole Miss, my mother and my favorite teacher both wanted me to become a minister of music. I decided to go to law school, which was like telling them I was going to go to hell. After I returned to Pascagoula to practice law, I became involved in the Mississippi gubernatorial campaign, where I met the local congressman from my district, a Democrat named Bill Colmer. Soon after, he asked me to come to Washington to work for him. I arrived in April 1968, and by August, I had crossed the Rubicon: I was a declared Republican. Colmer was a true Southern gentleman, never involved in race-baiting or anything distasteful, but he carried a very negative attitude about government. One thing we disagreed on was education. I've always believed there was a role for federal aid for education, mostly because my mother was a teacher. I voted with one of only four or five other Republicans in the House in the eighties for a separate Department of Education. I wrote a column and explained why I did it.

Colmer's favorite line was "Federal control follows federal funds." Four years later, he retired and I ran to succeed him, but as a member of the GOP.

I have come to believe that leaders are born not made—that visceral instinct is either there or it's not. But I also believe that you can be trained, and you can learn, to be a better leader. I'm an advocate of joining: I encourage my children, and now my grandchildren, to participate. And if you want to be in an organization, if you believe in it, you might as well strive to be the leader. That goes double for something as important as the United States Congress.

When I came to the Senate, I already had been whip in the House, which gave me a leg up in many respects. It ruffled some feathers among my colleagues when I ran against Alan Simpson for Senate whip and won (by one vote) in 1995. Some of them, including my future number two, Don Nickles, didn't like that I had jumped over some people.

There is a hierarchy and a system that needs to be respected, but I just don't believe in following it in lockstep, as in whoever is next in line automatically takes over; selecting a leader is too important to leave to things like habit or gravity. The Republican Party tends to follow this—sometimes to their detriment—in selecting a presidential nominee.

By the next year, when Bob Dole ran for president, they voted me in as their leader. I read all the books on LBJ, Howard Baker, Mansfield, Bob Dole, and I got to observe Dole and George Mitchell in person. Though I was considered something of a partisan warrior, it was Democratic leader Mike Mansfield whose style I responded to most. He led by letting others take charge on occasion, led by quiet persuasion, as opposed to LBJ's bullying approach, which I never thought was the best way.

I do believe in taking things head-on, and when I had a problem with members, Democrat or Republican, I'd go to their office and try to hash it out. As whip, I had "office hours" when members could come in and let me know issues or problems they were having. If there was a housing loan problem in their district, I'd call someone at HUD, or if there was a land issue, I'd call the Bureau of Land Management. When we would need their vote, they were a lot more willing to listen to me make my case. I also would collect mounds of information and learned how to tip certain members in my favor based on what I knew about them. For instance, I knew that if an issue had a biblical angle to it, I always could get a vote out of Robert C. Byrd.

Leadership is really about action—the determination to get up every day committed to improving your organization, whether that organization is the corner store or the United States Senate. True leadership manifests itself in the determination to get something done—against any kind of opposition, inertia, cynicism, and pressure. It'll rarely be perfect, but it's worth fighting for. My life and career are one long testimony to the fact that I believe that to be the case.

TOM: I was blessed with encouraging parents and some teachers who really made history come alive for me. I was especially drawn to American history, which I just gobbled up as a student. Those two influences, at a formative age, made all the difference in the world.

I was raised Catholic and I was in sixth grade when John Kennedy got elected—the first Catholic in the White House. One of the nuns at our school brought a black-and-white television set into the classroom so we could watch his inauguration. In 1961 that was a big deal, almost unheard-of at the time.

I had two great fears growing up—people and
heights—and I was determined to get rid of both. I
would stand on a ladder and look down, then I would
move farther and farther up until I had reached the top.
And I would actually practice having conversations with
people, just so I could get through one. It worked: asking
questions to invented people built up my confidence.
Ultimately, I'd like to think I overcame both fears: I
became a pilot and then a politician.

In 1972, while in the Air Force, I was serendipitously
stationed in Nebraska, an important primary state for
George McGovern in that election. He was an inspiring
figure to a lot of young men of my generation and I
decided to volunteer for his campaign. There was a
congressman from South Dakota named Jim Abourezk, a
surrogate for McGovern, whom I picked up a couple
times at the airport. He invited me to work on his
upcoming Senate campaign, which just sounded like such
an enticing opportunity. After he was elected to the
Senate, he asked me to handle all his defense issues and
foreign affairs. Jim was so generous, letting me come
back to South Dakota and serve as the first congressional
district director, which opened up my world and put me
in a position to get to know people. I had no network at
all when I started. He decided to serve only one term but
convinced me to run for an open House seat in South
Dakota, which I did. I got elected at age thirty by the
skin of my teeth: 139 votes.

I'm less sure that leaders are purely born, as Trent
maintains. Some of it is genetic and there are indeed
natural leaders and followers. There is undoubtedly a

comfort level that comes with leadership and some wear
it more naturally than others. But sometimes followers
have the capacity to become leaders if the right instincts
are drawn out. They may not realize it until that happens.

James MacGregor Burns writes that "leadership is
fired in the forge of ambition and opportunity,"[1] and I like
to believe that was true for me. Timing was a big factor in
my rise to Senate leadership. Trying to run earlier—
against an institution like Robert C. Byrd—would've been
crazy, but George Mitchell's retirement in 1995 brought an
open seat. I ran and ended up again squeaking by, beating
Chris Dodd for minority leader by a single vote. Chris
later became one of my closest friends in the Senate. He
once very kindly asserted that the Senate had made the
right choice. Coming from him, it meant a great deal.

A big motivator for me was that South Dakota was a
small state—one congressman, two senators, our
governor is never able to get any national traction; it
could benefit enormously from being on the national
stage. Seeing that opportunity, I went for it. I used to say
that I wanted to put South Dakota's agenda on the
national agenda. It was a campaign slogan but I meant it.

Like Mitchell, I tried to lead through inclusiveness.
Giving people a sense of ownership over their choices by
including them in the process is really the most effective
way to get them on board. People need to understand
what the vision is, what the thinking is behind your
decisions, and what their roles are and why.

Some leaders believe you shouldn't share information, because it is power. But I always thought that
the reverse was true: when information is shared, its

impact is multiplied. I took prodigious notes about every Democratic senator and made sure they never had to tell me twice about what mattered to them. I'd then bring it back up when I talked to them or, frankly, when I needed them on something. It was a form of horse-trading, but it also was persuasion.

There are times when you have to be strong and resolute, but that doesn't mean bullying. Bullying was just not my style; in fact, trying to bully a senator is a hard day's work. It's better to put the emphasis on inclusion, good information, and building bonds. Being a good leader requires you to not just respect people but to genuinely like them. Personal affection is an engine, a balm, and a catalyst in all arenas, politics included.

I always admired how Trent was such a keen political judge of circumstance. He could reach out not just to his own caucus but also to the Democrats and get a sense of which way the winds blew—even more than I could. You have to be a bit of a fortune-teller and a people reader. Obviously you always want to do the right thing, but timing and how you *frame* what the right thing is are all a part of that leadership calculation.

CHAPTER THIRTEEN

The Impeachment of William Jefferson Clinton

O NE of the biggest crucibles that the two of us—and the country—went through was President Clinton's Senate impeachment trial in January and February of 1999. The previous December, four articles of impeachment were brought to the House of Representatives, where the entire proceeding devolved into a circus. When it was over, two articles—perjury and obstruction of justice—were handed over to the Senate. It was our constitutional duty to decide whether or not we should remove the president from office. We were in a unique and historically weighty position. Robert Caro writes, "The House could accuse; only the Senate could judge, only the Senate convict."[1] All eyes were upon us. We also saw the moment as an opportunity to bring some dignity back to the U.S. Capitol.

> TRENT: Watching the House proceedings of President
> Clinton's impeachment was a low point for me as a
> lawmaker. Not just in terms of the president, whom
> everyone agreed had committed a "moral lapse"—in
> the words of former senator Dale Bumpers—but the

indignity with which the House of Representatives had handled it all. The American public seemed to agree: for all the outrage over his behavior, President Clinton's approval numbers actually increased after being impeached in the House. Democrats even gained five seats in the midterm elections that year. Of course the president had acted inappropriately—had sullied the office, in my opinion—but the House of Representatives had handled it all extremely poorly. They embarrassed themselves by playing politics with the issue. After two articles of impeachment passed in the House the weekend before Christmas, I called Tom on his cell phone while he was out doing errands.

"All right, it's in our lap now," I told him. "I don't wish we had to do this, but we do. And I think it's important to do it in the right way."

Tom replied as I would learn he always does when he's on the same page. "I couldn't agree more," he said.

I had been a young member of the House when President Nixon resigned in order to avoid impeachment. Almost twenty-five years had passed, but my memories of it all came back fierce during those weeks. Once again I was worried that the presidency itself would be damaged, perhaps irreparably. Tom and I both acutely felt the burden of history and our constitutional responsibility. Deciding on whether or not to remove a sitting president was a weighty proposition, and we agreed that it was up to us to depoliticize the experience to the greatest degree possible. That first phone call immediately framed the tone for the rest of our interactions during the trial. It was the beginning of a developing chemistry between the two of us that served us well throughout those tumultuous years.

I wanted to make sure that our system was preserved, that the American people would feel that we did the job that was required of us by the Constitution, and that we had not done damage to the fabric of the government and, by extension, the country. During the early haggling over process somebody in the Senate shouted out, "*We're* not on trial here!"

"Yes we are," I replied.

TOM: The impeachment trial in the Senate was perhaps the most intense thing I had experienced up to then as leader. It was not something that Trent or I wanted to deal with, but it had been thrust upon us. I couldn't help but wonder just how this was going to be perceived, not only in our country, but also by the rest of the world.

In that first call, we spoke about needing to reset the tone and how we were going to proceed. There were two things at work: how the Senate was going to vote, but also the process of reaching that vote. Both needed to be above reproach. Our chemistry strengthened as we talked it through, and we developed a mutual respect for each other along the way. The pressure from our respective caucuses was formidable, nearly overwhelming at times. Neither of us had an easy task; perhaps our initial bond came from recognizing what the other was going through. No one else but the two of us really knew.

As Democratic leader, I felt I needed to fend off some in the White House who, at times, appeared to want to utilize me and my staff for their defense. I resisted showing

visible support, including refusing to appear on the White
House South Lawn for a joint press conference after
the House impeachment vote. It was tough to shut the
president out—we'd had a close relationship until then—
but I had to remain impartial. I had to make sure the
message was conveyed that nothing about the Senate
trial was going to be managed from the White House.
The Senate was an independent entity and operated
as a coequal branch; our democracy depended on the
separation and balance between the two. It was important
that I draw a strong line in the sand with regard to our
objectivity and independence. Despite White House
attempts, including Clinton's misguided plan early on to get
thirty-four Senate Democrats to sign a pledge to vote
against conviction, I nixed any orchestrated effort.

The media attempted to frame it as one, but
Clinton's trial was never simply a partisan fight. Many
Democratic senators were just livid with the president;
some felt betrayed and wanted retribution. Senators like
Joe Lieberman and Robert Byrd went to the floor and
spoke very critically of the president. Some of us had
been given personal assurances from Clinton that the
accusations were not true. The president's betrayal cast a
wide net, and many of us were ensnared in it.

For the second time in the history of the United States, Articles of
Impeachment for the chief executive were being brought to the
Senate. The country was watching, the world was paying attention, and history was going to judge us on how we handled it. We
had to show that the system worked, that *justice* and *impartiality*
were not just empty terms.

Since our only precedent came from Andrew Johnson's seven-week Senate trial in 1868, we were flying nearly blind. We both went back to study the history in order to glean any direction, but Johnson's trial was a mess. Johnson had no vice president at the time, so the president pro tem of the Senate, Benjamin Wade—a vocal force for impeachment and a confirmed radical—was next in line to replace him. Historians argue that President Johnson was likely saved by a Senate that didn't want to put Wade in charge of the country. Nevertheless, Johnson avoided removal by the skin of his teeth—a single vote. We tried to retain the tradition and precedent set by the Johnson trial, but we were clearly dealing with an entirely different beast.

We asked Joe Lieberman and Slade Gorton, two thoughtful and experienced senators with legal backgrounds, to put together a proposal for an expedited process. They came back to us with a plan that did not include a full trial with witnesses, which the Republicans had been angling for. There was simply no need for more witness testimony; the thousands of hours of testimony already recorded were more than sufficient. Witnesses could serve no extra purpose outside of theater, which we were consciously trying to avoid. When Trent brought the proposal to the Republican conference, there was nearly a riot; some of his closest lieutenants, including Phil Gramm and Rick Santorum, were outraged. They claimed the plan gave short shrift to our duty, insulted the House managers, and let the president off too easily.

Rather than trying to ram it down their throats, Trent pulled back. He was ahead of his conference—something a leader needs to be conscious of—and the better part of valor was not trying to push it through. Some colleagues wanted testimony in the well from Betty Currie, Clinton's secretary, and Monica Lewinsky.

From day one we agreed that wasn't going to happen. We were not going to demean the institution by talking about a stained blue dress in the well of the Senate.

On that first day, January 7, 1999, after reading the charges and signing in as jurors, we had to immediately adjourn: we hadn't yet figured out how to proceed. The senators agreed to head down the hall and up to the second floor to a joint caucus in the historic Old Senate Chamber. Enough of us felt we had to discuss the matter away from the cameras and reporters, as it was an instance where transparency was just making it all the more difficult to proceed.

The Old Senate Chamber—the room had since been restored to its pre–Civil War appearance—is a neoclassical marvel. Underneath that magnificent half dome, among the marble columns, that gilded eagle, the famous Peale portrait of General Washington—we were hoping to be inspired by the solemnity of the room, the history of what had taken place there, and the matter before us. Senator Danny Akaka opened with a prayer, an invocation in effect: "Heavenly Father, we are in trouble and we need your help. We've come to a point where we don't know what to do."

Then Senator Robert Byrd gave a brief (in name only) on the history and our constitutional responsibility: "The White House has sullied itself," Byrd said. "The House has fallen into the black pit of partisan self-indulgence. The Senate is teetering on the brink of that same black pit . . . I implore us all to endeavor to lift our eyes to higher things. We can perform some much needed healing on the body politic."[2]

That meeting was the first indication that we were going to do as much as we could to reduce the partisan tension that was in danger of seeping in from the House of Representatives. In the two-hour discussion that followed, Senators Ted Kennedy and Phil Gramm, as philosophically opposed a pair of senators as you'll ever meet, each made recommendations that sounded awfully similar. We essentially combined the two and the Senate unanimously approved their plan.

Chief Justice William Rehnquist, seventy-four at the time and not in pristine health, presided over the trial. His presence helped to elevate the tone and keep the atmosphere decorous. The chief justice had a dignity about him that just commanded attention, as did the symbolic weight of his robe with those custom gold bars across the sleeves—though he was not afraid to inject some wry humor into the proceedings to break the tension.

Trent would say, "I think the Senate is ready for recess."

"No," the chief justice would deadpan. "I don't think we are." And we'd go on.

During some of the longer recesses, the chief justice even had a poker game going with some of the clerks, cash on the table. The sergeant at arms respectfully told them to put their money away.

Although history has treated Clinton's acquittal as a fait accompli, it was not at all predictable to those of us in the center of it what was going to happen, especially early on. We both had to fend off a great deal of pressure from our respective caucuses: there was a lot of internal turmoil as people tried to wrestle procedurally, personally, and legally with the president's actions.

The framers of the Constitution required that impeachment merit the vague standard of "high crimes and misdemeanors," words added by George Mason, who used "a seventeenth-century phrase that was already archaic in 1787 and has grown more opaque since," according to historian David O. Stewart.[3] Alexander

Hamilton attempted in *The Federalist Papers* to clarify by defining the impeachable act as one that emanated "from the abuse or violation of some public trust." But mores and values had shifted considerably in over two centuries. It was left to each individual senator's conscience and reasoning to determine if Clinton's actions applied. There was a great deal of introspection, a heightened level of tension, and a degree of anxiety among us all about how it would play out.

As the trial unfolded, Tom was able to pull back some of the angrier Democrats, like Lieberman and Byrd, from the precipice of removal. Byrd was something of a bellwether on the issue: the Republicans knew that he would be the leader of any Democratic charge to vote for the president's removal. When he released a statement announcing he was going to bring a motion to the floor to dismiss the charges, any chance of 67 votes coming together was sucked out of that chamber. The dismissal vote didn't pass but it was an indication to everyone, even to the Republican hopefuls, that the votes were simply not there.

To this day people walk up to Trent and tell him that he could have removed President Clinton from office if he had wanted to. Besides being an exaggeration of any single senator's influence, it's highly unlikely. The Senate had fifty-five Republicans at the time; even if all Republicans voted for the articles of impeachment, which they did not, twelve Democrats weren't going to join them, especially without Robert Byrd for cover. People often remember the history that suits them. But for the most part, people—including Chief Justice Rehnquist, whom Trent spoke to privately years later—felt we had handled ourselves appropriately.

We can honestly say we would not have acted differently if the vote was going to be close. Perhaps there would have been more pressure on each of us to wield partisan weapons—Tom's from the White House, Trent's from the House managers trying the case. In the end, we had to protect the dignity of the institution in the eyes of the American people and of history. It would exist long after we were gone.

The first article of impeachment, perjury, went down 55–45, with five Republicans voting for the president. On the second article, obstruction of justice, the Republicans almost got a majority of 51. It boiled down to Arlen Specter, the Republican from Pennsylvania. Trent was in the back of the chamber talking to him before his vote about the evidence and the importance of the symbolic majority. Specter then went to the floor and announced that he was voting "not proved" under Scottish law. (Despite his request to enter it that way, it was recorded as "not guilty.") Everybody started scratching their heads saying, "What is Scottish law and what does that have to do with anything?" It generated a lot of discussion and curiosity—a kind of *Where did that come from?* moment to end on.

Clinton's impeachment was a crisis for the country, but it was also the first "fire" that the two of us went through together. We established an open line of communication, and in the years that followed, that groundwork proved invaluable. Looking back, it was nearly an impossible set of circumstances, and we did our best to handle ourselves according to certain principles of fairness, respect, and dignity. After the final vote on that Friday afternoon and kind words from Senator John Chafee thanking us for guiding the Senate "through these very difficult times," we stepped in the middle of the aisle to shake hands, both relieved of the burden that we had carried all those months. The weight had been lifted, but we could not imagine the trials that lay ahead.

CHAPTER FOURTEEN

The World at Large

"North-America has become a new primary planet in the
system of the world, which while it takes its own course, in its
own orbit, must have effect on the orbit of every other planet,
and shift the common center of gravity of the whole system of
the European world . . . *[I]t is earth-born, and like a giant
ready to run its course.*"

—THOMAS POWNALL, 1780

D ESPITE the maxim, it's a myth that politics stops at the
water's edge. Vietnam, Korea, and both world wars all had
enormous political causes and implications. President Woodrow
Wilson's fight with Congress over the League of Nations was a
huge political maelstrom; in fact, it just about killed him.*

The perception that America is so clearly divided is a larger
tragedy because of what it means to the rest of the world. A
unified nation is a stronger nation; our dysfunction has elevated
itself into an international issue. We can never forget that the
world is always watching us. The lack of action and cohesion at
our highest levels sends all the wrong messages to the rest of the
world: our allies get concerned and our enemies get encouraged.

The global landscape has been shifting over time and America
has to reckon with other powers coming into their own. "Increasing

---

* Congress put up such a fight against it that he took it directly to the people.
He went on a barnstorming train tour of the country and had a massive stroke
about three weeks in, from which he never recovered.

power changes nations," Robert Kagan writes in *The World America Made*. "It changes their ambitions, their sense of themselves, and even their definition of their interests. It also has a way of bringing out qualities of character that may have been submerged or less visible when they were weaker."[1] We can't even imagine what a weakened America will do to the dynamics of the world's major players. Any predictions based on past behavior do not apply; we simply don't know how certain countries would behave if the United States wasn't stopping them, explicitly or implicitly.

Our failure to achieve collective action has very real national security implications. It seems obvious we are going to get tested, either by other countries or transnational forces. For one thing, it seems clear that Russia is testing us right now. Putin is operating based on an assumption of our present weakness, taking advantage of our internal division. He's certainly not going to be the only one.

We have both met Putin and he remains something of a wall, and something of a cipher: he struck us as steely-eyed and humorless in those settings. In fact, Tom skirted a little trouble with the Russian leader once by saying to an audience as they stood side by side in a meeting with other members of Congress: "President Putin and I see eye to eye on things in the world," using a hand gesture to reference their similarly short stature. The ex-KGB man was not amused.

In meeting with foreign leaders, ambassadors, dignitaries, and citizens over the years, it has become clear what a fixation and a fascination there is with America. We still speak to international groups and they now look at America with more concern: they ask what our international role will be going forward; they wonder about the problems with Congress and between its members and the president; and they ask outright if America is indeed in decline. It's bothersome and a little bit shocking how willing they are to do so. Just asking implies the answer.

Historically, the less Congress has its act together, the more power the president has—which is what has been happening recently. Congress may be at its weakest point in history, and because it's paralyzed, that void gets filled. Sometimes the president fills it with executive orders, as President Obama has in the later years of his administration, or the states do as much as they can to make up the difference. The more Congress is unable to act on its own, the more they're going to see that void filled and the less relevant they become.

This is especially true in foreign policy, where Congress has a constitutional role in approving treaties and declaring war.° There has been fierce debate in recent decades about war powers and what the president can do without congressional authority. It's an ever-evolving contest between presidents and the members of Congress of both parties. Congress has abdicated too much power and given too much latitude to the executive; its power continues to erode. It's slowly wearing away, year by year, and it's very difficult to get back if they don't assert their constitutional duty. If they can't unify on basic things, how are they going to take on something like reclaiming war powers from a president?

The °deep division between Congress and the president reached its apex with the letter that Congress wrote in 2015 to the Iranian leader—an example of the body asserting itself in the wrong way and at odds with its own executive. It's another example of domestic tension spilling dangerously over into foreign affairs and affecting our perception abroad.

° Although the last time Congress officially declared was when we entered World War II.

Congress went a step further when it then invited Israel's prime minister, Benjamin Netanyahu, to address Congress without the White House's consent, a nearly unprecedented move. In the past, there have been plenty of occasions when Congress differed vehemently with the president: the Vietnam War, the League of Nations, immigration, taxes. But it was always reactive; this is proactive, going around the president directly to the country involved. Debate is healthy, but this kind of move is dangerous: Congress can't unilaterally implement foreign policy.

A few years ago Trent was intimately involved in trying to get the South Korean free trade agreement through. Almost simultaneously with the vote, the president of South Korea was coming to the U.S. When Trent went to go see House Speaker John Boehner about arranging a meeting, the Speaker was very clear: he needed to get a request from the White House. That's the way it's always been done.

If this continues—if this becomes the practice going forward—it's a problem, because it sends very conflicting messages for the international community. How do they view this? Our president is saying one thing to these countries and the Congress is saying something else. That kind of confusion and division helps our enemies. It certainly does nothing to enhance our ability to conduct foreign policy. It's just not in the country's interest to handle foreign affairs this way.

Congress's dysfunction does not stay contained to the legislative branch; it spills into all these other areas. Somebody is making those decisions for them. In the case of foreign affairs, it's the administration. Sometimes it's the states or some other entity. No executive is going to willingly scale back his or her power; it just doesn't happen. Sometimes Congress conceded the power because the president was of the majority party. Other times it's because they couldn't get their act together sufficiently to stand up for their constitutional role. That's the thing about inaction: it doesn't just mean stalling. It almost always leads to a flurry of action from other forces.

"If history is a defense to an extent, it is also an indictment," writes Peter Baker in *Days of Fire: Bush and Cheney in the White House.* ". . . The most controversial actions of American presidents have proved more durable when they obtained buy-in from other sectors of society, particularly Congress."[2] Baker was writing about President George W. Bush's use of war powers, but it was not an isolated moment: it is part of a continuum that goes on in the face of a broken Congress.

We try to be optimists and paint the best picture we can, but it starts to stretch believability. You can't be so myopic that you lose all credibility by saying these things; there's no basis to assert them with any believability anymore. There is room for blame all around. The question is how to fix it. Either somebody has to lead in the right direction or something's going to happen that will force us into a relationship that's constructive. Crisis clearly presents an opportunity. It's unlikely that Congress or the president will be able to transcend their differences without a crisis forcing them to. Tom has always been convinced that what drives consensus more often than not is some kind of external threat, some sort of external crisis. Whether it's a hurricane or a threat from someplace abroad, it's what unifies us. It's unfortunate that it takes a crisis of a certain magnitude to trigger change.

Our next president will have a clean start and an opportunity to change the dynamics in Washington. Whether it's trade, foreign policy, or other neglected areas he or she works on, the new president should begin by reopening the lines of communication with Congress. There's simply too much at stake for him or her not to seize it. One thing the next administration will undoubtedly have to deal with is the current fatigue among the American public about foreign entanglements, especially after Iraq and Afghanistan.

The Cold War was essentially a standoff between two countries. Everyone was aligned with either the United States or the Soviet Union. Our current threat comes from transnational forces like ISIS. This threat has created an entirely new dynamic. Transnational forces are amorphous, making it easier for them to operate and harder for us to fight. They're more difficult to locate and to understand. They have no geographic boundaries, no legitimate government, no way with which to be truly identified beyond social media and the extraordinary damage they cause. These horrific videotaped beheadings that they send out are designed as recruiting tools, its own form of "marketing," in the words of former senator Mark Udall.[3]

On a variety of levels, our new circumstances demand a rethinking of how we address our national security concerns. Unfortunately, as with almost all these issues, this has become politicized. Of course, there are legitimate causes for debate that go beyond party affiliation. Should we arm the rebels in Syria? Should we send troops? Should we send military advisors? At what point do you draw the line? The debate in Congress is not just Republicans against Democrats—the divides are all over the place. There is Lindsey Graham and John McCain pressing for U.S. ground troops, isolationists like Rand Paul on the Republican side, hawks and doves on the Democratic side. President Obama has not handled it in a way that has given confidence to the people; it's clear that lashing he took in the 2014 midterms was partly a referendum on how he handled the threat. But the American people are ambivalent as well, neither wanting to ignore nor take it head-on.

Besides fatigue, there is also a belief that Europeans aren't doing enough of their fair share. Since World War II, Europe has relied on the United States to take the lead on most international threat issues. Burden sharing has always been a problem, but it's now a bigger one as the U.S. gets stretched thin and other countries remain reluctant. It's a common dynamic: offering yourself doesn't get you a pass the next time; it just makes others assume you'll do it again.

Our allies still shirk their role in international affairs, essentially telling the U.S., *That's your job.* They're quite open about it. In the 1990s, during the conflict in Kosovo, Trent was meeting with the president of Germany. "Germany is familiar with Kosovo from your history," Trent said. "You know more about it than we do. Why aren't you getting involved in that conflict?"

The German president's response was direct. "Well, you're the leader of the free world," he said. "It's your problem." Trent couldn't help but be struck by his bluntness.

That mentality is common across the globe. So when foreign countries see the United States dealing with such internal strife and dissonance, they're rightly concerned. After all, who else is going to occupy that space in the world? More importantly, are we willing to sit by and find out?

CHAPTER FIFTEEN

Leader of the Free World

P RESIDENT Obama was elected partly on the strength of two words: *hope* and *change*. Just the fact that he spoke about those ideas inspired people. He did so at a fragile time when the public most needed to hear it, and people responded. Whether he achieved those things is worthy of debate, but what he conveyed as a candidate was undeniable: a hopeful and positive message. For all the armchair quarterbacking about that election, it came down to the simple fact that the Republicans failed to do that. Hope is a mindset, so in some ways the president achieved what he set out to do on that front. But change is a different beast. Change is another matter altogether.

Barack Obama was attractive to huge parts of the electorate because he was going to change the culture in Washington. After the election was over, a lot of people—the two of us included— felt that he had a rare opportunity to do so. While he certainly gets credit for setting this as a priority, in certain ways he stumbled out of the gate. One mistake he made was to exclude people from his administration who brought both a passion for public policy and a great deal of experience to the table. Soon after the election, he announced a blanket ban on lobbyists and former lobbyists from serving in any capacity in his administration. Yet, some of these people could have been of great assistance to him with their vast networks and deep understanding of the regulatory, legislative, and political processes.

While he had people with enormous talent and understanding of governance like Pete Rouse, his senior counsel (and Tom's former chief of staff), he didn't have *enough*, in large part because of his self-imposed restrictions on hiring. We both know policy experts who could have been an enormous help to the president on a wide range of issues but were shut out because they had registered to lobby on matters about which they were passionate.

It is tough talk to ban lobbyists. But the term covers a wide variety of policy experts and political heavies in Washington. They have experience, knowledge, and contacts. Closing the door on all of them may appeal to some voters, but it comes at a high price. The president's decision to dial back the rhetoric and associate with some of these respected people in his second term seems a clear indication that he recognized his miscalculation.

On the macro level, to large swaths of the public, Obama the candidate connected. That was his great virtue and it was something to see. But the problem of his presidency seems to be that he has failed to connect on a micro level, with his colleagues and lawmakers in Washington. There's the famous line from New York governor Mario Cuomo: "You campaign in poetry. You govern in prose."[1] Obama seems to have too much of the poet in him.

For one thing, President Obama just doesn't seem to be much of an engager. He comes off as more aloof than his predecessors and doesn't seem to be encouraging good chemistry with either party. As much as the Senate leadership is responsible for the chemistry problems in Washington, the president is even more so. He's in a unique position to affect the climate by reaching out to Congress, communicating his plans, and bringing people in.

To be fair, Congress, beginning with the Republican leadership, has been decidedly hostile and partisan: right out of the gate, Mitch McConnell said that his main priority was to make Obama a one-term president. Similarly, former Speaker John Boehner did little to bridge the divide with the president, struggling to cater to the far right wing of his party, which has gained power. David Axelrod tells a funny but revealing anecdote in his book *Believer: My Forty Years in Politics.* The White House operator called and asked if he was available to speak to the president. When President Obama got on the line, Axelrod jokingly asked if anyone said they were *not* available for the president. "Only John Boehner," Obama said.[2]

In addition to a caustic attitude toward the president, Republicans have attempted on more than fifty occasions to repeal Obama's signature law on health care; they have sued him, and some have even called for his impeachment. The president can be criticized for not trying harder to foster a better relationship with Congress, but examples of Republican cooperation and civility have been few and far between.

In the final years of his presidency, Obama has been resigned to the fact that if he's going to do anything, it's going to have to be by executive order, in effect bypassing Congress: he did this with immigration, with the nuclear agreement with Iran, with the EPA. That just exacerbates the negative climate; even worse, all of those orders are reversible. Nothing he does by executive order is permanent. It's just a temporary solution. In fact, on their first day in office, most new presidents issue a slew of executive orders undoing a variety of executive orders from the previous term.

The American people are the ones who suffer when the highest levels of government don't trust or communicate with each other. Whatever the political battles between them and Congress—and there were many—Reagan, Clinton, and both Bushes all regularly met with congressional leaders. It kept the wheels turning.

That failure to communicate has created a giant hole—a gap of silence—between the most powerful people in the country. And this builds distrust and animosity, a dynamic not at all unique to the halls of power. It happens on all personal and professional levels: silence leads to information being acquired through secondhand sources. It's often jumbled, sometimes negative, and rarely accurate. It goes back to that phone the two of us had on our desks: we never had to wonder too much what the other was really thinking because we kept that line open.

The stakes are too high for the president not to connect to Congress. How many calls did Lyndon Johnson make as president to lawmakers to work a vote? Clinton, too, did it all the time, calling members of both parties. While working to pass NAFTA in 1993, he reached out regularly to Trent, trying to find out where the Republicans were and how to get the agreement through. Trent thought he could bring half the Republicans if the president could get half the Democrats, which is largely what happened.

The tendency with every president has been to build a comfort zone around himself, a fortress of people from his past: advisors and old friends. It has created a dangerous trend for the last twenty-five years, resulting in more centralization of authority in the West Wing. The cabinet, once a place for men and women of gravitas, has become a dumping ground for bureaucrats and administrators. They have few policy functions and limited time with the president. As an added insult, they have to get approval for everything from travel budgets to secretaries.

We have seen this developing throughout our entire careers in Washington. It goes back to President Nixon, who ran the State Department through Henry Kissinger at the White House. With every succeeding president, the centralization of authority in the West Wing has increased and the cabinet's function has decreased. Not long ago, the cabinet was well-known. The regular citizen could rattle off the names of Kennedy's cabinet because they had such high profiles; now you don't even see them on TV anymore. Nowadays, we doubt even the relatively well-informed person can name most of the current cabinet members.

The cabinet's lack of exposure and its members' inability to raise their profile is partly the president's fault: an aspect of his job is to elevate and promote those positions. The White House has taken more and more control over what should be some of the finest minds and the most powerful people in Washington. They've been stripped of their autonomy and don't have any latitude to do much beyond administrating the president's directives. Even John Kerry, who is doing the best he can to put out fires around the world, has been undermined by the West Wing. An unnamed White House official made a crack to a reporter about Kerry being his own satellite in orbit around the planet Earth. Weakening the secretary of state's public image like that is just ridiculous and it's reflective of a widening fissure that has developed between the White House and other departments.

The cabinet had historically been a place for powerful and independent thinkers. Lincoln famously brought a "team of rivals" into his cabinet, capable people who were his opponents in the election. FDR tried to do the same thing. In 2000, Trent stressed to then president-elect George W. Bush the importance of surrounding himself with competing voices, arguing that the tension would be beneficial. The new president chose not to take his advice. In fact, Colin Powell's disagreement with the rest of the circle was considered a giant problem, not a virtue. The battles between Powell and Donald Rumsfeld were certainly not something the Bush White House encouraged.

The tussle between Cheney, Rumsfeld, Powell, and Condoleezza Rice, who served as something of a referee, is well documented, most impressively by Peter Baker in *Days of Fire*. These were all strong personalities contributing to the making of big decisions; people in the country knew who they were, whether they liked them or agreed with their particular positions. Powell was ultimately pushed out because he wouldn't stay in line with the rest, but there are benefits in that tension, as we discussed in Part I. Those benefits extend to the executive branch, but recent presidents seem to resist that kind of conflict near their desk.

There's going to be an initiative by the next round of candidates to "run against Washington," which is common, especially after a two-term presidency. But we hope the winner realizes that there are a lot of capable, talented people *in* Washington that can help solve our institutionalized problems. We've seen it happen too many times: the Californians came in with Reagan, the Arkansans came in with Clinton, the Georgians came with Carter. A president brings in a circle of outsiders who are going to "fix" Washington, and it never succeeds. You simply cannot fix something with which you're not familiar. It would be too obvious to emphasize if we hadn't see it happen over and over again.

President Obama had a very short time in Congress, so he came into power quite unfamiliar with the day-to-day of it, the meat of it, the de facto way things happen. It's partly his lack of experience and partly just his personality. We hope the next person to hold the office is a more engaged president, one who understands the significance of the relationship between the legislative and executive branches. The country would benefit greatly from someone who listens to people outside of his or her own tight clique and taps into the capabilities and the talents that are available.

As we look toward the 2016 campaign and election, there are things we can't help but notice. First off, the names look quite familiar. We claim not to have—or not to want—dynasties in America. There's an enormous amount of fatigue now; after all, the Bush and Clinton names go all the way back to the 1980s. If you think of any product that dates back to the 1980s, whether it's a car or a computer, their brands have become quite old. Americans like newness and freshness. There's a level of fatigue in America now that's understandable and it says something about our political stagnation that is disconcerting.

We would advise the candidates to make better governance a campaign issue. It's clearly on the minds of a lot of voters. How can we right the ship? How can we end the deadlock? Obama campaigned on that in 2008, but just the opposite occurred. Given how the Obama presidency has unfolded, it would be hard for the public to trust that kind of rhetoric again.

As we write this, Hillary Clinton has distinguished herself by bringing forth a positive message. While everyone else is trying to blame her for Benghazi or for Obama's shortcomings, she has been focused on previous successes and future aspirations. She's talking optimistically about what can be done, which is a start.

But Hillary faces all kinds of challenges regarding the public's perception of both President Clinton and President Obama. She can distance herself from both of them only so much. Like many candidates before her, she's going to have to thread that needle. Often that's why the incumbent party loses: people are looking for change.

Hillary will want to take credit for the positives during the Clinton years, but invoking that also brings some bad memories as well. The same thing is true with her connection to President Obama: it'll be hard for her to take some of the credit without taking some of the blame. It's going to be a delicate dance, but she has proven nimble on her feet in that regard. Hillary and Jeb Bush have many of the same challenges. They come from different perspectives but they both have to be clearer on how they would distinguish themselves from their predecessors.

Hillary also needs to think more clearly about how she wants to be perceived. Some of the younger candidates, like Marco Rubio, are doing it for her. He's framing the election as a generational conflict: the new versus the old. And it's working, as it always does. People gravitate toward the younger candidate: they did for Obama, they did for Clinton, and they have historically done so. They're going to go for the younger, newer, fresher face if given the option.

It strains credulity for Hillary to present herself as the candidate of change. Her trickiest job will be framing her candidacy in a way that dispels the notion that she's a throwback. She has to re-establish her identity before the other side does it for her. But they have already started to and it's been effective. It's essential that she take control of the narrative and her image if she's going to be successful.

Trent has been saying for a long time that he was disappointed that the Republicans didn't have a message or any kind of vision in the 2014 midterm elections; all they did was run against Obama and hold their breath, hoping they'd hold the House and win the Senate. And it worked. Republicans in 2016 are not yet running on a vision or a message, which is a huge mistake. Clearly we're going to vote in different ways for president, but we both want candidates who will recognize that the nation needs vision and purpose. It will elevate the debate and hopefully end the tit for tat, maybe even break the vicious cycle we've been caught up in.

It would be wise for the candidates to pick two or three specific things that they are committed to doing, whether it's an energy bill, a defense bill, or the economy; obviously those are three things that affect everyone. And they need to stay specific. It's not going to be enough just to say they're going to be different from Obama. They can't just run an anti-Hillary or anti-Obama campaign and hope the country gets behind them. Republicans have to talk about what they would do differently; they need to have a message, an agenda, and a vision moving forward, or they'll be in serious trouble.

CHAPTER SIXTEEN

The Center of the Storm

"I am fairly out and you fairly in! See which of us will be happiest."

—GEORGE WASHINGTON TO JOHN ADAMS, 1797

THOMAS Jefferson said of the presidency, "No man will bring out of that office the reputation which carries him into it."[1] Jefferson was writing from personal experience, reflecting on how sullied his name became once he got involved in party and then presidential politics. He began his career as the brilliant and poetic mind behind our country's founding. His decision to leave any mention of his presidency off his gravestone reveals a great deal about how he felt about the position.

We've seen a lot of presidents up close: Trent started in Congress at the start of Richard Nixon's second term, Tom midway through Carter's presidency. As presidents make their way from the inaugural to their final years, they universally age before your eyes. They get grayer, as President Obama has. They get that exhaustion in their faces and in their walk, as President Clinton did. They carry the weight of war and tragedy, as George W. Bush did. Bush himself later said he felt toward the end of his presidency like "the captain of a sinking ship."[2] You could see it physically taking its toll on him.

They acquire the title on the first day and they gradually acquire the stature. The transformation develops over time, the result of being at the center of the storm, day in and day out. Even the quietest days as president would likely be the busiest days of most people's lives. A president's persona becomes magnified; part of it is the public's projection onto him, but it's a behavioral and physical thing as well. Up close you can see how they gain confidence and stature in the course of their terms. Tom is fond of that old line in politics: "Some grow with responsibility and others merely swell." U.S. presidents almost universally grow; there's a genuine gravity that comes with having to make the hard, heavy decisions like putting our military men's and women's lives on the line.

In private, these men have spoken passionately about how painful it is to know they're responsible for people's deaths. Most of them have had to speak to bereaved relatives after tragic events, like the families of those who died on the *Challenger*, 9/11 families, parents whose children died in Iraq or Afghanistan. It's more than a single person could ever really be prepared for. It is an incredibly burdensome and awesome responsibility that demands respect. Of course, over our years in Washington, we've had occasion to spend time with the presidents—sometimes personal, intimate time. No matter who held the office or what party he belonged to, we always felt a presence.

As the years went by, all of a sudden the presidents were our age or younger. They still carried that aura, but human nature kicks in when that happens. You think, *What's this guy doing as president? He should be my understudy.* Then you come back to down to earth.

Despite some perceptions, the U.S. president is not merely a figurehead who deals in speeches and ceremony: policywise, he's still the dominant figure. Although we have seen a diminished executive over the years, the president is still the agenda setter, the one who creates the tone for the nation, and America's primary personification all over the world.

Of course, we will always expect too much of presidents. But a president who can engage and who has a vision can have a profound effect not just on the direction but on the *confidence* of the country. A president shows us how we feel about ourselves. This is precisely what President Carter came up against toward the end of his term. Americans didn't like what he reflected back at them—"malaise,"* as it was labeled after his infamous speech to the nation—and they let it be known at the voting booth.

The stature and power of the presidency in American society is almost incalculable. In a one-on-one conversation, it's a formidable thing. Lyndon Johnson recorded nearly every conversation he had in the Oval Office, as well as on his Texas ranch. Those tapes reveal so much about how the man worked. Every call starts the same way: the person on the other line opens with a compliment, which is a fairly common way to start a conversation with the president of the United States.

Johnson often thanks them, adds a bit of self-deprecation, and then launches into what he needs. Former congresswoman Helen Gahagan Douglas calls to compliment him on his speech. After thanking her, he gets right to it: "I want you do to something for me," he says. "I want you to go as my representative to Liberia for their hundredth anniversary of the relations between the United States and Liberia. I'd like to go myself ... But I can't do it. It's this Saturday." It's three days away and

---

* Carter's famous "malaise" speech of July 15, 1979, actually never used that word.

she can't for the life of her get out of it. Johnson just won't let her.

Other times he'd announce something publicly just as a way to skip the asking part and avoid the risk of getting turned down. He did that with Sargent Shriver, who really didn't want to run his War on Poverty but had no choice. Shriver read in the news that he'd already accepted.

As president, Johnson only had one full caucus a year, because he put all his efforts on chemistry in the one-on-one. He had bonds that were unprecedented, including with powerful Democrat Richard Russell and Republican leader Everett Dirksen. "Let's get together for a drink and talk this over," Johnson said to Dirksen on one occasion.

Dirksen said, "Okay, I'll be down."

"No, no, I'll come to you," the president said.

Thirty minutes later the president was in the Capitol building. What they talked about may not have mattered as much as the very fact that they did it. The president treated the minority leader as worth that trip to the Capitol, which said volumes.

Of all the leaders in the modern era, Trent's hero was Ronald Reagan. One of Reagan's greatest strengths was how well he invited people in. He met with the leadership in Congress almost every week we were in session. Over the years he went from being very animated in these meetings to letting his attention waver. Sometimes the president would doodle while the rest of us yammered on. He'd be quiet when he was doodling and you would wonder, *Oh, shit, is he really paying attention?*—and then he'd come out with something that would really grab you and sum up where you were. He could be surprising that way.

One time Trent looked over and Reagan had drawn two lines representing two monetary policy alternatives. On the back of the paper was a doodle, this great drawing of a cowboy and a horse. Afterward, Trent asked him to autograph that picture and he kept it. It's now framed so that you can see both the doodle and the back.

Trent was invited a good deal to meet with Reagan, but even as a junior senator Tom got invited to the White House sometimes. Reagan was also wise enough to know what his strengths were and then had people around him to help make his vision a reality. "[Reagan saw] the world in terms of ideas," biographer Richard Reeves wrote. "He was an ideologue with a few ideas that he held with stubborn certainty."[3]

Reagan also had that magic touch with people, including an amazing chemistry with Democratic Speaker Tip O'Neill. They were on opposite ends of the spectrum, but the things they accomplished together are illustrative: you can be far apart policywise, but with chemistry and communication you can accomplish a great deal.

In spite of President Clinton's personal troubles, he could probably get reelected tomorrow. He took a page out of LBJ's book and did a lot of legwork cultivating relationships with leadership—although Clinton was a natural at that kind of thing. Tom was invited up to Camp David to have dinners, and Clinton would always invite the Daschles over for the holidays, regale them with stories, and give them a tour of the White House. He did all of that personally. He knew how it engendered the good chemistry that he would benefit from down the line.

Clinton was also a social caller, the only one among the presidents we knew. He would call both of us—at all hours of the night—often just to talk. He must've needed a mere four hours of sleep. He was just up rummaging around. Clinton said occasionally he would take a half-hour nap in the late afternoon and he was pretty disciplined about not having it last too long. Tom's wife, Linda, was running the FAA in the 1990s and a call after midnight at the Daschles meant one of two things: a plane crash or the president. Clinton always started the call the same way: "Hey, what are you up to?"

Tom would say, "What do you think I'm up to, Mr. President? It's one o'clock in the morning."

And he would just chat. Clinton would be playing solitaire on the phone while he talked and you'd hear him shuffle cards in the background.

He did it with the Republicans as well. Trent got those late-night calls too.

One time, about three years into Clinton's presidency, the phone rang at two in the morning at Trent's house. The phone was on Tricia's side of the bed, so she picked it up and handed it to Trent, telling him it was the president.

Trent started, "Mr. President, how are you doing . . . Yes, sir . . . I'd be glad to . . . Yes, sir . . . Well, I don't know. Let me work on that . . . " It kept going like that for about ten minutes.

Finally Trent gave the phone back to Tricia to hang up.

"What did he want?" Trisha asked.

"I really don't know," Trent said. "Something about Central America, I think." It was very unclear, but he seemed really concerned and he wanted to talk about it, so Trent obliged. That's just what you did when the president called, no matter what time of night. There was an unspoken assumption that the president didn't think anything about calling someone at two in the morning. You'd think it could wait until morning, but he was just itching to talk.

For all his faults, Clinton was charming and he had a sense of humor. He had the ability to turn some tense situations around with his personality and made a point of always being even friendlier to our wives than he was to us.

Clinton understood how much meeting with lawmakers mattered. "If I had to do it all over again I would block out significantly greater time . . . to just bring these guys in and let them say whatever the hell they want to say to me," Clinton told a reporter. "You know, most of these people are pretty smart. Most of them didn't get there by accident. Most of them love our country, and most of them have something to say. And I found that people that I ordinarily, superficially, would not have that much in common with would be quite helpful."[4]

President George W. Bush had a totally different lifestyle from Bill Clinton, in more ways than one. Bush was garrulous, too, to a degree. After Bush won the election, he came over to all the leadership offices to meet with each of us and ask for advice. We hadn't had a lot of opportunities to exchange any thoughts or ideas. Tom didn't know him well at all.

Tom made a suggestion to Bush that came from President Eisenhower, who used to meet with Lyndon Johnson and Everett Dirksen for breakfast. President Clinton wasn't a breakfast person—that wouldn't have worked for him—but Bush was. "I understand you're an early riser," Tom said to Bush, "and I think you should have breakfast with the leadership once a week." Nothing came of it right away; the president obviously was getting ramped up and had a full plate. He probably didn't feel like he had the time to do that.

But after 9/11, to Bush's credit, he called to remind Tom about it. "I wish we had done it sooner," he said, "but we're going to do it now."

That's how the breakfasts started. A few times a month, we'd meet at seven in the morning, bright and early, and have breakfast with the president: the two of us, Dick Gephardt, Dennis Hastert, sometimes Vice President Cheney. We picked up a lot of good information on what was going on in the world and where the administration was coming from. We'd sit down with President Bush and he would give us an around-the-world report, inviting us to ask questions. One of the first breakfast topics was the Authorization for Use of Military Force against terrorists, which launched the war in Afghanistan. Tom had some well-publicized reservations about it, as did others, and we were able to talk through it rather than resorting to battling through proxies and the media.

The breakfasts offered us a chance to get information on where the world was during that chaotic time and the administration's rationale for its choices. But something else happened as well. It built a relationship that created this chemistry, simply by meeting and talking. For a while there, we were a unit because of that regular contact. Those were not easy days, and having that foundation among us made a world of difference. For the most part, we came out of there unified. Sometimes we'd talk to the press outside; often we left and went back to work.

No one really told us what the rules of the breakfasts would be, but early on, Dick Gephardt, who doesn't like to wear a jacket, was carrying his over his shoulder. The president stopped him at the door. "Congressman, this is the Oval Office," Bush said. "I expect you to wear your jacket." Dick looked a little startled, but he put it on right there. Bush's White House set a tone that was

The Center of the Storm

consciously different from Clinton's, which was known for casual dress and eating pizza. Bush was likely just looking to reinforce the difference.

The best time to talk to President Bush was between seven and seven-thirty in the morning. Trent learned over the years to get around Andy Card or Karl Rove—that he could usually get the president on the phone if he called during that window. In that early-morning setting he was always a little more relaxed. Sometimes he'd just talk about things like sports, which was always easy with Bush because he was encyclopedic on that topic.

He once invited both Tom and Linda over to the White House residence for dinner. Before they arrived, Laura had to leave because one of the girls had gotten into some trouble. Tom offered to cancel, saying, "You've got more on your mind. We can do it another time."

"No, no, I really want you to come anyway," Bush replied.

So Linda and Tom had dinner with President Bush alone, which was a great way to get a sense of him as a person. Both Bush and President Clinton said the same thing about living in the White House: that they felt it was a little bit like a prison. Clinton was quoted as calling the White House "the crown jewel of the penal system." They felt holed up, with very little freedom of movement. Bush was lonely enough that he passed up a perfectly good excuse for canceling on the Democratic leader.

Somehow we always look at political leaders differently through the prism of history. Most often, the longer they're gone, the larger they become. John F. Kennedy was popular as president but he has become an icon, in large part because his chapter is an incomplete one in our history. He was young and attractive and his life was snuffed out too soon and so traumatically for any of us who remember it. Between his age, vigor, and the flux of the times, people often think about what would have been. That all gets projected onto President Kennedy's memory and image.

Then of course there are those whose images are indelible and completely locked, like the pre-Depression presidents: Harding, Coolidge, and Hoover. The criticism leveled against them may not be completely warranted, but their reputations have suffered as a result of the perception that they helped precipitate the Depression. President Carter left office quite unpopular but has built a second career since then. He did laudable work in Africa but he also stirred controversy that perhaps has distracted from his good work and intentions.

President George H. W. Bush has reemerged after almost becoming a footnote with his loss in 1992. He was obviously not that popular when he was defeated for reelection, but twenty-some years later he has become like the country's grandfather. He and his "other son," Bill Clinton, do work together now around the world. Gradually, the public has softened toward him. Bush Sr. has been the beneficiary of the long view of history. Some of that is due to the way he has conducted himself since he left; some of it has to do with his patrician role in his son's presidency.

George W. Bush left office with very low approval ratings but has seen a spike these last few years, as he has been quite deliberately out of the spotlight. He has also been viewed through a more forgiving lens with distance and as history starts to settle. Those men behave as if their office were permanent, and in a sense they're right: they are going to be written about until their final days, so they view their lives as bodies of work.

CHAPTER SEVENTEEN

9/11 and Its Aftermath

CONGRESS operates totally differently when there's a crisis of a certain magnitude. It really is the one unifier. On September 11 and in the aftermath of that tragedy, everything that separated us seemed small and unimportant. Our country has its issues, but America still unites around a crisis. A crisis can be catalytic in bringing people to a totally different perception of their roles. It is also a catalyst for leadership—or, rather, it can be. As Aaron David Miller points out, "Crisis only opens the door to the possibility of leadership, transformative change, and greatness; it certainly does not guarantee or mandate its inevitability."[1]

> TRENT: That morning I was in my Capitol office, watching the news coverage of the terrorist attacks in New York. At a quarter to ten, when the news came in about the crash at the Pentagon, I stood up and could see smoke billowing in the distance out of my window. I picked up the red phone to call Tom, who was majority leader at the time. "Tom, I think we're under attack," I said, "You

should order the building evacuated." Right then, my
security detail barged into my office to whisk me out.

"Okay, let me get my briefcase," I said.

"Hurry," he said.

We had no idea where we were going. The
congressional leadership—myself, Tom, Don Nickles,
Harry Reid—were rushed three blocks away to the top
floor of the police station. Our cell phones were all
jammed up and we couldn't get through to our wives or
family—and my daughter had just had a baby. While we
were there, news came through about the plane in
Pennsylvania; we didn't know if it was shot down or what
had happened. I turned to my security detail. "I think
this is dumb for us to be here," I said. "And I can't
communicate." I asked him to take me to Andrews Air
Force Base, where I knew I would be secure.

TOM: That morning John Glenn stopped by my leadership
office in the Capitol. We were having a cup of coffee and
I had my TV on in the background with the volume
turned low. At about the same time, we both noticed the
footage of the first tower on fire.

"My God, a pilot flew into the World Trade Center!"
I said.

And of course he knew: "That was no pilot," he said.

I began a leadership meeting in the Capitol, and
shortly after we started, Patty Murray looked out the
window and shouted, "Look at all that smoke!" Less than
three miles away, American Airlines Flight 77 had
crashed into the Pentagon. Security barged in and told us
to evacuate immediately and we rushed for all the doors.

I remember Robert Byrd was carrying what must have been five or six giant books that he felt were important enough to take with him.

We got to the top floor of the D.C. police station, where they pulled the shades down and we all stood in line to use one phone to call our families. While we were waiting, we worked on a joint statement from both parties. Concentrating all of the leadership in one tight spot—three blocks from the Capitol—was a terrible idea. Trent and I spoke about how disturbing it was that there was really no plan at all. It shows how completely invincible everyone felt back then from all the troubles in the world.

I got out of there and went over to a nearby colleague's apartment. While I was there, security called. "We changed our mind again," they told me. "We want to evacuate you to a secret undisclosed location. Meet on the West Lawn of the Capitol and there'll be a helicopter waiting for you there."

We all met up back at the Capitol and piled into a helicopter, and as we were lifting off I heard on my headphones, "Could you pick up Senator Lott out at Andrews Air Force Base?" After picking up Trent, we flew just north of the Pentagon. I'll never in my life forget looking out the window of that helicopter and seeing the smoke, the plane still burning there, that fuselage half buried into the side of the building. I vividly remember all that smoke billowing and all those firemen surrounding it.

We carpooled by helicopter out to the secret undisclosed location; we hadn't an inkling of where we were going. After we arrived, I had a conference call with

the Democrats. Soon after, Trent and I began to feel
increasingly uncomfortable there. We were in a protective
environment, all our colleagues were still out there, and
our families were still vulnerable.

TRENT: By early afternoon we were all assembled in a room
at the underground site. The first call we got was from
Dick Cheney. I then got a call from Kay Bailey
Hutchinson. "Where are you?" she said. "We're going to
have a meeting of the Senate Republican Conference in
the police station. We want to know what to do." Tom and
I both figured we should be available and we talked to
our respective caucuses.

Shortly thereafter, I had another teleconference with
Vice President Cheney. I told him that I wanted to get back
to the Capitol. "My son is on the Hill," I said. "Our people
are there and they don't know what to expect. They need
us; send the helicopter back to get us." He was having none
of it, basically telling me "No chance." I got agitated and
called my security guy and said, "Get a car and come get
me." But soon after we got a call to tell us the helicopter
would be back to pick us up and land us at the west front of
the Capitol. We arrived back there and the House and
Senate had assembled on the east front and came around to
meet us. We hadn't expected them to be there.

There was a growing consensus that we needed to demonstrate
defiance and show that we weren't going to be shut down. We had
to negotiate with both the administration and security; neither
wanted us anywhere near the Capitol, which was likely the terrorists' fourth target that day. But it was important to show our

citizens—and the world—that the United States government was going to keep functioning, do it personally, and do it on live television, from those steps. How could the public believe us if we were hiding ourselves? When word got out that we were going to speak, most of the Senate and House members came over to stand with us. It was quite a scene: it looked like an armed camp out there with security, wires, and equipment all over the Capitol steps. After Speaker Denny Hastert said a few words, Tom spoke:

> *Today's despicable acts were an assault on our people and on our freedom.*
>
> *As the representatives of the people, we are here to declare that our resolve has not been weakened by these horrific and cowardly acts.*
>
> *Congress will convene tomorrow.*
>
> *And we will speak with one voice to condemn these attacks, to comfort the victims and their families, to commit our full support to the effort to bring those responsible to justice.*
>
> *We, Republicans and Democrats, House and Senate, stand strongly united behind the president, and we'll work together to ensure that the full resources of the government are brought to bear in these efforts.*

As we both got to the far end of the steps, someone began singing "God Bless America." It started spontaneously with a few scattered voices and then we all joined in. It was a small gesture, but it was such a troubling time and people seemed to take comfort in that sign of unity. More than anything, the purpose of the joint statement was to say we're continuing to function and we're going to be back the next morning doing the country's work.

And we did. With a few scares—we had to evacuate the Capitol a couple of times in the next few days—we went about our business.

For all the horror of that day and the uncertainty that was its aftermath, there was some positive outgrowth. The sense of patriotism and community among lawmakers in those months was just inspiring. Senators came to the floor and said, "I'm not a Democrat or Republican, I'm an American." Not incidentally, that period was one of the most productive periods that we'd had in the Senate; we even had our highest approval rating in its history: 84 percent. It stayed in the 70s into 2002—remarkably high for Congress.

During that period, we had to take up some very difficult issues. The public saw us passing bills, helping New York, rescuing the airlines, and protecting citizens. We were all caucusing together, occasionally in the Senate cafeteria, which was big enough to hold everyone. We had very candid conversations and went around committees when we needed to. It was a complete departure from past practice. As always, there were philosophical differences between parties about what to do and how to do it, but they weren't *politically* motivated. No one was for or against things simply because of the president's party. In fact, it didn't get political for a long time.

The first issue that became political was the Bush tax cuts. We had been going around the committees a lot in those days; that's how we were getting things done so fast. We were also having leadership breakfasts with President Bush, which helped keep our communication lines open. The Speaker returned to regular order because the majority rule in the House favored the Republicans. Around that time, not coincidentally, the breakfasts with Bush tapered off and then ended. The administration correctly assumed that while they could count on Tom and the

Democrats working with them on post-9/11 issues, this was something else. They understood that they were going to have to fight to get those through, and Tom was probably not going to be part of the winning equation.[°]

> TOM: Because of the tension and pressure in those days, I had been having severe headaches. I started to get concerned that it might've been more than just stress. In October, I went out to Bethesda Naval Hospital to get an MRI. The report came back that there was absolutely nothing medically wrong and it was probably just stress-related. After the report, I was feeling relieved on my way back in to work. I walked into the office and Pete Rouse, my chief of staff, met me immediately.
>
> "We've got a serious problem," he said. "A young woman was just exposed to anthrax. Twenty-seven other people in the area have all been exposed."
>
> After getting briefed on the details, I wanted to go into my office but they wouldn't let me; they had to quarantine everybody. Twenty-eight staff members had been exposed and their survival was my primary concern. My staff and I called their families, every parent; some of the exposed were young interns. On top of that were the logistical problems. The anthrax circulated very quickly because it got into the ventilation system, so they found traces of it all over the building. No one had any idea how to clean it out. We were fortunate that everyone in my

---

[°] The vote on the 2003 tax proposal was 50–50 in the Senate, with Vice President Cheney breaking the tie.

office survived; by the end of the month, five people in
Florida and New York would die from anthrax inhalation.

President Bush and I had been talking on a daily
basis in those days, so I called him just to let him know
what was going on. He was on his way into a press
conference and it was on his mind, so he casually
mentioned it to reporters. Immediately afterward, three
hundred people showed up outside our office door, just
clamoring for information. The president called me right
after that to apologize.

"You know what," he said. "That was probably not the
smartest thing to do. There was just so much on my mind."

I didn't blame him; I probably would've done
the same thing. In those days we had such a good
relationship. I told him I appreciated the sympathy and
his willingness to help in any way.

"We'll do whatever it takes," he said.

That was as close as President Bush and I ever got.

TRENT: In the immediate aftermath of 9/11, there was an
atmosphere of vulnerability that everyone felt, even the
White House. You obviously can't always protect against an
incoming missile or incoming airplane. After the anthrax
attacks in Tom's office, we all became concerned about our
staff being exposed. The Capitol essentially had to be
quarantined for a while. We found out later there was
another letter directed toward Senator Leahy in the mail
system. After that, we started to basically irradiate all the
mail.

But it was gratifying to discover how generous
people were, to witness their willingness to help out. It

was chaotic, but there was also great camaraderie and
generosity. Republicans and Democrats were sharing
office space in the Russell Senate Office Building;
committees would go open up rooms to let people's staff
work. Everyone wanted to play the Good Samaritan. The
government wouldn't have been able to function without
people offering up space, sacrificing, and giving what
they could. It was happening all over the country in
various ways and for a time, it happened here.
Washington became a community again.

We didn't know who was responsible for the anthrax attack but,
like most Americans, we assumed it was part of a larger effort. We
thought it could easily become a pattern, something that could
go on for quite some time. Al Qaeda was just becoming better
understood, and there was no way of knowing how far or deeply
their operation reached. Everyone, in and out of government, just
assumed that more attacks were coming. For all the arguments
and controversy about the government's methods of protecting
its citizens—and we each have issues, looking back—the fact
remains: we still haven't had another incident. But all these years
later we're still struggling with the balance between freedom and
security.

As part of the so-called Gang of Eight,* we were both informed
very early, in October 2001, about the "warrantless" wiretaps that
were part of the Patriot Act. The most controversial aspect of the

---

* The Gang of Eight is made up of the Senate and House leaders from both
parties, plus the chairs and ranking members of the Senate and House
Intelligence Committees.

program—which came to light a few years later—was the communication surveillance of Americans in the U.S.

There's a process of notification where we would get on a
garbled phone—a classified phone line—and get briefings regarding
security matters. Afterward, we were not even allowed to talk to our
staff about it, which was really difficult, especially with something
controversial like spying on Americans. We also had to make
decisions based on what we were told, without the benefit of any real
review on our end. It was an uncertain time; all we could do was rely
on the sources of information that we had, with Vice President
Cheney presenting the most forceful case. We've now come to
understand that some of that information was not accurate.

> TOM: What I always ask people to remember is how
> uncertain everything was at the time. Vice President
> Cheney, in particular, was pretty adamant about the
> dangers out there and what needed to be done. Colin
> Powell's assertions and presentation to the UN were a
> big factor for me. There was the collective judgment on
> the part of the Bush administration, British intelligence,
> and others. There was a certain set of threat criteria
> that in my view, in those early stages, had been met. We
> were trying to make the best decisions based on the
> information we had. Looking back, I would have made
> the same decisions, because you have to go based on
> what you're given. Now we have the luxury of hindsight,
> and it's obviously a different picture.

> TRENT: When you're a member of Congress, especially
> when you're in the leadership or on the Intelligence
> Committee, and there's a serious national security issue,

you're being informed of certain possible threats. The threats we were getting in 2001 and 2002 were numerous and rarely specific. You err on the side of doing what you're told is necessary by the administration or the National Security team. At that point we had no idea what was going to happen next or where the threats were going to come from. We were being told by the Justice Department, by the vice president, by those in the position to know, that they needed this authority.

Looking back on it, I think we probably did go too far, but we needed to be able to trace these people in every way possible. We erred on the side of caution, giving the various agencies the powers they needed. In subsequent legislation, over the years, we dialed back what the NSA is able to do.

Trent was on the Senate Intelligence Committee at the time. In the hearings and investigations, it became clear that the FBI and the intelligence community—and various entities within the intelligence communities—were simply not communicating with each other. There were fourteen different entities within the intelligence community, everything from the Coast Guard to the Department of Defense. Each was very protective of its intelligence operation and not open to working with the CIA. The law has clear guidelines about where the FBI's purview ends and the CIA's begins; too often they were not communicating at that handoff. At the time, there was a reorganization of the entire intelligence community, with a director of intelligence put in charge of it all. Part of it was an institutionalized increase in sharing between entities, the establishment of the Transportation Security Administration, and the creation of the Department of Homeland Security.

It was a classic case of far too much siloing. Sharing information was just much harder than it should have been. We think we're
still struggling with that, and we're not alone. Donald Rumsfeld
recently stated, "To my regret, a fundamental rethinking of
America's national security apparatus has still not occurred."[2]

TOM: The Iraq War vote was bitterly divided on the
    Democratic side. The tally in our caucus was 29–21, but
    in reality it was much closer. I was torn by it, but at the
    same time I had to be sensitive to what information
    I'd been given. The dilemma was that if the Saddam
    Hussein regime really did have access to weapons of
    mass destruction and used them against us, God forbid
    I had voted against stopping him. When I framed it like
    that to myself, I voted for it, reluctantly, with a fairly
    clear conscious. It was a very emotional and extremely
    contentious caucus debate that we went through over
    and over again; it lasted for weeks. The Republicans
    seemed more unified on invading Iraq, but it was very
    divisive on our side.

        After the vote passed, President Bush asked me to
    join him in the Rose Garden to announce the resolution,
    but I declined. I decided I was going to support the
    president but I was skeptical about the motivation of the
    press conference. I wanted to hold off on making it look
    political and stay sensitive to the other side, especially
    considering how divisive an issue it was. It smelled a
    bit too much like politics to me, which didn't seem
    appropriate. Politics should be absent from some issues.

CHAPTER EIGHTEEN

The Humility and the Audacity

"Courage is the first of human virtues because it makes all others possible."

—ARISTOTLE

"No event in American history which was so improbable at the time has seemed so inevitable in retrospect as the American Revolution,"[1] writes Joseph J. Ellis. Good fortune played a role, but if not for the courage of certain men and women, the story of our nation would have turned out much differently. More likely there would be no America at all. The somewhat fossilized narrative of our independence, the nineteenth-century claims of Manifest Destiny, and our country's fortunate rise in the twentieth century can combine to blind us to how unlikely it all was. In actuality, it was people who made it happen.

Most of Ellis's books on our Founding Fathers are fascinating in how they confront the myth of America's inevitability. "What in retrospect has the look of a foreordained unfolding of God's will," he wrote, "was in reality an improvisational affair in which sheer chance, pure luck—both good and bad—and specific decisions made in the crucible of specific military and political crises determined the outcome."[2]

Washington, Jefferson, and Hamilton could just as likely have ended up in English textbooks as infamous traitors to the British

Empire who were executed for their failed rebellion against King George. That they were the heroes of one story and not the footnote of another is due to their collective bravery in the face of overwhelming opposition. That opposition came from all fronts: military, political, historical, and geographical. Some of it came from within their own ranks. John Dickinson, a key delegate to the Continental Congresses and the Constitutional Convention and author of previous tracts against the king, famously refused to sign the Declaration of Independence. It would be suicide, he argued. From the floor he told his colleagues that he refused to "brave the storm in a skiff made of paper."[3]

The battles fought in the name of American independence were both large and small, political and physical, personal and philosophical. James Madison, who had abandoned religion as an adult (partly because the Bible called his epilepsy the devil's work), battled any efforts to suppress freedom of religion in the new land. Years before he wrote the Bill of Rights, which provided for religious freedom right at the top, Madison frequently took the lead to defend the religiously persecuted.[4] He had no personal fondness for Baptists, or any group he defended, but he understood that America required that such fights be fought.

John Adams was a feisty and fearless political warrior, repeatedly thumbing his nose at the very idea of popularity, to the detriment of his career. In continuing to keep the peace with France despite enormous pressure from his own party, he abandoned the Federalists (and killed his political future) to protect what he knew was a fragile adolescent nation: "Adams derived deep personal satisfaction from singular acts of principle that defied the agendas of both political parties," Ellis writes. "The fact that the decision . . . rendered him unpopular, that it struck most observers as political suicide, only confirmed for him that it must be right."[5] Of all things our founders teach us, perhaps none was as important as this: if the courageous choices didn't come at an enormous cost, we would never define them as such.

In 1838, in Springfield, Illinois, a twenty-eight-year-old newcomer spoke to a town hall meeting about our nation's Founding Fathers:

> *If they succeeded, they were to be immortalized; their names were to be transferred to counties and cities, and rivers and mountains; and to be revered and sung, and toasted through all time. If they failed, they were to be called knaves and fools, and fanatics for a fleeting hour; then to sink and be forgotten. They succeeded. The experiment is successful; and thousands have won their deathless names in making it so.*[6]

Twenty-three years later, as president, that man would preside over our nation's biggest crucible and the deadliest conflict in our nation's history. The Civil War, which nearly split the union, was always in doubt—so much bloodshed made it unclear if there'd be anything left that resembled victory at all. In 1864, President Lincoln was repeatedly told by advisors that dropping the Emancipation Proclamation would ensure his reelection, but he refused. "You think I don't know I am going to be beaten, *but I do . . .*" he said, "badly beaten."[7] Lincoln held fast to his unpopular position, the epitome of having the courage of one's convictions.

Henry Clay's son met with Lincoln during this time and asked him to heed the famed senator's maxim: "I'd rather be right than be president,"[8] a motto Clay literally lived by. It went beyond politics for Lincoln as well, if it was ever about that. Even once it became obvious that his life was in danger, Lincoln refused to give in. Death threats were common, he had been shot at before, and he and his wife had premonitions about his assassination. Lincoln is but one example but perhaps the quintessential one: our country remains not because of fate or fortune. People fought and died for it, and we had leaders to make sure it survived, even when they themselves did not.

Seventy-five years after Lincoln's death, we were enormous underdogs in the Second World War. It is no exaggeration to say our victory in that conflict literally changed the course of world events. The quote that opens this chapter was one of Churchill's favorite sayings and its poignancy comes from its simplicity: without courage, it doesn't matter what else you have; you need courage for the rest of what you have to matter.

Historian Richard Beeman writes of the "humility and the audacity of those men who came together in Philadelphia to effect the revolution of 1787."[9] The tension between those two traits—a naïveté to think you can make an impact and the boldness to try—creates that third thing we call courage.

Patriotism and hindsight can sometimes make us paint the country's Founding Fathers as saints or pure heroes, but historian Michael Beschloss reminds us they were just men, "anxious, self-protective politicians [who] tried to escape having to walk through the fire."[10] They would have avoided some of the battles if they were not necessary. No leader opts to face a crisis, but neither does he walk away from it.

Beschloss, in the preface to his book *Presidential Courage: Brave Leaders and How They Changed America, 1789–1989*, writes:

> *At times of crisis and urgent national need, it has been*
> *important for Presidents to summon the courage to dismiss*

what is merely popular—and the wisdom to do that for
causes that later Americans will come to admire.[11]

"For causes that later Americans will *come to admire*." A true
leader reads the future, demonstrating foresight that can look to
the present like foolishness or stubbornness. The leader steps out
before there is a floor underneath or a crowd to catch him—with
the trust that when the time comes there will be.

One of the monikers given to our Constitution is the "Civil
Bible," which is reminiscent of David McCullough's line about the
Capitol building being the national temple. The Constitution
binds us in civic society the way our holy books do in the spiritual
one. It is a living, breathing document that has sustained our
government through 228 years of enormous change of which that
first generation could not possibly have conceived.

It's hard for the modern American to imagine how risky their
actions were: demanding rights, declaring independence, fighting
to achieve it, and then daring to create a democratic experiment
on this vast land. Washington recognized they were on "untrod-
den ground."[12] Madison said they were in "wilderness without a
single footstep to guide us."[13]

Adams knew how in over their heads they were, but argued
they nonetheless must forge ahead: "We are deficient in genius,
education, in travel, fortune—in everything," he wrote to his wife,
Abigail.[14] Adams was a realist, but he underestimated the value of
what they could do collectively.

It goes back to Barney Frank's point about the self-reflexive
aspect of a democracy. Former congressman Rush Holt put it
this way: "A self-governing country works only if we believe it
does."[15] That's the brilliance of our democracy: the system itself
is a self-fulfilling prophecy. We do have ultimate faith in the

good judgment of the American people. As writer Alain de Botton has recently written: "Central to modern politics is the majestic and beautiful idea that every citizen is—in a small but highly significant way—the ruler of his or her own nation."[16]

Throughout history, America has proven it can rise above insurmountable conflict and drive on through the stagnation. As they have been for each successive generation, Adams's words speak to us: we may be deficient, there are things we may lack, but the best reason to charge forward is the most obvious one—*there is only us.*

Leadership is not about corralling cattle or driving a herd; it depends upon a symbiotic relationship. Leaders are chosen and accepted. They require the humility to listen to the people and the bravery to step ahead of them—as well as knowing which is needed when. The one thing a dictator can never be is a leader. They operate based on the currency of fear; no matter how intimidating, the strongest dictator will never be more than a "power holder."

True leaders know that people need a sense of ownership, a reason to be invested in the outcome. Once people have hope, they will add to the leader's courage with courage of their own. Once this happens, so can the process of change. Transformation does not occur without a strong catalyst; courageous leaders provide that catalyst, and then they embody it.

Courage is sometimes mistaken for disloyalty because it requires a willingness to paddle farther from shore than one's peers. Teddy Roosevelt, thrust into the presidency after President McKinley's assassination in 1901, was quite unpopular in his own party—so much so that he would run as a third-party candidate in 1912. The enmity mostly stemmed from T.R.'s crusade for workers' rights, the environment, and against corporate monopolies. Roosevelt knew that "the trusts are crushing the life out of the small men,"[17] and although many regular voters idolized him for it, the party bosses and Gilded Age moneymen who controlled much of politics at the turn of the century did not. Roosevelt risked his presidency, and ultimately his political career, on the fight against the same behemoths.

"Teddy Roosevelt genuinely thought of himself as a gladiator against evil," Beschloss writes in *Presidential Courage*. "Resembling John Adams, making people angry made him feel principled."[18] Roosevelt was a self-described "rough and tumble man"[19] who showed physical courage in countless ways: taking a bullet during a speech and not missing a beat, leading his famed Rough Riders in the Spanish-American War, and steering an expedition into the Amazonian jungle. But it's his political courage that put him on Mount Rushmore. "Aggressive fighting for the right," Roosevelt maintained, "is the greatest sport the world knows."

> "One of the countless drawbacks of being in Congress is that I am compelled to receive impertinent letters from a jackass like you in which you say I promised to have the Sierra Madre mountains reforested and I have been in Congress two months and I haven't done it. Will you please take two running jumps and go to hell."
>
> —LETTER FROM CONGRESSMAN JOHN STEVEN McGROARTY OF CALIFORNIA TO A CONSTITUENT, 1935

Lincoln claimed a leader must be far enough ahead to drive his people forward, but not so far that when he turns around there's nobody in sight. It's a wise observation—and of course he would know better than anyone. "The voice of the people is not always the voice of God," the young Teddy Roosevelt said, "and when it happens to be the voice of the devil, then it is a man's clear duty to defy its behests."[20]

In politics, a leader must get the pulse of the collective: this only comes by being a good listener within your party and especially with the other party. What's possible? What isn't? How far out am I? Trent was clearly too far ahead of his caucus with the original impeachment proposal for President Clinton; he had no choice but to change course. Tom did not always naturally occupy the middle ground of his caucus; he often had to figure out where that was. An effective political leader is constantly making those calculations.

In Trent's case, especially when he was in the House, he didn't have to guess what his constituents believed; ninety-nine times out of a hundred he was right there with them. Tom may have been more liberal than some of his fellow South Dakotans, but he had lived there his whole life and had a strong grasp of his district's needs.

But senators are responsible for entire states, huge contingents of people who couldn't possibly agree with us on everything. Even a relatively homogenous state is home to millions of people with various jobs, philosophies, histories, and perspectives. A man who can speak for all men speaks for none of them. Sometimes we were the political minority back home. When Tom represented South Dakota, it was a decidedly red state; and when Trent first joined the House, Mississippi was a historically blue one. Balancing our personal convictions with those of our states could mean walking a tightrope.

The classic civics question, which young people frequently ask us, is how we proceeded when our convictions dictated one vote and our constituents another. That tension is a key part of politics. We say we'd listen to our constituents, consider our states' needs, and in the final analysis we had to vote our consciences. Otherwise, we'd be sacrificing everything. Edmund Burke said, "Your representative owes you, not his industry only, but his judgment; and he betrays, instead of serving you, if he sacrifices it to your opinion."[21]

Senators' six-year terms and large constituencies were explicitly designed to free the upper body from unfettered public whims. (Hamilton actually lobbied for lifetime tenures.) This concept took some time to catch on. Senators were originally chosen by state legislatures, and dating back to colonial times constituents felt they had a right to give their senators explicit instructions on how to vote. "When they disagreed, however," Senate historian Richard A. Baker notes, "they faced a choice: they could ignore the instructions, or they could resign."[22] Senator Humphrey Marshall of Kentucky talked his way out of being thrown in the Kentucky River for supporting the Jay Treaty*, although he couldn't avoid being stoned in the state capital.[23] With time and with the passing of the Seventeenth Amendment providing for direct election of senators, the public began to embrace their senators' independent judgment.

Our system relies on feedback to work: if the voters feel the gap is too wide between you and them, they are given the opportunity to express their displeasure and vote you out. Leaders must be cognizant of the size of that gap, balance themselves, and adjust to it where appropriate. But as an elected official in a

---

* The Jay Treaty was a controversial agreement with the British signed by President Washington in 1794 and negotiated by Supreme Court Chief Justice John Jay. Jeffersonian Democrats viewed it as far too favorable to our former British enemies; they also bristled at how it tied America's economic futures so closely to a country against whom we had just fought a war.

democracy, you have to accept the possibility of being moved. Your very existence is to protect, embody, and honor that choice. It's reminiscent of the famous line: "I disapprove of what you say, but I will defend to the death your right to say it."[*]

There's an old expression we used to have in the Senate: "This guy is going to vote his mail." A senator would count the letters he received on each side of an issue and then vote based on the higher stack. That bellwether has fallen by the wayside since the onset of hyper-orchestrated issue campaigns. Coordinated campaigns are not new, of course, but they've become ubiquitous, partly as a response to the modern media environment.

The mail isn't necessarily reflective of your constituency anymore, so you can't trust it. A vocal, organized group can look like a majority. Astroturfing, it's now called, as in fake grassroots. Of course, it's rarely regular mail anymore; it's floods of e-mails and phone calls. Trent experienced a quite intense example of this during the last attempt to pass immigration reform in 2007.

> TRENT: Like all institutions, the U.S. Congress is constantly
> shifting—even more so because its makeup changes
> every two years. Besides elections, it's affected by the
> times and the tides; it evolves and devolves; it sheds its
> skin and then grows a new one.
>
> In my final years in the Senate—after Tom had
> already left—I reemerged in the leadership as majority
> whip again. I couldn't help but notice the increased
> difficulty of getting even basic things done: the caucus

---

[*] The famous line was written by Voltaire biographer Evelyn Beatrice Hall in an attempt to explain her subject's belief system. (*Friends of Voltaire*, 199)

was almost allergic to the idea of consensus and my colleagues were getting noticeably meaner. Battles had gone way beyond winning a vote or an election. What had taken root was an equation of destruction.

In addition, every vote or statement was going to be the subject of a thirty-second commercial from a future opponent. You didn't know which vote or statement was going to frame those ads, but you knew they were coming. Suffice it to say I began to lose interest in an institution to which I had dedicated my life. The body seemed to have stopped working—or, rather, it was working, just toward things I couldn't get behind, hijacked by purely political agendas.

My frustrations came to a head in 2007 over the Comprehensive Immigration Reform Act. My embarrassment and disgust in how that bill was handled was one of the main reasons I retired when I did. The level of cowardice I witnessed was unprecedented. An enormously important issue was long overdue for reform—and yet, we still couldn't make it work. What most frustrated me is that we did what you're supposed to do: we had built a consensus on both sides. At the time we had the full spectrum of philosophical differences as well as both parties' leaders on board: myself, Jon Kyl, and Lindsey Graham on the Republican side and Ted Kennedy, Dianne Feinstein, and Harry Reid on the Democratic side.

Besides support on both sides of the aisle, the public was mostly with us, and the country desperately needed it. Incredibly, in the end, it didn't even get to be voted on; it went down on a procedural vote. The bill didn't pass the threshold for cloture to end the filibuster—an ignominious demise if there ever was one.*

The bill's chances were auspicious for quite some time, but it fractured, and once that happened the crack just widened and widened. Interests on both the far left and the far right began to fight it, but I put the blame squarely on Rush Limbaugh. He irresponsibly labeled it "amnesty" at a critical moment over the weekend. Limbaugh had an enormous and vocal constituency at the time, and his words instantly changed a lot of Republicans' attitudes. After that, the whole atmosphere shifted in a heartbeat.† Besides the pressure calls from within my party, I had to fend off Limbaugh listeners, who jammed up my phones for over a week; I even received three death threats—one from my home state. All for just daring to work on immigration reform.

It got out of hand. Sometimes, when the phone would ring in my office before my assistant arrived, I would just pick it up and say, "Hello, this is Trent Lott." That would throw them off. It gave me a chance to talk to them—person to person. Sometimes I even got somewhere with them. One doctor from Oregon told me at the end of our conversation, "Well, I'm glad I talked to you. You completely changed my mind."

Seeing immigration reform become a political football in the years since has been a huge disappointment. Having been involved with immigration issues going back to the

---

* It actually lost *three* cloture votes.

† Senator Obama cast one of the deciding votes against cloture.

mid-eighties, it was all somewhat déjà vu for me. As whip in the House in 1986, I helped pass the last immigration reform, Simpson-Mazzoli, a bipartisan bill signed by President Reagan. It had its merits but it didn't go far enough. Toward the end of his second term, I was with a small group in the Cabinet Room with President Reagan. I approached him afterward. "Mr. President," I said, "we're not doing what we're supposed to do to secure the border. It's getting worse, and we have to do something." I even made some suggestions—none of which he ever did. I watched president after president get into that office and none ever made a serious effort to secure the border. Then in the 2000s we woke up to over eleven million illegal immigrants living here.

Some Americans are vocally and effusively against any path to citizenship, but the lack of sensible immigration solution—or even an attempt at it—is one of America's greatest failures. President Obama recently took executive action to push through reform, which was a huge mistake and likely illegal. Unilateral action just exacerbates the tension with Congress, putting an even heavier wet blanket over any chance of permanent reform. On top of this, any executive action is immediately reversible by the new president. By the same token, the Republican response—trying to use the Homeland Security appropriations bill as a way to reverse the executive order—was a tactical mistake. Neither side was going to succeed through those kinds of hardball methods.

Both Republicans and Democrats are at fault in not moving to have broad-based immigration reform. But we need not just illegal immigration reform but *legal* immigration reform. A lot of people who want to come in the country that have something to offer find it very difficult to get through the maze to get in here legally. I've been involved a few times with the obstacles in getting people to my home state. I've tried to help a female physicist from Sweden get into the NASA facility in Mississippi for a specific program—even on a temporary basis—and it was very difficult.

A few years back, I worked to get a couple of Canadian doctors into the small town of Picayune, Mississippi. They wanted to come, and the community desperately needed them. Incredibly, it took months. With a vested interest in letting these people into our country, you'd think it'd be easy. But it was impossible; making it happen was an absolute nightmare. You would have thought we were trying to smuggle in Saddam Hussein.

CHAPTER NINETEEN

Courage and Memory in the United States Senate

"Courage may be in scarce supply, but the demand appears down as well. And we have come to grade courage on the curve."

—JOHN McCAIN

SENATOR AS INSTITUTION: ROBERT C. BYRD

At fifty-one years, five months, and twenty-six days, Robert C. Byrd was the longest serving senator in United States history. Majority leader, minority leader, majority whip, chairman of the powerful Appropriations Committee, president pro tem of the Senate—Byrd served many roles during his half century tenure. He cast the most votes in Senate history (more than eighteen thousand) and served every president from Eisenhower to Obama: the changes and events he witnessed—and participated in—made Byrd an institution in and of himself.

There are objects, places, and rituals that tie the Senate back to the past, but Byrd was a living, breathing example of it. He had such gravitas and dignity, in look, in speech, and in action. One Senate historian reverently noted "his immaculately styled silver-white hair, his dark blue three-piece suit framing a carefully chosen silk necktie, and his dignified bearing convey[ing] the modern image of an ancient Roman senator."[1] Byrd was almost regal looking, someone whose image you'd find on an antique coin or in a classical painting.

Close to the end of the Clinton impeachment trial, when votes were about to be taken, Senator Byrd asked Tom to come down to his office each morning before they began the session. Tom obliged and he and Byrd would read and discuss biblical passages that were applicable to the issues of the trial. They'd carve out that time together because Byrd felt it was important. It's just the kind of thing you did when Bob Byrd asked.

Senator Byrd also took it upon himself to be the Senate historian. Not only did he write the volumes, but he also spoke them from the floor on Friday afternoons. As a young senator Tom was called upon to preside quite frequently, as the junior senators are required to do. From that post he'd have the opportunity to listen to Byrd go on at great length. Trent attended those sessions as well, sometimes even taking notes as Byrd detailed some important or forgotten event in Senate history. Byrd's grasp of the long arc of the Senate's story, its fluidness and its solidity, was unmatched. Those speeches became four huge books on Senate history, beautifully bound volumes of seven hundred to eight hundred pages each.

Byrd had an instinctive understanding of the Senate, both its larger purpose and its inner workings. He revered it but he also used it to his advantage, becoming such a master of rules and procedure that he had an edge over just about any other senator. Famously, Bob also liked to take his time, and often others'. He respected the fact that the upper chamber sometimes moved glacially. A senator in the model of Clay and Webster, men who regularly spoke for three hours on the floor, Byrd saw virtue in neither speed nor brevity. "The Senate is often soundly castigated for its inefficiency," Byrd once said, "but in fact, it was never

intended to be efficient. Its purpose was and is to examine, consider, protect, and to be a totally independent source of wisdom and
judgment."

He was as unlikely as anyone to become a United States
senator, much less its majority leader, growing up poor and mostly
self-educated in the hardscrabble coal country of West Virginia.
In his first campaign, "with country folk in the hills, much like a
preacher, he talked the Old Time religion. Afterward he brought
out his fiddle and entertained the crowd . . ."[2]

Byrd was a tender and gracious man as well, often making
gestures to his colleagues that would permanently endear them
to him. We each had the experience of being in the Senate
chamber when Robert Byrd took to the floor to honor the birth
of our first grandchildren: he said a few words and then recited
a poem, which was put in the *Congressional Record*. We had
the poems framed and hung in our grandchildren's bedrooms.
It's something that connects them both to their proud grandfathers and even further back—to the old Senate giants like
Robert Byrd.

Of course, he wasn't all softhearted gesture. He honored
Senator Don Nickles's grandchild, too, but did not miss the opportunity to add: "I could not help myself in reminding Budget
Chairman Nickles that, given his support for a budget that
embraces record deficits, his sweet grandchild was born owing
$24,000 on the national debt."

Byrd was literally encyclopedic on all kinds of history:
American, Roman, European. One night at a White House
dinner he boasted to Queen Elizabeth that he could recite the
royalty of England chronologically, all the way from the beginning. "That's impossible," the queen replied. Byrd took the
challenge. Throughout the night he made his way through the

list until she finally told him, exasperated, "Enough already. I believe you."

Tom once asked Byrd what his secret was in learning and retaining so much—including poetry, which he was able to recite from memory. Bob said that he hated the drive from Washington to West Virginia and he needed to occupy himself. His staff would drive him there and he would sit and learn poetry. It was his goal to learn a new poem on every trip—and he did. His mind just held things like a trap.

It was about more than just memorization. Byrd's knowledge was about reverence for the past and the wisdom of our ancestors, pride in our country's story, a connection to the accomplishments of men and women long gone—all of which continued through him. In fact, it has become clear to us that Robert Byrd was the living embodiment of those very things.

> "I made up my mind to risk myself on a proposition for a general pacification. I resolved to push my skiff from the shore alone . . ."
>
> —DANIEL WEBSTER

SENATOR AS SURVIVOR: JOHN MCCAIN

There's an iconic photograph of the two of us sitting in Tom's office next to John McCain. Both of us are pleading with him with our hands out and John's got this familiar look on his face, the one that says: *I'm not buying it.* McCain is a tough man to please, but the Senate is so much stronger with him in it. Harry Reid recently told us that John has become one of the most important players on either side of the Senate chamber. That's tough for anyone to become; to be a man of principle and passion and still be valued on both sides is just incredibly rare. But John pulls it off. And if you were going to pick the Republican that Democrats respect the most, it would likely be John.

John is a true throwback: he knows how the Senate works, how it used to work (he was once Navy liaison to the Senate), and how relationships keep it running. Some of the younger senators and congressmen don't seem to understand the value in that. The institutional memory he brings is invaluable and getting exceedingly rare as John's generation retires. We'd hate to see it become extinct.

John is dogged but not bound by territorial notions of party or role; he'll rummage around on both sides of the aisle, heading over to the Democratic leader in a heartbeat if he feels the need to. Of course, he manages to regularly make both sides mad too. "We should be careful to distinguish between outrage and anger, a distinction I've often missed,"[3] he once wrote. He can be volatile for sure, but he is always tenacious, and admirably so. McCain-Feingold—the Bipartisan Campaign Reform Act of 2002—took years to push through and faced countless obstacles along the way. It was finally passed through John's sheer force of will. We've had issues with its consequences, but its passage could not have happened without John's bulldog determination.

A key part of John McCain's legacy is how he handled himself *after* he lost two elections: the 2000 Republican primary and the 2008 presidential election. In 2000 he was enraged about the negative tactics the Bush campaign used against him in the South Carolina primary. After McCain dropped out, Tom talked to him several times about jumping ship and coming to the other side. He almost pulled the trigger: people have no idea how close John was to becoming an Independent who would have caucused with the Democrats. He would've been a force to be reckoned with if he had. But he remained and returned with gusto, as he did after losing the general election in 2008.

Win or lose, history always judges the party's nominee more favorably. George McGovern lost by a landslide in 1972, but history shines on him to an extent because he was the Democratic nominee for president of the United States and because of all of his extraordinary accomplishments after his defeat. The nominee doesn't just vanish; he is still the leader of the party, and John has held that role admirably. It doesn't mean we agree with all of John's choices—we're both still baffled by his choice of running mate—but his stature and legacy is assured. The fact that he has become an even bigger factor upon his return says a great deal about what kind of man he is.

After running for president and returning to the Senate—ostensibly a body of equals—a senator has to reestablish him- or herself. It's quite a transition to go from being the center of national attention to being just one of the caucus again. Both McCain and John Kerry have done it admirably, because they didn't rest on their laurels nor did they act above the work. They rolled up their sleeves and contributed.

In McCain's book *Why Courage Matters: The Way to a Braver Life*, he writes with wisdom and experience about the concept: the kind he admired as a young man in the military and the kind he respects as an older man in the Senate.

> *Without courage, all virtue is fragile: admired, sought, professed, but held cheaply and surrendered without a fight . . . That's what we mean by the courage of our convictions. Not that our convictions possess an innate courage, but that if we lack the courage to hold them . . . against threatening opposition, in the moment of their*

*testing, they're superficial, vain things that add nothing
to our self-respect or our society's respect for the virtues
we profess . . . [W]ithout courage we are corruptible.*[4]

In addition to just knowing how the Senate works, John implicitly understands the value of persistence there. It is often the thing that keeps issues alive. This is true both with your colleagues and with the public. Richard Nixon said, "About the time you are writing a line you have written so often that you want to throw up—that is the first time the American people will hear it."[5] A truer line about politics has not been said.

John, like Ted Kennedy, just worked to wear you down; to be honest, sometimes you gave in because you didn't want to have to deal with it anymore. McCain is like Teddy in the sense that they both had strong, even historic second acts in their careers. They seemed to be finished, were written off by most people, and then came back even stronger.

Washington can be a "powerful reinvention canvas," Mark Leibovich noted in his book about modern-day Washington, *This Town: Two Parties and a Funeral—Plus, Plenty of Valet Parking!—in America's Gilded Capital*. "The city is filled with proving grounds that double as sanctuaries, like the Senate floor."[6] His book may be cynical regarding the way the city operates, but the author is dead right about the way Congress can be both an arena for blood sport and a temple of rebirth.

CHAPTER TWENTY

Fear and Loathing in the U.S. Congress

"One man with courage makes a majority."

—ATTRIBUTED TO ANDREW JACKSON

IN stark contrast to the role that courage has played in our country's history, the operative trait in today's U.S. government is fear. In Congress, so much emphasis and energy is placed on being in control that it leads to the obvious question: What's the point of even being in the majority? Is its purpose just to sustain itself? With elections occurring every other year and the off season getting shorter and shorter, it certainly seems that way.

Last fall before the midterms, Trent had lunch with a senator in the Republican leadership. "Okay, suppose you do get the majority," Trent said to him. "You're still not going to have sixty votes. Are you going to produce anything?" The senator, a veteran politician, gave him a blank stare. Trent's question seemed to be beside the point.

The Republicans ended up winning that majority, but right off the bat they did little but contribute to the stalemate, especially in their interaction with the president. The atmosphere and the gridlock simply carried over. The challenge is for the Republicans to prove they can govern. When they began, they moved two bills in two months—a disappointing start. They need to start moving bills that are less controversial and more inclined to get bipartisan support, like energy and education.

We'd rather be in a productive minority than a stunted majority, which today is just heresy. You could get killed in this town for saying something like that. During our time in the leadership we didn't view producing as a zero-sum game. We sensed that if something got done, there'd be plenty of credit to go around. That kind of shared credit is tough now, because wins are defined by the other party's loss. The very act of sharing a win now seems to negate it.

Defensive governing, such as not letting things come to the floor for a vote or preventing the minority from offering amendments ("filling the tree"), may yield a short-term victory but it creates substantial long-term problems. The protective action invariably triggers a reaction from the other side, adding to the distrust, the tension, and the caustic environment. It's a unifying tactic for the minority too: nothing makes it easier for a leader to rally his troops than being shut off from the process.

One of the main reasons the Constitutional Convention in Philadelphia was kept secret—even the shades in the room were drawn—was so no delegate had to answer for changing his mind. James Madison, who was present for every session that summer, later told a historian that secrecy was essential: "No Constitution would ever have been adopted by the Convention if the debates had been made public."[1]

Explaining the secrecy to Jefferson in a letter, Madison argued, "It was thought expedient in order to secure the unbiased discussion within doors, and to prevent misconceptions and misconstructions without."[2] People debate, positions evolve, and sticking to your original belief for its own sake is not a virtue in itself. In some situations the courageous thing is to admit to a mistake or that you changed your mind.

Nowadays we have a term for it: it is called flip-flopping and it's the scarlet letter of politics. Its ascension was in the 2004 campaign against John Kerry, who tried to explain how he had voted both for and against the use of force in Iraq. He had his reasons but he did a poor job explaining it, and the label stuck. We have both been accused of flip-flopping in our careers; it comes with the territory. It's not a completely fair term, because an active mind is a working mind, and sometimes that means an evolving mind. As John Maynard Keynes is famously misquoted as saying: "When the facts change, I change my mind. What do you do, sir?"*

You want to try to avoid taking on more water than you have to, but there are times when you absorb the hits because it's part of the job. Some finesse it better than others, but it happens to every single elected official we know. Obviously, a thick skin is required in politics. It's messy, it can be dirty, and you don't belong there if you can't accept that. The best you can do is have a sound basis for changing your mind and to explain yourself to your constituents—something we both always tried to do.

As a senator, John Kennedy wrote about the high expectations of those in public office, and the oft-narrow judgment of the public. "In no other occupation but politics is it expected that a man will sacrifice honors, prestige and his chosen career on a single issue," he wrote in *Profiles in Courage*.

Lawyers, businessmen, teachers, doctors, all face difficult personal decisions involving their integrity—but few, if

---

* The actual quote is: "When my information changes, I alter my conclusions. What do you do, sir?" (A *Treatise of Melancholie* by Timothie Bright, 1940)

any, face them in the glare of the spotlight as do those in
public office. . . . [W]hen the roll is called he cannot hide, he
cannot equivocate, he cannot delay—and he senses that his
constituency, like the Raven in Poe's poem, is perched there
on his Senate desk, croaking "Nevermore" as he casts the
vote that stakes his political future.[3]

It's very windy at the top in Washington, Trent likes to remind people, especially those who think it'll be smooth sailing when they get there. Everyone is gunning for the leader—your enemies always and your subordinates sometimes. Over the last forty years a large percentage of congressional leaders were pushed out. Tom Foley was defeated, Jim Wright had difficulties, Newt Gingrich resigned. Of course, we each had our own problems.

But you can't lead from a defensive posture, fearful that you're going to get taken out. You need to use the time that you have productively. As Trent has said, if you're going to get your head chopped off politically, why not get something done in the process? To work so many years to become a leader and then to spend that time shoring up your walls—it just doesn't seem worth it. Is this what holding the highest offices in the land is all about? We certainly don't think so. Every generation of political leaders aspires to rise to the standard set by a certain number of our predecessors. That is a high bar. The question really comes down to whether we have it in us to do it. Some do and some don't. But it is critical we remember that there is only us.

Part IV

Vision

"The greatness of America lies not in being more enlightened than any other nation, but rather in her ability to repair her faults."

—ALEXIS DE TOCQUEVILLE,
DEMOCRACY IN AMERICA (1835)

CHAPTER TWENTY-ONE

Writing the Future

"I like the dreams of the future better than the history of
the past."

—THOMAS JEFFERSON TO JOHN ADAMS,
AUGUST 1, 1816

THOMAS Jefferson had reservations about the very idea of a
permanent constitution. He was ambassador to France—
what was then called minister plenipotentiary—while the document was being conceived, debated, and written. His friend James
Madison wrote letters to keep him apprised of its progress. Often
the idealist to Madison's pragmatist, Jefferson expressed his
doubts. "No society can make a perpetual constitution or even a
perpetual law," he wrote to Madison. "The earth belongs always
to the living generation: they may manage it then, and what
proceeds from it, as they please . . ."[1]

Jefferson went so far as to suggest that each generation—
every nineteen years—should write a new Constitution, wresting
itself free from the choices and mind-sets of the old and the dead.
The country's laws should be free to evolve along with its people,
he argued. Madison convinced his friend of the impracticality of
such an idea. Laws bind a civil society; they cannot be repeatedly
thrown out.[2]

Jefferson would die penniless and in debt (partly inherited
from his deceased wife's family), so his ideas were likely influenced

by both personal hardship and philosophical conviction.°[3] But his reasons seem less important than his point, that "each generation is sovereign and that the dead cannot govern the living."[4] The present had a duty to the future just as the past had a duty to them.

Jefferson was not alone. Others involved in our country's creation were decidedly mindful of how future generations would be affected by their work. Virginia delegate George Mason, Madison's collaborator on the Bill of Rights, was one of them. "The influence which the [government] now proposed may have upon the happiness or misery of millions yet unborn," he wrote to his son from the Constitutional Convention, "is an object of such magnitude, as absorbs, and in a manner suspends, the operations of the human understanding."[5]

Twenty-five years later, wiser but no less a dreamer, Jefferson would still harp on the concept of an evolving society, one unshackled to the past. "Laws and institutions must go hand in hand with the progress of the human mind," he wrote, words that today grace the Jefferson Memorial. "As that becomes more developed, more enlightened, as new discoveries are made, new truths disclosed, and manners and opinions change with the change of circumstances, institutions must advance also, and keep pace with the times."[6]

Each generation is indeed responsible to the next and, as Jefferson believed, morally forbidden from laying unnecessary burdens on the unborn. This philosophy ran through a great deal

---

° In 1814 a nearly bankrupt Jefferson sold his books to the U.S. government for $23,950, which became the foundation for the new Library of Congress. (Richard A. Baker, 200 Notable Days: Senate Stories, 1787–2002, Washington, D.C.: U.S. Government Printing Office, 2006)

of Jefferson's thinking—thinking that conceived some of our country's most lasting ideas. Nowadays, with so much uncertainty facing our descendants, Jefferson's belief could not be more important.

We've met a great number of young people during our time in Congress and since leaving office. Interacting with them is one of the immense benefits of our work, and we believe it's our duty to encourage their participation. Few things give us more optimism than meeting intelligent and engaged young people. They recognize our country's virtues as well as its shortcomings, and are motivated for action. Their curiosity, patriotism, and enthusiasm about getting involved make those experiences some of the most rewarding work we do.

They ask how we got started, because our stories could be their stories: neither of us had money or connections—just the desire to get involved. It gives them the sense of what's possible. We also try to offer some on-the-ground insight that they may not pick up in books or classrooms, which they always enjoy. We get notes thanking us for inspiring them, but that feeling goes even stronger the other way.

The quality of their questions is impressive: What principles do you stand for? What are the toughest decisions you've had to make? What is the fundamental difference between the Republican and Democratic Parties? How hard a job is this, really? Their desire for three-sentence answers presents a challenge as well, but we oblige: curiosity is an essential part of a mind at work. But they're also seeking answers to the same questions we're asking: Why have things become so dysfunctional in Washington?

Despite all the easy reasons for negativity, our young leaders are not deterred. This alone bodes well for our future. Plenty of

armchair critics denigrate this generation, condemning their electronic devices and attention spans, but our experience on the
ground does not bear out that stereotype.

Arguably the next generation will have a leg up in that they've
had firsthand experience of what they don't like. They also benefit
from having been taught, and having learned, social responsibility, a feature that makes their generation unique. It'll be fascinating to see how that will play out in their lives.

The younger ones have no memory of our country not being
at war. For the older ones, in college or entering the job market,
9/11 was a formative event, a collective horror at an impressionable age. Perhaps their seriousness of purpose is tied to that. Like
those too young to fight in World War II, they witnessed a terror-
ist attack on their homeland, followed by a display of great unity
and purpose among the people. Like the young Lincoln, their
cause is not yet defined. But we have faith they will face it with
commitment, poise, and wisdom.

"We are shaping the world faster than we can change ourselves,"
Winston Churchill warned our parents' generation, "and we are
applying to the present the habits of the past." Like so many
things Churchill said, these words span the decades and speak
directly to our current times. We have to be able to adapt and
evolve, as Jefferson said our government must. This next generation is going to be both the beneficiary and the victim of incred-
ible technological change that will continue to dramatically shrink
our globe. With that erasing of distance comes enormous opportunity and enormous risk.

A prime example of that risk is that at some point, certainly
in the lifetime of our children, the United States is going to experience a major cybersecurity crisis. We've seen early signs of this

already, with recent hacks on corporations like Target, Home Depot, and Sony.° Our businesses, our banks, and our military are all in danger of suffering an enormously destructive breach. A cyberattack is a terrifying proposition for which we have not adequately prepared. What happens when it's not stolen credit card numbers but military coordinates or the locations of nuclear weapons? We have become so enamored and accustomed to our technological landscape that we forget how permeable it all is.

One of the great failures of the Congress over the last few years has been its inability to pass cybersecurity legislation. When first introduced, it looked possible. There was the necessary movement for something of its size and complexity to pass. However, it fizzled out completely, killed by the special-interest pressures on all sides. All the entities affected by the Internet dug in their heels: the U.S. Chamber of Commerce, the cable and phone companies, the entertainment industry. The Obama administration, which showed leadership on the issue, just could not get any side to compromise. Once things like that fade, it takes moving mountains to bring it back. The great tragedy would be if it took a crippling attack for something to get done.

Tom has a "five-alarm-fire" theory of Congress: only when the problem is raging out of control does Congress act. But they spend so much time putting out five-alarm fires that they never get to fire *prevention*. We've seen this in recent years with raising the debt ceiling, with passing a budget, and with funding the Department of Homeland Security. They end up acting at the eleventh hour. But some issues demand preventive action because

---

° In March 2015 the former director of national intelligence said that "The Chinese have penetrated every major corporation of any consequence in the United States . . . " (*CNN Money* 3/13/15)

putting out the fire is just a nightmare, especially in the intangible and mobile space of the digital world.

After a prayer breakfast a couple years ago, Trent saw an unlikely group of senators huddled at a table off to the side: Jon Kyl and Dan Coates, two very conservative Republicans, were talking with Sheldon Whitehouse and Chris Coons, two very liberal Democrats. Curious, Trent went over and found them talking about passing a cybersecurity bill together. It was an encouraging sight: *This is the answer,* Trent thought. The senators were looking to create a third way that reconciled the two versions that came out of committee. Not long after, the senators were outed, cornered, and told to back away. It's why Trent found them huddled in the first place: compromises these days tend to dissolve in the light. Those bipartisan meetings have to be kept under close wraps at least until they have enough support to stand up on their own.

This sequence is replicated again and again in Washington. While the wheels of government seem to move slower and slower, these dangerous and preventable issues are picking up steam. Those senators were on the right track, though: with many issues that desperately require congressional action, a bipartisan solution is as close to a silver bullet as we'll ever be able to fire.

A Bipartisan Answer

IN 2007, Tom joined three other former Senate majority leaders—fellow Democrat George Mitchell and Republicans Howard Baker and Bob Dole—in founding the Bipartisan Policy Center. The BPC is a venue for exploring common ground on the most significant issues facing our country, among them health, energy, national security, transportation, and housing.

The goal was to gather public policy veterans and advocates, leaders, academics, experts in various fields, and former elected and appointed officials to study the issues and produce common ground policy solutions. One of its first projects was a comprehensive health plan that looked very similar to the Affordable Care Act that was signed into law.

Going beyond the traditional think tank model of passive "white papers," the BPC gets involved in the nuts and bolts of legislation and does the legwork necessary to get momentum for its recommendations. Using its extensive network of connections, the BPC meets with members of Congress and the administration to advocate for practical measures, works to engage affected organizations to join its work, and coordinates with appropriate media to ensure public awareness and collective action.

Currently the only D.C. think tank that actively promotes bipartisan solutions, the BPC recognizes the value in both process and product when competing sides work together. The BPC's goal is not to ask its participants to give up their ideological identities but rather to *reflect* them in their contribution to the whole. Since the environment is less politically heated than Congress, the partisan views at the BPC are treated as valuable, not as elements of discord. The BPC works with the kind of positive tension utilized by our country's early leaders, offering solutions that were forged in fire rather than destroyed by it. As we discussed in Part I, that tension can create something beyond division. In a Darwinian sense, the solutions evolve out of it.

The initial impact of the BPC and its high-profile participants brought in a broad selection of contributors, all looking for constructive ways to work on public policy. Trent began to work with the BPC soon after our initial year. Our work comes from an aspirational place, but it is also born from a concern regarding modern trends in government and politics. We were both driven by our frustration with an increasingly polarized and politicized environment and our concern about its effect on governance. The work stemmed from our firm conviction that finding common ground was no longer just an ideal or an attractive option: it has become the only option. The organization's work is never without fierce debate and disagreement, but that's the point. It wouldn't work any other way.

One of our largest projects to date, which we cochaired, is the BPC Commission on Political Reform. Its goal was to examine the partisan divide in our country and advocate for sensible reforms that could work within the current political landscape.

Along with BPC president Jason Grumet and the other cochairs—Olympia Snowe, former secretary of agriculture Dan Glickman, and former secretary of the interior Dick Kempthorne— we assembled a diverse team. Our goal was to work out common-ground solutions concerning the electoral process and Senate rules and practice, as well as to present ways to promote a sense of civic duty and encourage service, especially among young people.

The recommendations range from the easy, to the possible, to the nearly impossible but worth discussing. There are common-sensical changes that require little more than the leaders simply deciding to make them; those goals require no statutory or consti-tutional reform. The second group of changes, harder than the first, can reasonably happen with rule changes—nothing unpre-cedented. The last group includes suggestions that require sweep-ing change, usually a constitutional amendment. Whatever the difficulty in enacting this last category of changes, their need can't be ignored: they are systemic issues and the conversation has to happen. Classifying these as impossible is actually misguided, because putting ideas on the table and discussing and debating them is a start. If enough people in power can talk about the impossible, then it ceases to become so.

On multiple occasions we both have had to deal with what at the outset looked like impossible tasks but revealed themselves not to be as we got closer. Once you embark on the long road of action, that wall begins to crumble. As Google cofounder Larry Page is fond of saying, you have to have "a healthy disregard for the impossible."[1] That's the audacious part of courage.

We released the BPC's recommendations for political reform in June 2014 and were surprised by the mostly positive response; we didn't receive nearly the criticism we expected, especially from the current leadership. The favorable press was encouraging because it proved that there is a yearning for reform. With so much skepticism in the air about government, people were starving for someone from the inside to speak out. The lack of a political agenda or overt partisanship in the recommendations gave them credibility as well. We were freed from the prison of political infighting and maneuvering. We weren't pushing a single viewpoint, just a unified one.

CHAPTER TWENTY-THREE

Electoral and Campaign Reform

"Don't vote. It only encourages them."

—UNKNOWN

THERE'S endemic frustration and cynicism about politics, some of which is justified. A good portion of it is directed at the very process of how we select our leaders. The drawn-out campaigns end up turning off potential voters, especially in the final stretch, when the ads are ubiquitous and the negatives are sky-high. The over-targeting and incessant polling cause people to stay home out of exhaustion. Some end up voting for the least offensive candidate or make a protest vote. The time, money, and effort that goes into influencing the electorate has poisoned the well so entirely that everyone comes out of Election Day feeling like they've been put through the wringer. And they have.

Those who get on the November ballot in the first place are often selected through an unfair and lopsided primary process. A smaller and smaller percentage of both parties have increasing power to select the candidates, and a handful of wealthy organizations profoundly influence the outcome. Our current primary system came about in the late 1960s as a remedy to the "smoke-filled back rooms" where party leaders got together, made deals, and handpicked the nominees. The state primaries were designed

as a democratic replacement for those rooms, but we have come
full circle: nominees are again selected through the monopolized
power of the few.

We still have fundamental faith in the people's vote making the
difference, but turnout in state primaries is an abysmal 15 percent
of eligible voters, sometimes less. And that 15 percent is not a
random sampling of America: it's a motivated and well-funded base,
not the "people" in any literal sense of the word. With so many
voters staying home, it doesn't take that many people to tip a
primary, especially in a sparsely populated state.

Our democracy requires a better primary system, one that
encourages greater participation. One recommendation that
would educate the public, focus their attention, and decrease
fatigue would be condensing the state primaries into a single day.

A National Primary Day would be reminiscent of Super
Tuesday, the day in March when eleven states' primaries are held.
Super Tuesday serves as a visible marker during the campaign
season and its primaries receive better coverage. Partly it's the
branding of the day, and partly it's just the sheer number of primaries: all that volume fills up the networks, cable news, the airwaves,
and the blogosphere. A National Primary Day would help to
elevate the attention and priority of all the primaries. The ideal
result would be a more informed and motivated voting populace.

Since the Iowa Caucus and the New Hampshire and South
Carolina primaries are always first on the calendar, those states
wield a great deal of power. If a frontrunner gets clobbered or a
dark horse makes a strong showing in those early states, the whole
electoral landscape shifts. Those states would obviously push back
on anything that would take away their influence, especially a
leveling of the entire schedule. But there's little merit in keeping
the control in their hands: those states are simply not reflective

of the country as a whole. Of course, no one who needs to be elected could ever say such a thing, which is part of the problem. One of Republican candidate Scott Walker's aides had to resign for making such comments before Walker's presidential campaign even began. The hoops that candidates go through in order to endear themselves to those states turn the early primaries into something of a circus act.

The primaries for the November election start in January and go all the way into June. Besides the exhaustion created by such a marathon schedule, the system is a mishmash: people don't even know the primary elections are taking place until it's too late. A single day would raise the profile of those primaries that get ignored; as part of the larger picture, they'd end up getting national attention. On paper, separating the states' primaries should give each one of them attention. But the opposite happens. There's a finite amount of focus out there, and the primaries just don't soak it up. Some don't even make a dent in the newscast; they're trees falling silently in a forest. However, if the public is invested in a compressed and immediate way on that one day—and watches the results on that one night—the momentum and energy would increase the turnout.

In presidential election years especially, the primaries are treated like the early round of the playoffs: casual voters stay home and tune in later in the season. But if we created an environment of focus and (dare we say it) excitement around the primaries, more people would participate. The change would benefit no single interest group except one: the American public. The candidates and nominees would be more reflective of the desires of the whole. We would begin to elect leaders who represent the best our nation has to offer. It's astounding that we've become accustomed to so much less.

Of course, implementing such a plan would be no cakewalk. Each state gets to decide on the details of its primary. State party officials run elections, and they are likely benefiting in some capacity from their current systems. Those early-primary states would no doubt put up a fight: their citizens act as though voting first is their birthright, when in fact the schedule was determined quite randomly.

Realistically, a national primary would require more unanimity than is likely achievable. Mandating it at the federal level is not ideal, but the federal government could incentivize the states to do it. Positive reinforcement from Uncle Sam always seems to work better than his demands. There are less drastic options that would still pull us in the right direction. Senator Slade Gorton cosponsored a bill with Senator Joe Lieberman in 1999 that would have set up four different regional primaries, one a month throughout the spring. Each Tuesday would be for a different region: the Southern primary, the Midwestern primary, the New England primary, and the Western primary. Overriding the states proved to be too difficult and the bill died. The National Association of Secretaries of State proposed a similar plan around the same time (fifteen years later, they continue to push for it) and a regional primary plan failed to get through Congress in the decade before Gorton's bill.

Such institutional changes never happen quickly; they begin with a motivated force, then a groundswell, and finally a critical mass demanding action. Even then it takes some time. We have to care enough to stay at it, because the benefits—to both the democratic process and in the final product of our elections—would be enormous.

November's general election has a higher turnout than the primaries but still lures a frustratingly low percentage of voters. In the

2014 midterms, 36.4 percent of eligible voters made it to the polls for the general election, the lowest number since World War II. Even during presidential election years, the turnout rarely gets above 55 percent. Despite the variety of ways that it has been made easier over the years, one in four eligible voters—51 million Americans—aren't even registered to vote.[1]

In this citadel of freedom and democracy, we should all find this shameful. It stands in contrast to how Americans like to see themselves. To put the number in perspective, the 2014 Scottish independence vote brought out 85 percent of the voters. Even though there are only 5.7 million people in Scotland, that percentage reflects an engaged and passionate citizenry. Something major was at stake for the Scottish people, and they responded in droves.

One reason for the low turnout is logistical: we vote during the workweek and those who get home late or have other responsibilities don't always make it a priority to get to the polls. The practice of voting the first Tuesday in November dates to 1845, when Congress tried to select a convenient time for a mostly rural society. By November, the harvest was usually over but harsh weather hadn't yet set in. Saturday was a workday for farmers, Sunday was for church, and Wednesday was market day. Considering it might take a full day to travel by horse to a polling station, Tuesday in early November became the choice, where it remains to this day.[2] It would be wise for us to revisit this antiquated logic. A good start would be moving Election Day to the weekend.

In addition, polling places are not in the most convenient locations or the easiest to access for some people, especially in rural areas where they have to drive quite some distance. Low turnout isn't always a matter of attitude; sometimes it's a physical issue. Tom knows plenty of South Dakotans—the elderly, Native

American voters who never had a car—who face a variety of obstacles to voting.

It's inexcusable: one of the most basic precepts of the American idea is guaranteeing people's ability to vote. Precincts in poorer, rural, elderly, and minority communities are not given priority. There are plenty of improvements that could be made on the state level. For one thing, local voting officials could go to assisted-care facilities, get seniors registered to vote, and organize them on Election Day. It's such a basic right, and when we fail those voters, we undermine our own institutions.

Electronic voting has been gaining steam as an option, and it's a method that Tom supports. We already do our banking, shopping, and taxes online. Trent worries about the increase of fraud under such a system, although he agrees we're inevitably heading toward electronic voting. There has been progress as states move away from one-size-fits-all voting and adapt to the makeup of their citizenry. Ten states and the District of Columbia already have same-day voter registration.[3] In Oregon, there are no polling places at all—they *only* have mail-in voting—and elections there have been virtually fraud-free. In the twenty-first century, the practice of voting in person within a ten-hour window is outdated and no longer suits our society's needs. It's time we modernized one of the most essential—if not *the* most essential—institution in our democracy.

Recent reforms aimed at fixing the electoral process have done nothing but strip authority away from the political parties. Parties once served as the anchors, the focal points of the action, but campaign finance reform has made the parties powerless during campaign season. In an attempt to block "soft money," federal law closed up the wrong end—the receiving end. The giving side is freer than it has ever been, having found a way to do an end around to the candidates, who are no longer even picked by the parties.

Candidates used to need the support of committeemen and precinct captains to get elected. That has all vanished. The modern candidate puts his own people together, raises the money on his own and through outside groups, and then buys as much media as possible. The party doesn't even have the capacity to help. We've created a twisted situation and turned campaigns into something of a free-for-all—all in the name of so-called reform.

There is a direct correlation between time and money. One of the reasons today's races are so expensive is that they're longer than they've ever been. We now start almost two years out, virtually from the end of the previous election. The biggest beneficiaries of the long campaign season are neither the candidates nor the voters but the media. A close second are the consultants and the campaign strategists who make their livings off the campaigns. Their salaries and reputations depend on long, brutal elections. Since consultants are paid a percentage of the media buy, they have a huge dog in a bitter fight. They get rich off of keeping the election season long and conflict-heavy.

Trent witnessed the election in Great Britain when Margaret Thatcher was running for prime minister for the first time back in the 1970s. By law, the campaign there has a fixed starting point a few months out and it runs within a limited time frame. Trent went to both parties' headquarters to talk about the election; the differences between what he saw there and what he knew from home were considerable. Of course, that was a long time ago and there was much less money involved, but it's an instructive example. The United Kingdom's elections still operate on that principle. A positive by-product of that tightened season is the level of knowledge and interest among the populace: everyone from the bus drivers to the street vendors was discussing that election.

The United States could benefit a great deal from a version of the British system. The UK currently has a "long" and a "short" campaign season, each with its own time frame and its own spending limits. If the U.S. campaign season were condensed, it would decrease the money and increase public interest and turnout in one fell swoop. The quality of the campaign would improve dramatically, and there'd be less space and time to go negative. A shortened season would also help the incumbents in Congress running for reelection; they wouldn't have to be campaigning and traveling half the year. We never wanted to be part of such a long campaign season; it's a necessary evil, to some extent.

Blocking the influx of money is a nearly impossible task, and the Supreme Court has recently made it even harder. The federal government should give up trying to control the money, which has been fruitless and counterproductive, and attempt to limit the time frame in which the candidates can use that money. It's a thousand times easier to enforce that, since the ads, by definition, are public and only so much money could flood in during the tighter window. Money and time are the two most important levers controlling elections in this country. Tinkering with the second is worth a study, because the Supreme Court has already weighed in on the first.

The Money Problem

I N any discussion of campaign reform, money sits there like an eight-hundred-pound gorilla. From the perspective of time, influence, and fairness, nothing else has become as toxic to our democracy. Advocates of unlimited money view it as a freedom issue; consequently, they argue that the flow of money should remain unfettered. The United States Supreme Court has recently agreed with them. However, as the history of the First Amendment has shown, freedom can be a double-edged sword.

In 2010 the Supreme Court ruled in the Citizens United case that money equals speech, a momentous decision that changed the way campaigns are run. It has also left only two options if we want to limit the influx of campaign money. The first is to incentivize candidates to limit their "speech" through public financing, something that was attempted at the presidential level in 2008, with disastrous results. The other option is a constitutional amendment, which requires the support of two-thirds of both chambers of Congress and has no chance of passing. Since neither option is tenable, we face an impasse. Tom's favorite metaphor is that campaign money is like a river that flows through various fingers into a delta. Whenever we plug up one of the delta's fingers, the money just flows through the others. This has become the predictable result of every attempt at campaign finance reform.

In the struggle to find a solution for the money problem in politics, we seem to be stymied by two factors: our inability to limit spending and the shackles we've put on the parties. It's not just the sheer volume of the money that is troubling but the concentration of it in the hands of fewer and fewer sources. Each election cycle, their power is consolidated and increases at an alarming rate. The backing of wealthy donors—not the party— is the most important factor in determining which candidate becomes the frontrunner. For instance, billionaires Charles and David Koch pledged $900 million across various conservative organizations for the 2016 campaign, which will be only part of the most expensive campaign in history.[1] Their stated goal is to have finances "on par" with the two political parties; in fact, former Obama aide David Axelrod argued that "In many ways, they have superseded the party."[2] A recent study found that 60 percent of the money spent by super PACs on both sides in the last three election cycles—$600 million—came from fewer than *two hundred* donors.[3]

On top of what the candidates and the super PACs raise on their own, the House and Senate campaign committees each had close to $200 million in the bank for the 2014 midterms. Of course, this money doesn't just appear: it takes legwork and man-hours to raise it. Even the party leader can't raise a hundred million dollars in a Senate race (as Mitch McConnell recently did) without a lot of heavy lifting.

When candidates have to devote so much of their time to chasing money, priorities get shifted, interests are compromised, and conflicts of interest arise. It's a natural outgrowth of our current system. Tom travels a lot for the National Democratic Institute, which talks about governance to other countries. When he discusses the need for transparency with other nations, they push right back. "You're talking to *us* about money?" they say. "With *your* system? Give us a break." He has trouble responding, because they have a point. There is a certain hypocrisy to our efforts to lead in this regard.

Perhaps unsurprisingly we have different positions on the role of money in politics, but we both share the view that it is becoming increasingly problematic. Our key disagreement revolves around whether or not money can be legally characterized as speech, as the Supreme Court has ruled in two recent major cases.

> TOM: The prospect that money equates with speech is absolutely and unequivocally wrong. We already do limit money in government in very specific ways: you can't accept or solicit political money on federal property, you can't give money to an unelected official, and you can't walk up to a bureaucrat and try to hand him money—that's called a bribe, and it's a federal crime. Some argue that the limit on campaign spending is too tough to set, but we already limit political money in a variety of ways. The Citizens United ruling seems to have ignored that fact.
>
> As a corollary, many states argue that the Second Amendment allows you to carry a gun almost anywhere. But you can't take a gun on an airplane and you certainly can't take a gun into the Capitol building. We've decided that there are certain pragmatic limits on the right to have a gun. That has expanded quite a bit over the years, but we almost all agree that some limit needs to exist in a

functioning society. It's hard to understand why money can't also be subject to a pragmatic limit. "There never will be no money," veteran reporter Jill Lepore argues, "but, for the public to have faith in government, the law has to be something a great deal stronger than: anything goes."[4]

Society can both recognize money as a form of speech but not allow it to flow 100 percent freely. Does it really make sense, as we saw, to spend $100 million in a Senate race in Kentucky? Are we okay with $300 million in 2024? Is there a billion-dollar Senate race in our future? When do we reach the sensible limit of our constitutional rights?

The idea that money can't be limited because it's a form of speech is a hollow argument because even actual speech is restricted. The Supreme Court has ruled that it is illegal to yell *fire* in a theater because of the danger it poses to others. Nor can you threaten the life of the president, or anyone for that matter. So we even put limits on actual speech. There's a practical appreciation for the fact that you can't just do whatever you want in a free society; political money needs to be part of that precedent.

TRENT: I'm inclined to honor the Supreme Court's decision and agree that money is speech, although I am concerned with some implications of the Citizens United ruling. I understand the impetus of wanting to limit campaign money, but what troubles me is the execution of it. I'm not against the proposition of limits, but the devil of it is all in the *how*. What is the limit for how much you can spend on a Senate seat in Kentucky? How would you determine that? How would you enforce that? Would that be just for the candidates themselves or is that for all money, including outside money? That's not a small detail to me—how the limit is set and what it is. It's a major problem, but I think it's important to have a spirited debate about it and consider options.

However, the super PACs, as currently practiced and designed, violate the basic rules and ethics of disclosure, transparency, and immediacy. Any fund where the contributors are not known is simply corrosive to democracy. Super PACs have become screens for negativity, designed to distance the candidate from the mudslinging—though no one is fooled.

Disclosure of money needs to be 100 percent transparent because that's partly what a quality democracy is all about. Candidates should have to identify where their money is coming from instantly— certainly before the election. I don't like or trust any fund where the contributors are hidden. This is America: Lay it all out there and let the people draw their own conclusions about whether the money would inappropriately influence policy.

If Congress only responds to five-alarm fires, then this is going to have to become one before Congress weighs in. What Trent has always argued is that we don't need campaign finance reform so much as we need *campaign* reform. The finance reforms have always caused more problems than they have solved.

The last congressional attempt at campaign finance reform was the McCain-Feingold bill in 2002. While well intentioned, it has been a major disappointment in practice. McCain-Feingold was designed to end "soft" money—unlimited money sent to the parties for organizational purposes rather than to a specific candidate. At that time money to the parties was the only reservoir of unregulated funds; limiting that path seemed the smart way to end soft money. It was a laudable goal, but the problem was that both sides just created other unregulated outlets, specifically the super PACs. They just dig new trenches for the money to flow through, fingers that are bigger and more unwieldy than the one they closed up.

Today's unregulated money is likely ten times what it was before McCain-Feingold tried to ban it. The bill was destructive on two ends: it weakened the parties and empowered the outside groups. Even John McCain himself, who spent years fighting for it, would admit it hasn't worked. As it always does, the water found other ways through.

And the issue is not just the amount of money raised: the time, effort, and conflicts of interest involved in raising the money are also huge problems, and their effect on legislating has been pernicious. In his provocatively titled article in *Foreign Affairs*, "America in Decay: The Sources of Political Dysfunction," political theorist Francis Fukuyama calls the influx of money into politics a form of "reciprocal altruism" and argues that it is "rampant in Washington and is the primary channel through which interest groups have succeeded in corrupting government."[5]

The money chase has become time-consuming and—in appearance at least—morally questionable. There's an unseemliness of having a fund-raiser at a restaurant on Capitol Hill held by a group that may be affected by a vote you just made. Nor is this strictly a campaign season problem: it has reached year-round proportions. Heading over to the Senate Campaign Committee and making calls to donors is a big part of the job:

senator as telemarketer. We don't blame voters and pundits for being turned off: This is how you run for office in the world's greatest democracy?

It's not just the four or five members of the leadership, either: brand-new senators are instructed to hit up donors as well. A House member told us recently that when he arrived he was told to plan on spending thirty hours *per week* on the phone—plus ten hours doing events in his district—before he did anything else. That's forty hours per week, the base of his schedule. Only after that could he get to his other work: legislating.

Leadership PACs, which help to raise money for other candidates, became popular as a result of the decisions made by the Supreme Court, in particular, *Citizens United.* They have become ubiquitous and much more broadly used, partly because they're such a rich source of campaign money. *Leadership* is a misnomer: those PACS have nothing to do with leadership anymore. It's just a huge loophole. We'd guess that close to all one hundred senators have leadership PACs. They're attractive because the limits on donations are considerably higher. An elected official can get $2,600 from individuals but $10,000 for his or her leadership PACs ($5,000 for primary, $5,000 for general). The leadership PACs have exploded as a result. One recommendation we have at the BPC is to limit them to the actual leaders— the top three congressional leaders on each side.

In the House and Senate, chairmen of high-profile committees are told frankly by leadership to use their position to raise money, mostly as a way to offset the super PAC money coming from the other side. So the cycle continues. Candidates need the PACs and they need to constantly raise money in order to be competitive in this environment. It has all the features and dynamics of an arms race.

In the same *Foreign Affairs* article, Fukuyama explains the heart of both the money and the primary problem in politics. It comes down to "distorted representation" and the widening between what our country claims it is about and the reality behind that curtain:

> *The interest groups that contend for the attention of Congress represent not the whole American people but the best-organized and (what often amounts to the same thing) most richly endowed parts of American society. This tends to work against the interests of the unorganized, who are often poor, poorly educated, or otherwise marginalized.*[6]

There are steps we can take, both as individual citizens and as a collective, to fix this discrepancy. Part of it is making voting more urgent, popular, and straightforward. Part of it is advocating for leaders who can inspire trust. Part of it is participating in our community or getting involved in public service in our own way. The BPC recommendations build off of these three pillars in the hopes that a new America—one that takes into account where we've been, where we are, and where we should be going—can grow from this foundation.

CHAPTER TWENTY-FIVE

Congressional Reform

"The country needs and, unless I mistake its temper, the country demands bold, persistent experimentation. It is common sense to take a method and try it; if it fails, admit it frankly and try another. But above all, try something . . ."

—FRANKLIN DELANO ROOSEVELT

CONGRESS operates from a foundation of tradition, prescribed rules, and current practice. Some things are embedded in its DNA, part and parcel of the body's soul since the "saucer-that-cools-the-tea" time of our Founding Fathers. Others, like the number of votes required or procedural rules, have been updated through the years to adhere to practical needs. Still others are habits that flow in and out of favor based on the climate in Washington and who's in power.

In February 2015, while the Republican Congress was threatening to defund the Department of Homeland Security, essentially holding it hostage in an effort to block President Obama's executive action on immigration, George Packer wrote:

> [I]nternal forces have steadily weakened the defenses of the body politic, leaving . . . a strategy of total war on every issue that comes before Congress, and a national government that is the last place you'd look to for solutions to the country's most corrosive problems.[1]

Faith in that body politic has never been lower because of that "strategy of total war." There are techniques that are part of how Congress operates and there are others that pass the line of good taste, the public's well-being, and common sense. Our leaders need to act responsibly with the extremely powerful weapons that they wield. Recommendations in the BPC report regarding congressional practices look to instill common sense and responsibility in the daily work of the Congress.

As we discussed, the airplane has been one of the more corrosive modern influences on government. Congress crunches the bulk of its schedule into the middle of the week to accommodate the travel of its members, whose families invariably live back home. Of course, the airplane is a modern convenience that isn't going anywhere. However, there are ways to counteract its effect on the way government operates.

One of the most commonsensical recommendations in the BPC report—it requires nothing more than the leaders simply doing it—is instituting the five-day workweek in Congress. There can be no mandate on where lawmakers live, but a five-day workweek will shift their schedules in a way that encourages, if not demands, D.C. residency. Representatives argue that their time back home is not vacation, as they're working in their congressional offices. That's valid work, but there is also a country that is not being run. There are decisions on national policy that simply can't be made from places like Pierre, South Dakota.

The five-day workweek is an elegant solution, direct and simple. It comes from long-standing precedent and practice, one with which all Americans are familiar. It will also set off a snowball effect and address other issues of transience: the lack of community, minimal interaction among lawmakers, and the slow pace of legislation. We guarantee that a poll of Americans would overwhelmingly support a five-day workweek for Congress; however, aversion to Washington remains so high that this same majority would invariably *not* support their representatives living there.

Besides the infrequency of days in session (an average of nine days a month), what adds to the current inertia is the lack of coordination between the two chambers of Congress: the House of Representatives is in two weeks and out two weeks, while the Senate is even more haphazardly scheduled. Since bills need to make their way through both houses, this is a real problem. Another BPC recommendation is that both houses maintain the same three-week-on, one-week-off schedule; it would help create the necessary momentum needed to get anything done at the federal level. Legislators will get time in their respective districts, but in what seems like an obvious fix, *it will all be the same time.* Momentum is such a key element in lawmaking, yet it's nearly impossible these days to pick up enough steam to move anything through. Changing the schedule would do wonders for both the nuts and bolts of legislation and the intangible chemistry issues that are as much a part of Washington as anything carved in stone.

Most legislation in Congress begins in committee: a bipartisan group of members who carefully study the respective issues, hold hearings, commission studies, and make a recommendation to the whole body. "Standing" or permanent committees have been around for about two hundred years. When a bill is produced for the whole body to debate, amend, and vote on, it is known as "making it out of committee." A powerful chairman, by the same token, can prevent something from ever making it out of committee.

Committees play an obvious logistical role, but too many members of Congress are suffering from committee overload—for reasons unrelated to legislation. Congressional members try to get on the most visible or influential committees, partly for their legislative power and partly for the fund-raising platform. As a result, the committee piling has gotten out of control. Committees like Finance and Appropriations have enormous influence and grant their members substantial visibility. Spots on these committees are highly coveted, and entire careers are spent waiting for their chairmanships.

The right committee position can be a huge boost to someone's fund-raising. In 2014, Tom was invited to at least ten fund-raisers for a single chairman of an important committee—who wasn't even up for reelection. Congressmen and senators stretch themselves way too thin by sitting on five or six committees. In the House, chairmen have begun to keep track of attendance to discourage this. Congressmen literally poke their heads in or sit down for thirty seconds to avoid being marked absent, like high school students. Trent's clients call him and ask, "Will you please call Senator X and get him to show up for a subcommittee hearing?" They literally can't get enough members there to get a quorum.

It's the modern dilemma: lawmakers have more to do and less time in Washington to do it. Besides strengthening the committees and giving the chairmen more autonomy, the BPC recommends that they pull the reins on all the overloading: senators should be limited to serving on one major and one minor committee.

When the Affordable Care Act was up for a vote in Congress, House members caught a lot of flak over the fact that they didn't really know what it contained. "We have to pass it to find out what's in it," they said—an absurd but accurate statement. The

BPC recommends a simple fix: bills should be posted a minimum of three days in advance of a vote to allow sufficient time for lawmakers (and the public) to read and discuss the measures. The public has a right to expect their representatives be allowed the time to learn what's in a bill.

At a minimum, this rule would give staff time to see what their bosses are about to vote on. We each had the experience of having to vote on things we didn't have time to read. With bills that often run on for hundreds of pages and limited time, it's an occupational hazard. However, like with a lot of issues in Congress, there are practical ways to address the problem.

One of the most fundamental rules of the Senate is unanimous consent: all one hundred members theoretically need to agree for the body to move on. The rule essentially gives each senator a veto. If there is an objection, the Senate has to work through its mechanisms to address it.

Therein lies an enormous amount of leverage for each individual senator, because any senator can put a hold on a nomination or a piece of legislation. Tom once had a bill on the Mni Wiconi water pipeline, which was an important project in South Dakota. One evening John McCain went to the cloakroom, put a hold on it, went to the airport, and flew to Phoenix. Trent tracked him down, and when John landed, Trent got him on the phone. "John, you can't do this," he argued. "This is something that's in South Dakota, it's a big deal to the Democratic leader, and you just gotta take that hold off." Without a lot of argument, McCain agreed. The hold, we should add, had nothing to do with the pipeline. It says something about the relationship the two of us had as leaders, but it also shows how easy it is to stop anything if a senator feels like it.

The filibuster (from the Dutch for *pirate*) is not a rule but rather a practice that has been in the Senate for two hundred years. It gives a single senator the right to talk endlessly from the floor, preventing anything from coming up for a vote. It takes 60 votes for cloture, the mechanism that can end the filibuster. Since the majority almost never has 60, the filibuster has become a pervasive and dependable weapon for the minority.

Filibusters are painless in modern times, because no one has to hold the floor anymore. They once required physical stamina and commitment; the difficulty in filibustering—as well as the disruption it caused—was precisely what limited its usage. Now all a senator needs to do is have his staff call and essentially threaten to filibuster, which is called a hold. Sometimes the hold is related to the bill itself; oftentimes it has absolutely nothing to do with it. Senators are using that notification of objection as leverage to get something they want—and it's enormously effective.

As a result, the number of holds (which can be measured in the number of cloture votes) has skyrocketed in recent years. There were 196 cloture votes in the 2014 Congress. To put it in perspective, between 1955 and 1961 there was *one* cloture vote: the Civil Rights Act of 1957. And the fact that we can easily name it says a lot about what a big deal it used to be when cloture vote was taken. Now it's daily business.

One of our recommendations is to return to the requirement that a senator literally be there in person to hold the floor in order to filibuster. Such a requirement would substantially limit the filibuster's usage, which is exactly the point. Back when senators had to actually talk and hold the floor to filibuster, it was a whole process. They used to bring cots into the cloakrooms and the Marble Room of the Capitol because the vote could be at any time.

There is something about wearing people down physically that serves its purpose, reducing the length and frequency of that practice.

George Mitchell tells a famous story about an old-fashioned filibuster where they brought out the cots. He had given up a cushy job to be in the Senate, and it was two in the morning and he was complaining to himself: *What am I doing here? I gave up my dream job for* this? He found a cot in the middle of the crowded room next to John Warner. Mitchell realized Warner could've been home sleeping with his wife, Elizabeth Taylor, so what was *he* complaining about?

Another thing that has pulled the fangs out of the filibuster is dual tracking—something started by Robert Byrd. Dual tracking prevents the filibuster from actually holding things up because it allows for two bills to move through at the same time. Filibusters used to clog up Senate business. Again, it's what made them so rare. Since dual tracking is a practice, not a rule, the majority leader can simply choose to abolish it.

The filibuster didn't always offer so much leverage. Senators weren't as prepared to go to the floor to filibuster something as frequently as they are today—because now they don't have to literally do it. We've made it so easy that you get a handful of holds every single day—a dramatic increase that has adversely affected all Senate business. Until recently you could put a hold on legislation or a nomination without even having to acknowledge who you were. The holds are less anonymous than they used to be but they're still not entirely transparent.[*]

---

[*] There was a vote in the 112th Congress in 2011 to end anonymous holds, but in practice some still do it through other means of circumvention, like "tag-team holding."

Making all holds public wouldn't necessarily reduce them anyway, because in many cases senators *want* them public: they're doing it for the publicity. It's a badge of honor, something to campaign on. They would love nothing more than for their constituents to say, *My senator's holding up the whole Senate because he thinks it's that important.* It's a motivation rather than an impediment. In addition, the hold notification is done staff to staff. One remedy—or deterrent—would be to require the member to actually come to the floor to announce a hold or to object. We bet that holds would plummet with such a requirement.

There's also a rolling hold: somebody announces a hold, the Senate addresses his or her concern, and then that senator transfers that hold to somebody else, passing it like a baton. Quite often Trent had to chase the rolling holds around his own caucus. He would find out which Republican had the hold and go and try to convince that person to get off of it. Suddenly somebody else would have the hold, and then he'd have to track it down again. One time he was tracking a hold and got in the cloakroom and found out it was his! His staff got overzealous and put a hold in his name and he had no idea. (The Capitol is a heady place: senior Senate staff can get caught up and sometimes forget they're not senators.)

In theory, the minority is allowed to offer amendments to legislation as a way to temper, adjust, or counteract the bill on the floor. A bill has a limited number of amendments that can be attached to it. According to Senate rules, "Depending on the kinds of amendments that Senators offer and the order in which they are recognized to offer their amendments, Senators can offer anywhere from 3 to 11 amendments before the Senate has to vote on any of them."[2] However, the majority leader gets first crack at offering amendments, and he has no limit. Very often, in order to prevent the minority party's amendments from being stuck to the bill—amendments designed to weaken it or force senators to vote for or against something politically damaging—the majority leader uses all of them. This is called "filling the tree." Like holds and filibusters, its use has multiplied astronomically in recent years.

As the minority is repeatedly blocked from offering amendments, anger and resentment lead to pushback—and the only recourse is yet another hold, a threat to filibuster. This is the normal way that the cycle operates, with both sides laying blame at the other's feet. The way to end it would be to guarantee the minority the ability to offer a certain number of amendments; the BPC recommends ten.

Tom was at the prayer breakfast in 2014 when a veteran Republican senator told him that while in the minority they had been allowed seven total amendments on the floor all year—which strikes us as an abuse of the system. We need to emphasize that the practice isn't new. Byrd used it, and he may have even perfected it; Dole did it some; Mitchell did it some. Trent did it twelve times over a six-and-a-half-year period. Tom did it once between 2001 and 2003. Bill Frist filled the tree fifteen times between 2003 and 2007.

After that, as with the filibuster, things went haywire. As majority leader, Harry Reid filled the tree a full seventy times between 2007 and 2013, an enormous increase.[3] Quantity affects quality, as Hegel said. It's not just about frequency; it's about how much the entire system is now at the mercy of such tactics. The filibusters have reached that limit as well, because each time the tree is filled, there's a filibuster in the offing.

Amendments are regularly offered in order to politically jam opponents, so filling the tree is the majority leader's way of protecting vulnerable members. But there are other ways to protect members and still accommodate the legislative process. For one thing, the leader can offer an alternative. You give the members something they can vote for so they don't have to vote exclusively against something politically damaging. Apparently that has lost favor as an option, but that's what we used to do as majority leaders. As for all the defensive tactics, they have gotten out of hand. Trent would push back on members and say: "Why are we here? You get a six-year term in what is supposedly the greatest deliberative body in the world, and you don't want to vote on a tough issue. I don't understand."

We do have to give credit to current majority leader Mitch McConnell, who gets better marks than Harry Reid does in this role. McConnell has opened up the process and actually gotten some things done, like approving the Trade Promotion Authority and passing the Iran resolution. He is also allowing many amendments to the National Defense Authorization Act and, wisely, has done a good job returning to regular order.

As we've said, there's nothing that unites a minority more than the feeling that they're getting shut out. Constantly filling the tree causes two types of dysfunction: first, it creates gridlock, because nothing gets passed. Second, it unites the opposition, because out of indignation they band together. This dynamic is visible in all kinds of institutions and transcends all issues. If you can convince people that they've been treated unfairly, it doesn't matter what the issue is: you can persuade them to line up behind you and charge.

CHAPTER TWENTY-SIX

A Call to Service

"Do your nearest duty."

—JOHANN WOLFGANG VON GOETHE

WE try to remind audiences, young people especially, that this country and its institutions are much more fragile than people realize—far too fragile to take for granted. From the outside they may look permanent, as solid as the monuments to our leaders, but history tells a different story.

"History shows that world orders, including our own, are transient," Robert Kagan writes in *The World America Made.*[1] Our institutions, our country's stability, and our place in the world are not set fixtures. None of it just happened on its own and none of it will remain in place on its own. It is just when we assume such things will always be there that they start to deteriorate on us, victims of our neglect or our assumptions about their permanence. They are durable, of course, but they were created by people, are kept running by people, and need people to continue and flourish.

The final section of the BPC recommendations focus on launching "an era of big citizenship." As this generation of public servants retires, our institutions require an influx of dedicated and able men and women to take over, breathe new life into them, and shepherd them through the next century. Civic participation has always been an integral element of American society—Tocqueville praised Americans' civic engagement during his visit in the early nineteenth century—but recent decades have seen it wane. Historians note that it peaked during and after World War II and has been in steady decline ever since. The problem may not be a new one, but with each passing decade we put our future at greater risk.

Apathy, exhaustion, and cynicism about government are in danger of pushing away the next generation of public servants and participants. The BPC report references a surprising poll: if given the opportunity, just one in ten college students would serve as mayor for a day—even if the pay were on a par with typical jobs in business or sales. Statistics like these reveal a cultural and generational aversion to government work that, if left unchecked, can drain the public sector of the kind of talent needed to keep it running. To paraphrase John Adams, if the pipeline is not filled with the best and the brightest, then it will be filled with others.

A different BPC/USA *Today* poll found similar assumptions. When asked if "the best way to make major positive changes in our society is through local, state, and federal governments [or] through community involvement," responders chose community involvement by a two-to-one margin.[2] These and other studies reveal more of a cultural bias against government work than even the most cynical among us would assume. The problem has no silver bullet; it involves a complex mix of increasing resources and changing mind-sets, the latter perhaps being more crucial. The BPC report attests: "By making public service a cultural norm . . . we can promote a more positive attitude toward the political system, thereby reducing the level of polarization and increasing participation."

George Washington was a champion of duty throughout his life, viewing his military and political tenures as forms of service to his country. Washington was universally praised during his lifetime and venerated in every era afterward because of his stolid commitment to service. He would leave what he considered his primary job at Mount Vernon to answer the call when he was needed and his example has set the standard for many leaders who followed. Our early presidents didn't overtly campaign for office, because by tradition they were supposed to respond when the public needed them. This was a bit of theater, to be sure, but it still revealed a solemnity and duty in how they viewed public office.

The modern-day aversion to public service is not a problem limited to city halls, town councils, and local politics; it has ramifications that ripple through the population at large. The BPC report concluded that the "decline in civic engagement . . . could be contributing to today's more polarized society."[3] It follows that the less involved citizens are in the public space, the more likely they are to distrust others. Studies bear this out. If you are exposed only to the views in your silo or the ideas that bounce around your echo chamber, your opinions about others are unlikely to change. In fact, they're more apt to become further cemented into place. The result is further polarization. That animus flows back into the feedback loop, turning people off from any kind of public service and contributing to the dangerous cycle.

As the top of each successive cohort of college graduates opt for the private sector, the nation must treat it as a mission to lure those future leaders into the public sphere. We benefit as a collective citizenry by their involvement and we need to find effective ways to draw them into public work. Plenty of these capable men and women have the skills and interest in public service but turn away—or, incredibly, are turned away—for reasons we can control.

The BPC recommendations call for a more engaged citizenry at all levels of the public sphere and at all stages of citizens' lives. The first one is the most consequential and controversial: requiring a year of national service—military, civilian, or volunteer through nonprofits or religious institutions—for Americans ages 18 to 28. Polling shows that the American public is in favor of such an idea by a large majority; as the advocate organization ServiceNation notes, "It's the rare issue supported by huge majorities of Democrats, Republicans, and independents."[4] Resistance to such a mandate would still be strong in this country, but we've reached such a drastic point in our nation's history that perhaps it is time for such methods. Our freedoms only work if they operate in conjunction with a responsibility to each other and the whole.

A sense of collective responsibility—and a form of sacrifice—should become an integral part of being an adult in this country. The BPC recommendation offers options that fit with the uniqueness of the individuals. Previous generations had to give their lives; now we'd be asking young people to give one year of their earning potential. Any kind of federal mandate is likely pie in the sky, but there are incentive-based methods that could work, practical trade-offs that invest in our future. Society would benefit from the contributions of that age group, and they, in turn, would benefit from the experience. Ideally, it would inform their attitude and perspective throughout their life. That sense of caring for the whole, being part of a larger community and nation, would remain with them long after that year is up.

A pragmatic way to start a national service program would be through trade-offs on an important issue directly tied to that age group. Recently, we gave a talk at Tom's alma mater, South Dakota

State University, where Tom suggested using national service as a way to forgive U.S. student debt, which has skyrocketed to more than a trillion dollars and is in danger of hobbling the next generation. The idea of linking service to student debt has been around for years—John McCain has advocated for it, as have others—and there are limited versions of it out there.

We need to broaden such programs: our country cannot allow a tuition system to continue that has no responsible limit on loans and no practical way to pay it back. It's not just a student or family's financial problem; it's a societal one. We are breaking the backs of young people before they even have a chance to climb out on their own. Just as we feel they have a responsibility to the country, we have a responsibility to them. The debt/service trade-off seems like a natural solution to both issues.

Forgiving debt would not be an expense; it's a long-term investment in the future of the country, a way for people to simultaneously serve and get an education in the process. Young men and women would get the benefit of the training as well as the education at a reduced cost. The value would be immeasurable and the productivity differences would be phenomenal. An investment in education is a deal that each and every one of us should be willing to make, as we all end up paying for it anyway.

We were both fortunate to have the kind of parents who stressed education in our homes, and we reaped the benefits of their long-term thinking.

TRENT: My father dropped out of high school after the ninth grade. He made a decent living as a blue-collar worker, but his lack of formal schooling limited what he could do. He had a complex about it his whole life. As a teenager, I remember coming home late one night from the Frostop root beer stand as he was coming in from the second shift in the shipyard. I told him I thought maybe I'd skip college and come out to the shipyard with him. He came over to me as if he was going to hit me and I stood up to receive his blow. "You listen to me, young man," he said. "You're going to college. I dropped out of high school. You're *not* going to make that mistake." That was enough; I never again discussed that prospect with him.

TOM: I once had a cabdriver tell me, "My biggest problem is that I had a fifteen-year-old deciding what my life was going to be." Those early decisions have so much weight. My father was an artist who lost all of his paintings in a fire early in his career. He never painted again, becoming a minimum-wage bookkeeper and staying there for forty-five years. We were talking about my future once when I was in high school and he said, "I had one year of college and I've been a bookkeeper all my life. And I'll be a bookkeeper the rest of my life. You need college if you want to be anything beyond that." That conversation had an enormous impact on me. That was it—that was all I needed to know. He instilled in us that an education was the only way to have control over your life.

We can all make an investment in the future in both big and small ways. Trent and his wife, Tricia, sponsor scholarships to the Trent Lott Leadership Institute at the University of Mississippi. They're involved in the selection process, evaluating the applicants' essays and helping to choose the recipients. Reading the applicants' essays about why they want to go into a public policy and leadership program, what their aspirations are, and how they feel about government service is nothing short of inspiring. It's a close-up look of what the best and brightest could be—if we give them the opportunity and the tools.

Whenever we have a platform to speak these days, we both emphasize the necessity of keeping this democracy strong. Tom regularly presses for what he calls "the Four Pillars of Democracy": tolerance, respect for the rule of law, leadership, and participation.

The importance of participation is grossly underestimated, evidenced by the 15 percent turnout in the primaries and the 34 percent in the general election, which CNN pointed out means 144 million voters—more than the population of Russia[5]—stayed home. Those numbers reflect something of an epidemic of nonparticipation in this country—evidence of too many people shirking their most basic communal responsibility.

President Obama recently made some waves when he mentioned that perhaps it's time we considered mandatory voting, a reflection of his frustration with the low numbers more than a practical solution. Although some countries, like Belgium, Argentina, and Australia, indeed fine citizens for not voting, it's unlikely any form of mandated voting would gain traction in this country, nor would we support it. It's a drastic measure that infringes on basic freedoms; forcing people to vote also sends the wrong message and doesn't really solve the problem. The low turnout is a symptom, not a cause. Besides, it's not taking responsibility if you do it under threat of penalty. It's hard to value something that you're forced to do.

We don't talk nearly enough about responsibility across the board, whether it's responsibility for our health, for our community, or for our democracy. True, there is always going to be a contingent of motivated young people who care enough to get involved, as there has been in every generation. There was a whole legion of people motivated for different reasons when we were finding our callings in the 1960s. Tom was motivated by the palpable excitement of the Kennedys and the ripple of change that characterized that era.

It's imperative that we encourage a form of commitment to country for young people, even if it's only a year. The more we can motivate people to take responsibility and the more we promote and encourage that mind-set, the more solid a foundation we will have in our future. Tom has five grandkids and he already has had conversations with them about how important it is that they understand this responsibility. Trent has emphasized the same things to his children and grandchildren. It's a family-based value, because it starts at home. At all levels—home, school, church, work, social circles, community—we as a nation need to continually instill that sense of responsibility if we want it to sink in and endure.

Freedom is an American value—some would argue our primary one—but every right comes with a responsibility; some are constitutional, some are moral. But these rights are not automatic, nor are they bottomless. We have to take the initiative to protect those rights and ensure their continuation. There will always be a debate in this country about what should be mandated, what should be incentivized, and what should be voluntary; that debate is healthy. As we maintained in Part I, the argument itself strengthens our democracy. But we need to discuss these things in the public sphere. How much freedom is a God-given right and how much requires active involvement and commitment? In a country of 319 million people, a vast majority need to take responsibility for the larger picture or that larger picture will shift. We have to defend the country, pay our taxes, take care of our health, our families. It's morally egregious for us to ask others to be responsible for our irresponsibility, but when you let your health go, ignore your community's needs, or stay home during elections, you're doing just that.

There are a variety of ways we can motivate, encourage, and reward those who have an interest in public service—at all stages in life. One of our recommendations is to reimplement mandatory civics courses in high schools across the country. Our schools do not teach the role of government as thoroughly and as prominently as they should. There has been some inkling that civics may be making a comeback, with Arizona and North Dakota signing laws that will make them the first two states to require that high school students pass a citizenship test to graduate.[6] We took civics classes in high school as a required part of our public education, and that need for civic responsibility should be reintroduced in school. We currently emphasize math and science— which are important—but we do it at the expense of other areas that are just as significant to our children's future, if not more so. As North Dakota governor Jack Dalrymple rightly noted when he signed the law, "Understanding our civic rights and duties empowers us all to bring about positive change . . ."[7]

It's not just an education issue; it's about the application of that knowledge, which spreads into other areas of young citizens' lives. Civics classes are a way to introduce a career in government to an impressionable group of students who are already thinking about their future, their role in society, and their career paths. Such intervention could help create our next generation of public servants, elected officials, and leaders. At the very least, it would help shore up a generation of dedicated and involved citizens.

The executive and legislative branches can also use their considerable platforms to highlight and celebrate extraordinary civil servants whose stories and accomplishments can inspire the public at large. Our heroes tell us a lot about who we are; if we honor our most impressive public servants and participants, we don't just show appreciation to those who dedicate their lives to the public sphere; we also promote to the young what we value as a society. We need to encourage and publicize that career path to youngsters looking for one. Civil service is noticeably absent at career and college fairs, and an increase in visibility there could go a long way toward bringing qualified and interested applicants into the field. Public service needs to be incorporated in- and outside the classroom in order to become one of those intriguing paths that our brightest young people consider exploring.

Our nation's future requires that we stem the tide of intelligent and dedicated young leaders ignoring public life and only choosing the private sector. We need to encourage more civic participation both by raising the incentives and tearing down the entrenched obstacles. Another way to get high schoolers involved is through student government, which could be broader and more inclusive than it is at most schools. It's a ripe area in which to introduce a sense of responsibility and engender an early interest in public policy. As the BPC report notes, "Schools should increase dramatically the opportunities for students to participate in student government and other leadership roles, which research shows leads to greater participation in public service later in life."[8] We are often drawn in life to that which got to us at a malleable age. Advertisers and corporations have known this for decades— public service needs to take advantage of that.

Once students get to college, they are given enormous freedom and options regarding their majors, their electives, their extracurricular activities, and their career paths. But universities also need to recognize the public good in promoting service.

College campuses are the ideal environment to motivate an active citizenry—a place to attract young leaders and divert them toward public service when they are open to such ideas and considering their options. It is a ripe time in their lives for such a decision: they are intimately involved in their communities and can effect change on a canvas that's manageable enough for them to see the results.

Incredibly, as we learned in putting together the BPC report, service programs like AmeriCorps VISTA and the Peace Corps are *turning away* eager and qualified applicants every year because they don't have the resources to include them. Six hundred thousand Americans apply to these programs each year but a staggering 80 percent are turned away because of a lack of openings.[9] This is a shame and easily fixable. We need to increase funding and resources to these kinds of service programs, which are such valuable arms in any democracy.

Once these young leaders and citizens go out into the world, enter the job market, start families, and join communities, there are numerous ways we can help them to get involved. Both Republicans and Democrats would benefit enormously from training young potential leaders to run for office. The executive branch can follow suit and work to train and educate college recruits for the variety of starting floor positions available. We recommend that the federal government expand the number of openings available to recent graduates looking for a fulfilling career path.

Once men and women begin their careers, there is no reason not to give them opportunities to get involved on a volunteer or part-time basis. The BPC recommends that the private sector provide for service-sabbatical opportunities, in which they can use the skills they've acquired in their careers to contribute to society's needs, benefiting their communities and their country.

It's likely there are many citizens who would like to get involved but simply cannot manage it with their work schedules.

Another untapped area is the enormous number of baby boomer retirees (78 million) who still have the motivation, skill, and verve to do good work. People are living longer than ever and retirees still have plenty of years and energy left. The government should work harder to entice this group into service. Perhaps they are looking to fill their free time; perhaps their careers satisfied them only financially; perhaps they feel anxious about the world they're leaving behind for future generations. Whatever their motivation, we'd be wise to tap that healthy and expanding population.

Plenty of people these days sneer at government, mock politicians, and are ignorant or apathetic about public policy; but we have found in our lives working in the Congress, *for* the Congress (because it is a form of service), to be enormously fulfilling.

People often ask us if it was worth it. When you're in elective office, you do give up a great deal: you don't make a lot of money and you live on a fixed income. If you came from a blue-collar or poorer family and if you're honest, you certainly won't get rich at the job. You also have to sacrifice time away from the people you love. You have your name and your reputation on the line every day, because, after all, you are human and you make mistakes.

Public service is one of the highest callings in a democracy. The fulfillment you get in believing you can make a difference is a powerful motivation. In spite of the sacrifices, it was well worth it, trying to effect change and long-term results for our states and for our country.

After our careers and at our ages, we could sit on boards and take lighter schedules, but we're both still very motivated and passionate about public work and good governance. We currently have vehicles that allow us, with limited influence, to bring about a national dialogue that we believe is critical. We work on public policy issues that we care deeply about in an effort to continue the agendas that we had for most of our professional lives. Our venues have changed, our roles have changed, but our passion and interest hasn't.

You don't spend a lifetime in the public arena and then just come to full stop. Tom was defeated when he was relatively young and found there was so much more he wanted to do. After thirty-nine years of working in the Congress, Trent wasn't going to call it a day, go home, and sit on a porch and rock. He had enough sense to quit while he could walk out the door instead of being carried out.

Conclusion: Duty

A FTER the attack on Pearl Harbor and our entry into World War II, Winston Churchill (quoting British foreign secretary Sir Edward Grey) announced that the United States was like "a gigantic boiler. Once the fire is lighted under it there is no limit to the power it can generate."[1] And he was right: not just militarily, but across the board, our nation awoke to an opportunity and seized it.

In their book *That Used to Be Us: How America Fell Behind in the World It Invented and How We Can Come Back*, authors Thomas L. Friedman and Michael Mandelbaum look beyond our country's documents and laws to a set of practices that are unique to our nation: *those*, they argue, are what made the American experiment a continued success. They call it the "American formula" and argue that the Constitution was "necessary but not sufficient" for our grand experiment here to endure. The formula still works: we have to maintain faith in its durability and be strong enough to adapt it to changing times and circumstances.

The term *melting pot*, so often used to describe the United States, is a misnomer, because we haven't really melted together at all.

Our country is something closer to borscht: we keep our unique identities and cultures and toss them into the mix of American experience. That's part of the American formula. Our country believes in opportunity and innovation because we remain open to the new—both in people and in ideas.

Risk is in America's DNA. It ran through the blood of those who came here and those who have built their lives here. That risk taking has been handed down for generations and has lodged itself into our collective consciousness. It continues to be a rich and healthy part of the American psyche and the American idea. The worst bet anyone could have made was one against American ingenuity. Misconceptions abound that we as a country have lost this important trait, but they're unfounded, premature, and false.

In the 1830s Alexis de Tocqueville, who was fascinated at how the American experiment was playing out, wrote in *Democracy in America*: "Every American is eaten up with longing to rise."[2] Until now, each generation of American parents could expect that their children would have greater successes than they did. Previous generations have been able to promise a better education, economic security, and a higher quality of life for their children and grandchildren. That is no longer a guarantee. We must act to preserve what's worth saving, change what is hindering us from progress, and exercise the wisdom to know which is which.[3]

We need to ask ourselves: Are we still supporting the ideas that give Americans the opportunity to rise? If not, how do we get back to doing that? We cannot forget how we got here or what allows us to remain in this great republic—through the blood, sacrifice, and hard work of others.

There's a powerful poem called "The Young Dead Soldiers Do Not Speak" by Archibald MacLeish. MacLeish was the

Librarian of Congress at the time and asked that it be published anonymously. It reads in part:

> *They say, We were young. We have died. Remember us.*
> *They say, We have done what we could but until it is*
> *finished it is not done.*
> *They say, We have given our lives but until it is finished no*
> *one can know what our lives gave.*
> *They say, Our deaths are not ours: they are yours: they will*
> *mean what you make them.*
> *They say, Whether our lives and our deaths were for peace*
> *and a new hope or for nothing we cannot say: it is you*
> *who must say this.*
> *They say, We leave you our deaths: give them their*
> *meaning . . .*[4]

We leave you our deaths: give them their meaning . . . Forgetting the great many sacrifices on which our nation was built would be shameful; when we cannot find common ground, or refuse to in the name of politics, we are doing just that. There are so many people that have given the ultimate sacrifice. For the rest of us, the only way to honor them and to give their deaths meaning is to take responsibility for what they fought for. We pay them back by not letting them die in vain, and we do that by working to make our democracy strong enough to endure. That's what gives those sacrifices their meaning.

They did their jobs; we need to do ours. The future of our country depends on courageous leaders bringing the sides together, governing through hope rather than fear, and presenting a vision for the country.

"American history isn't something in the past, it's continuing," said activist Reverend Malcolm Boyd, "so we are a part of it. Tape is rolling on American history."[5] It is within our power, as individual citizens and as a collective citizenry, to change our course. The Founders had a vision for this nation and laid the groundwork for it to grow. We must keep digging and continue that work. We must rebuild what we have lost and create anew what the times demand. It will begin when we harness the natural tension of politics in a productive way, creating an environment that allows for chemistry and compromise. That process requires leadership and courage in the face of habitual inertia, entrenched differences, and petty squabbling. Once we embrace a shared vision for our future, we can then work to make it a reality.

"I think we are born into this world and inherit all the grudges and rivalries and hatreds and sins of the past," President Obama recently said. "But we also inherit the beauty and the joy and goodness of our forebears. And we're on this planet a pretty short time, so that we cannot remake the world entirely during this little stretch that we have. But I think our decisions matter.

"At the end of the day, we're part of a long-running story. We just try to get our paragraph right."[6]

It is not only within our power to change things, it is our duty: we must work at it and fight for it. We are not just former lawmakers but fathers and grandfathers, and we recognize how critical it is that we serve as stewards for the next generation. In some respects we don't have the confidence that we're leaving them a better place. But there's no way we will give up. There is too much at stake. We no longer have that luxury of petulance. We have the tools, we have the resilience, and we have the motivation. It is in our hands.

Acknowledgments

THE authors would like to thank Anton Mueller, who has been an insightful editor and visionary for the project, along with publisher George Gibson, Rachel Mannheimer, Nancy Miller, Marie Coolman, Sara Kitchen, David Chesanow, Summer Smith, and the entire wonderful team at Bloomsbury Publishing. Special thanks also goes to Veronica Pollock, Jennifer Roberts, and Kelly Dockham for their help.

Trent and Tom want to express their heartfelt thanks to Jon Sternfeld for his extraordinary efforts throughout this entire project. It has been a real pleasure to work with him. He has been invaluable to us from the very beginning. Trent would also like to thank his wife, Tricia, who has been a loyal partner for fifty-one years. Tom would like to thank his wife, Linda, for all of her encouragement, love, and support for more than three decades.

Jon would like to thank Jason Grumet at the Bipartisan Policy Center and Marc Dunkelman. He is especially grateful for the support of his wife, Lydia, along with the rest of his family: Lucy, Arlo, Josh, Dad, and Mom.

Notes

FOREWORD

1 Steve Coll, "The D.N.C. and the Summer of Discontent," *New Yorker*, Aug. 8 & 15, 2016, http://www.newyorker.com/magazine/2016/08/08/the-dnc-proved-that-hillary-clinton-is-deeply-qualified-to-serve-as-president.

2 Ted Barrett, "Senate Resumes Gridlock as Zika Funding Vote Fails," CNN.com, Sept. 6, 2016, http://www.cnn.com/2016/09/06/politics/senate-zika-funding-vote-fails.

3 "Beyond Distrust: How Americans View Their Government," Pew Research Center, Nov. 23, 2015, http://www.people-press.org/2015/11/23/1-trust-in-government-1958-2015.

4 *Meet the Press*, NBC.com, Aug. 28, 2016, http://www.nbcnews.com/meet-the-press/meet-press-august-28-2016-n639011.

5 "The Run-Up," Episode 5, "The Syringe and the Truth," *New York Times*, http://www.nytimes.com/2016/08/23/podcasts/media-truth-charlie-sykes.html.

INTRODUCTION

1 Jonathan Wiseman and Ashley Parker, "Congress Off for the Exits, but Few Cheer," *New York Times*, Aug. 1, 2014.

2 Mark Preston, "CNN/ORC Poll: Most Think Congress Is Worst in Their Lifetime," CNN.com, Sept. 9, 2014, http://www.cnn.com/2014/09/09/politics/cnn-poll-congress/index.html.

3 John Lloyd and John Mitchinson, *If Ignorance Is Bliss, Why Aren't There More Happy People?: Smart Quotes for Dumb Times* (New York: Crown, 2009), 235.

CHAPTER ONE: THE 228-YEAR ARGUMENT

1 Eric Lane and Michael Oreskes, *The Genius of America: How the Constitution Saved Our Country—and Why It Can Again* (New York: Bloomsbury, 2007), 4.

2 David O. Stewart, *Summer of 1787: The Men Who Invented the Constitution* (New York: Simon & Schuster, 2007), 45.

3 Joseph J. Ellis, *Founding Brothers: The Revolutionary Generation* (New York: Knopf, 2000), 16.

4 Lane and Oreskes, *The Genius of America*, 48.

5 Ibid., 199.

6 Hamilton-Madison-Jay, *Federalist Papers*, "Federalist 10" (New York: Signet, 2003); Ed. Clinton Rossiter, 78.

7 Lynne Cheney, *James Madison: A Life Reconsidered* (New York: Viking, 2014), 5.

8 Hamilton-Madison-Jay, *Federalist Papers*, "Federalist 10" (New York: Signet, 2003); Ed. Clinton Rossiter, 74.

9 James Madison, *Notes on the Debates of the Federal Convention of 1787* (1787), http://avalon.law.yale.edu/18th_century/yates.asp.

10 Ron Chernow, *Alexander Hamilton* (New York: Penguin Press, 2004), 284.

11 Excerpt from George Washington's Farewell Address, Sept. 19, 1796.

12 Ellis, *Founding Brothers*, 16.

13 James MacGregor Burns, *Transforming Leadership* (New York: Atlantic Monthly Books, 2003), 127, 170.

14 Ellis, *Founding Brothers*, 197.

CHAPTER TWO: THE PULLING

1 Joseph J. Ellis, *Founding Brothers: The Revolutionary Generation* (New York: Knopf, 2000), 15.

2 Papers of James Madison, Congressional Series, 14:370–72, "A Candid State of Parties," *National Gazette*, Sept. 22, 1792.

3 Donald Rumsfeld, *Rumsfeld's Rules: Leadership Lessons in Business, Politics, War, and Life* (New York: Broadside Books, 2013), Appendix B.

4 E. J. Dionne, *Our Divided Political Heart: The Battle for the American Idea in an Age of Discontent* (New York: Bloomsbury, 2002), 4–5.

CHAPTER THREE: THE PERMANENT CAMPAIGN

1 Joslyn Pine ed., *Wit and Wisdom of the American Presidents: A Book of Quotations* (Dover: Dover Publications, 2000), 69–70.

2 Amy Gutmann and Dennis Thompson, *The Spirit of Compromise: Why Governing Demands It and Campaigning Undermines It* (Princeton, N.J.: Princeton University Press, 2002), 2.

3 David Dayen, "The Electoral-Industrial Complex: Fortunes Made by Consultants on Campaign Spending," *Firedoglake*, Nov. 12, 2012, http://firedoglake.com/2012/11/12/the-electoral-industrial-complex-fortunes-made-by-consultants-on-campaign-spending/.

4 John F. Kennedy, *Profiles in Courage* (New York: Harper, 1956), 18.

5 David Brooks, "Ryan's Biggest Mistake," *New York Times*, Aug. 3, 2012, http://www.nytimes.com/2012/08/24/opinion/brooks-ryans-biggest-mistake.html.

6 Dan Heuchert, *University of Virginia Magazine*, "Running on Respect," Spring 2007.

7 American Presidency Project, http://www.presidency.ucsb.edu/data/turnout.php, Compiled by Gerhard Peters from data obtained from the Federal Election Commission.

8 Holly Yan, "Obama, Maybe It's Time for Mandatory Voting," CNN.com, March 9, 2015, http://www.cnn.com/2015/03/19/politics/obama-mandatory-voting/index.html.

9 David S. Joachim, "First Draft," *New York Times*, Oct. 23, 2014, http://www.nytimes.com/politics/first-draft/2014/10/23/today-in-politics-22/?entry=mb-3.

10 Thomas E. Mann and Norman J. Ornstein, *It's Even Worse Than It Looks: How the American Constitutional System Collided with the New Politics of Extremism* (New York: Basic Books, 2012), 101.

11 Marc Dunkelman, *The Vanishing Neighbor: The Transformation of American Community* (New York: W. W. Norton, 2014), 189.

12 Ira Shapiro, *The Last Great Senate: Courage and Statesmanship in Times of Crisis* (New York: Public Affairs, 2012), xviii.

CHAPTER FOUR: DOWN THE WELL

1 *Isaac Bassett: A Senate Memoir*, "Sixth Massachusetts Regiment," Senate.gov, http://www.senate.gov/artandhistory/art/special/Bassett/tde tail.cfm?id=20.

2 Ken Burns, *The Congress*, PBS Paramount; 2004.

3 Hamilton-Madison-Jay, *Federalist Papers*, "Federalist 10" (New York: Signet, 2003); Ed. Clinton Rossiter, 383.

4 Robert Caro, *Master of the Senate: The Years of Lyndon Johnson* (New York: Knopf, 2002), 11.

5 George Packer, "The Empty Chamber," *New Yorker*, Aug. 9, 2010, http://www.newyorker.com/magazine/2010/08/09/the-empty-chamber.

6 Ashley Parker, "From Mid-Atlantic to Midwest, Voters Express Frustration and Fatigue," *New York Times*, Oct. 10, 2014, http://www.nytimes.com/2014/10/11/us/politics/from-mid-atlantic-to-midwest-voters-express-frustration-and-fatigue.html?_r=0.

7 John F. Kennedy, *Profiles in Courage* (New York: Harper, 1956), 2.

8 Ron Brownstein, *The Second Civil War: How Extreme Partisanship Has Paralyzed Washington and Polarized America* (New York: Penguin Press, 2007), 367.

9 Olympia Snowe, *Fighting for Common Ground: How We Can Fix the Stalemate in Congress* (New York: Weinstein Books, 2013), 128.

10 Ira Shapiro, *The Last Great Senate*, 361.

11 John F. Kennedy, *Profiles in Courage* (New York: Harper, 1956), 26.

12 Richard A. Baker, *200 Notable Days Senate Stories 1787–2002* (Washington, D.C.: Senate Historical Office, 2006), 30.

13 Thomas Jefferson, *A Manual of Parliamentary Practice for the Use of the Senate of the United States*, Washington, D.C., 1801.

14 Baker, *200 Notable Days: Senate Stories*, 61.

15 Joanne Freeman, "Alexander Hamilton and the Idea of Honor," Alexander Hamilton Awareness Society, July 14, 2014, Trinity Church, Lecture. http://www.c-span.org/video/?320292-1/alexander-hamilton-idea-honor.

16 Doris Kearns Goodwin, *The Bully Pulpit: Theodore Roosevelt, William Howard Taft, and the Golden Age of Journalism* (New York: Simon & Schuster, 2013), 382.

CHAPTER FIVE: THE MEDIA EFFECT

1 "Decode DC," Episode 42, "Exit Interview," Jim Moran, NPR. http://www.decodedc.com/home/2014/7/10/episode-42-exit-interview-rep-jim-moran.html.

2 Aaron David Miller, *The End of Greatness: Why America Can't Have (and Doesn't Want) Another Great President* (New York: Palgrave Macmillan, 2014), 7.

3 "First Draft," *New York Times,* Feb. 27, 2015.

4 Ron Brownstein, *The Second Civil War: How Extreme Partisanship Has Paralyzed Washington and Polarized America* (New York: Penguin Press, 2007), 369.

5 Michael R. Beschloss, *Presidential Courage: Brave Leaders and How They Changed America, 1789–1989* (New York: Simon & Schuster, 2007), 328.

6 Doris Kearns Goodwin, *The Bully Pulpit: Theodore Roosevelt, William Howard Taft, and the Golden Age of Journalism* (New York: Simon & Schuster, 2013), xi.

7 Ibid., 323.

8 David Brooks, "Snap Out of It," *New York Times,* Sept. 22, 2014, http://www.nytimes.com/2014/09/23/opinion/david-brooks-snap-out-of-it.html.

9 Emerging Technology from the arXiv, "How to Burst the 'Filter Bubble' That Protects Us from Opposing Views," *MIT Technology Review,* Nov. 29, 2013, http://www.technologyreview.com/view/522111/how-to-burst-the-filter-bubble-that-protects-us-from-opposing-views/.

10 Bill Bishop, *The Big Sort: Why the Clustering of Like-Minded America is Tearing Us Apart* (New York: Mariner Books, 2008), 304.

11 Ibid., 68.

12 Ibid., 71.

13 Ibid., 68.

14 Patrick Henry, "Shall Liberty or Empire be Sought," 1788, *The World's Most Famous Orations: America: I* (1761–1837), 1906. http://www.bartleby.com/268/8/14.html.

CHAPTER SIX: A NATION OF MEN AND WOMEN

1 Mike Lofgren, *The Party is Over: How Republicans Went Crazy, Democrats Became Useless, and the Middle Class Got Shafted* (New York: Viking, 2012), 7.
2 Eric Lane and Michael Oreskes, *The Genius of America: How the Constitution Saved Our Country—and Why It Can Again* (New York: Bloomsbury, 2007), 49.
3 Joseph J. Ellis, *Founding Brothers: The Revolutionary Generation* (New York: Knopf, 2000), 17.
4 Lane and Oreskes, *The Genius of America*, 7.
5 John F. Kennedy, *Profiles in Courage* (New York: Harper, 1956), 18.
6 Chris Matthews, *Tip and the Gipper: When Politics Worked* (New York: Simon & Schuster, 2013), 251.
7 Ibid., 37.
8 Ellis, *Founding Brothers*, 17.

CHAPTER EIGHT: ROADBLOCKS TO CHEMISTRY

1 Joseph J. Ellis, *American Creation: Triumphs and Tragedies at the Founding of the Republic* (New York: Knopf, 2007), 22.
2 Marc Dunkelman, *The Vanishing Neighbor* (New York: W. W. Norton, 2014), 25.
3 Paul Wesslund, "Ex-Senators: Congress Remains Stuck," Feb. 24, 2015, Ect.coop. http://www.ect.coop/editors-pick/ex-senators-congress-remains-stuck/78622.
4 Walter Isaacson, *Steve Jobs* (New York: Simon & Schuster, 2011), 431.

CHAPTER NINE: EXPERIENCE AND TRANSPARENCY

1 Dana Bash, "The Death of Horse Trading on the Hill," CNN.com, Dec. 12, 2014, http://www.cnn.com/2014/12/12/politics/horsetrading/index.html?hpt=hp_t2.
2 Walter Isaacson, *Profiles in Leadership: Historians on the Elusive Quality of Greatness* (New York: W. W. Norton, 2010), 12.
3 George J. Mitchell, Interview by Richard Norton Smith, Robert J. Dole Institute of Politics, *Robert J. Dole Oral History Project,* April 11, 2007, https://docs.google.com/gview?url=http://dolearchivecollections.ku.edu/collections/oral_history/pdf/mitchell_george_2007-04-11.pdf.

4 Walter Isaacson, *Profiles in Leadership*, 12.

5 Marc Dunkelman, *The Vanishing Neighbor: The Transformation of American Community* (New York: W. W. Norton, 2014), 190.

6 Cass Sunstein, *Simpler: The Future of Government* (New York: Simon & Schuster, 2013), 13.

7 Ellis, *Founding Brothers*, 180.

8 Ibid., 182–83.

CHAPTER TEN: IN THEIR OWN WORDS

1 Sam Tanenhaus, "The Blight of Bipartisanship," *New Yorker*, Jan. 19, 2015.

2 Don Oberdorfer, *Senator Mansfield: The Extraordinary Life of a Great American Statesman and Diplomat* (Washington D.C.: Smithsonian Books, 2003), 12.

3 Robert A. Caro, *The Passage to Power: The Years of Lyndon Johnson* (New York: Knopf, 2012), 167–69.

4 *The Speaker's Quote Book: Over 5,000 Illustrations and Quotations for All Occasions*, ed. Roy B. Zuck (Grand Rapids: Kregel, 1997), 225.

5 Address by Senator Mike Mansfield, Leader's Lecture Series, U.S. Senate, March 24, 1998. http://www.senate.gov/artandhistory/history/common/generic/Leaders_Lecture_Series_Mansfield.htm.

6 Oberdorfer, *Senator Mansfield*, ix.

7 Address by Senator Howard Baker, Leader's Lecture Series, U.S. Senate, July 14, 1998. http://www.senate.gov/artandhistory/history/common/generic/Leaders_Lecture_Series_Baker.htm.

8 "The Dole Institute Oral History Project," Robert J. Dole Archive and Special Collections, Interview with Howard Baker, May 7, 2007, http://www.c-span.org/video/?289735-1/howard-baker-jr-oral-history.

9 David Stout, "Howard H. Baker Jr., 'Great Conciliator' of the Senate, Dies at 88," *New York Times*, June 26, 2014, http://www.nytimes.com/2014/06/27/us/politics/howard-h-baker-jr-great-conciliator-of-senate-dies-at-88.html.

10 Ibid.

11 James Gerstenzang, "Sen. Howard Baker Dies at 88; Majority Leader and Reagan's Chief of Staff," *Washington Post*, June 26, 2014, http://www.washingtonpost.com/national/sen-howard-baker-majority-leader-

and-reagans-chief-of-staff-dies-at-88/2014/06/26/2e84ff30-c5da-11df-
94e1-c5afa35a9e59_story.html.

CHAPTER ELEVEN: THE LEADERSHIP HOLE

1 James MacGregor Burns, *Transforming Leadership* (New York: Atlantic
   Monthly Books, 2003), 76.
2 Interview with Stephen J. Dubner, Freakonomics Radio, "Is There a
   Better Way to Fight Terrorism?" Feb. 3, 2015.
3 Aaron David Miller, *The End of Greatness: Why America Can't Have
   (and Doesn't Want) Another Great President* (New York: Palgrave
   Macmillan, 2014), 111.
4 Speech by Ambassador Adolf Berle, May 1945, Itamaraty, Brazil.
5 Miller, *The End of Greatness*, 3.
6 Burns, *Transforming Leadership*, 2.
7 Jonathan Martin, "Long Shots Loom as Spoilers in Tight November
   Races Across Nation," *New York Times*, Sept. 27, 2014, http://www
   .nytimes.com/2014/09/28/us/politics/3rd-party-names-may-tip-scale-
   as-2-parties-battle-for-control-.html.
8 *Esquire*: Oct. 15, 2014, "The Report: How to Fix Congress Now."
9 Ken Burns, *The Congress*, Florentine Films, 1988.
10 Nai Issa and Louis Jacobson, "Congress Has 11% Approval Ratings but
   96% Incumbent Reelection Rate, Meme Says," Politifact, Nov. 11, 2014,
   http://www.politifact.com/truth-o-meter/statements/2014/nov/11/
   facebook-posts/congress-has-11-approval-ratings-96-incumbent-re-e/.
11 David Axelrod, "Fresh Air with Terry Gross," WHYY Radio, Philadelphia,
   Feb. 10, 2015.
12 Burns, *Transforming Leadership*, 2.
13 Miller, *The End of Greatness*, 4.

CHAPTER TWELVE: TRENT AND TOM

1 Burns, *Transforming Leadership*, 126.

CHAPTER THIRTEEN: THE IMPEACHMENT OF
WILLIAM JEFFERSON CLINTON

1 Robert Caro, *Master of the Senate: The Years of Lyndon Johnson* (New
   York: Knopf, 2002), 7.

2 Congressional Record: 106th Congress (1999–2000); Remarks of Senator Robert C. Byrd—Bipartisan Conference in the Old Senate Chamber, January 8.

3 David O. Stewart, *The Summer of 1787: The Men Who Invented the Constitution*, 215.

CHAPTER FOURTEEN: THE WORLD AT LARGE

1 Robert Kagan, *The World America Made* (New York: Vintage, 2012), 88.

2 Peter Baker, *Days of Fire: Bush and Cheney in the White House* (New York: Doubleday, 2013), 609, 645.

3 Scott Raab, "What Happened Broke Faith in the Constitution. . . . And It Is Morally Repugnant. When This Report Is Declassified, People Will Abhor What They Read. They're Gonna Be Disgusted," *Esquire*, Dec. 11, 2014, http://www.esquire.com/news-politics/a31502/mark-udall-0115/.

CHAPTER FIFTEEN: LEADER OF THE FREE WORLD

1 *The New Republic*, April 4, 1985.

2 David Axelrod, *Believer: My Forty Years in Politics* (New York: Penguin, 2015), 7.

CHAPTER SIXTEEN: THE CENTER OF THE STORM

1 Thomas Jefferson to James Madison, Jan. 16, 1797; Julian P. Boyd, Charles T. Cullen, John Catanzariti, Barbara B. Oberg, et al., eds. *The Papers of Thomas Jefferson* (Princeton: Princeton University Press, 1950), 29:232.

2 Peter Baker, *Days of Fire: Bush and Cheney in the White House* (New York: Doubleday, 2013), 609.

3 Richard Reeves, *President Reagan: The Triumph of Imagination* (New York: Simon & Schuster, 2005), xii.

4 Ron Brownstein, *The Second Civil War: How Extreme Partisanship Has Paralyzed Washington and Polarized America* (New York: Penguin Press, 2007), 406, 407. Brownstein interview with Bill Clinton, Oct. 4, 2006.

CHAPTER SEVENTEEN: 9/11 AND ITS AFTERMATH

1 Aaron David Miller, *The End of Greatness: Why America Can't Have*

(and Doesn't Want) Another Great President (New York: Palgrave Macmillan, 2014), 43.

2 Donald Rumsfeld, *Rumsfeld's Rules: Leadership Lessons in Business, Politics, War, and Life*, 14.

CHAPTER EIGHTEEN: THE HUMILITY AND THE AUDACITY

1 Joseph J. Ellis, *Founding Brothers: The Revolutionary Generation* (New York: Knopf, 2000), 6.

2 Ibid., 5.

3 Jack Rakove, "The Patriot Who Refused to Sign the Declaration of Independence," Historynet, June 3, 2010, http://www.historynet.com/the-patriot-who-refused-to-sign-the-declaration-of-independence.htm.

4 Lynne Cheney, *James Madison: A Life Reconsidered* (New York: Viking, 2014), 32, 40.

5 Ellis, *Founding Brothers*, 194–195.

6 Abraham Lincoln, "The Perpetuation of Our Political Institutions: Address Before the Young Men's Lyceum of Springfield, Illinois, January 27, 1838." www.abrahamlincolnonline.org/lincoln/speeches/lyceum.htm.

7 Michael R. Beschloss, *Presidential Courage: Brave Leaders and How They Changed America, 1789–1989* (New York: Simon & Schuster, 2007), 96.

8 Ibid., 101.

9 Richard Beeman, *Plain, Honest Men: The Making of the American Constitution* (New York: Random House, 2009), xiv.

10 Ibid., ix.

11 Ibid.

12 Letter to Catherine Macaulay Graham; New York; January 9, 1790, http://teachingamericanhistory.org/library/document/letter-to-catherine-macaulay-graham/.

13 To James Madison Sr., July 5, 1789, Library of Congress, http://www.gwu.edu/~ffcp/exhibit/p8/p8_1.html.

14 David McCullough, *John Adams* (New York: Simon & Schuster, 2001), 9.

15 "Decode DC," Episode 44, "Exit Interview," Rush Holt, NPR. http://www.decodedc.com/home/2014/7/24/episode-44-exit-interview-rep-rush-holt.html.

16 Alain de Botton, *News: A User's Manual* (New York: Pantheon, 2014), 7.

17 Beschloss, *Presidential Courage*, 131.

18 Ibid., 135.

19 Ibid., 146.

20 Theodore Roosevelt, "The Duties of American Citizenship," Buffalo, N.Y. Jan. 26, 1883, speech. http://www.pbs.org/wgbh/americanexperience/features/primary-resources/tr-citizen/?flavour=mobile.

21 Edmund Burke, "Speech to the Electors of Bristol," Nov. 1774, *Works* 1:446–48, speech. http://press-pubs.uchicago.edu/founders/documents/v1ch13s7.html.

22 Richard A. Baker, *200 Notable Days: Senate Stories, 1787 to 2002* (Washington, D.C.: Senate Historical Office, 2006), 19.

23 Ibid.

CHAPTER NINETEEN: COURAGE AND MEMORY IN THE UNITED STATES SENATE

1 Neil MacNeil and Richard A. Baker, *The American Senate: An Inside History* (New York: Oxford University Press, 2013), 3.

2 Ibid., 33.

3 John McCain, *Why Courage Matters: The Way to a Braver Life* (New York: Random House, 2004), 139.

4 Ibid., 38–39.

5 Howard E. Gardner and Emma Laskin, *Leading Minds: An Anatomy of Leadership* (New York: Basic Books, 1995), 12.

6 Mark Leibovich, *This Town: Two Parties and a Funeral—Plus, Plenty of Valet Parking!—in America's Gilded Capital* (New York: Blue Rider Press, 2013), 79.

CHAPTER TWENTY: FEAR AND LOATHING IN THE U.S. CONGRESS

1 Lynne Cheney, *James Madison: A Life Reconsidered* (New York: Viking, 2014), 128.

2 *The Writings of James Madison*, Vol. 1: 1769–1783, edited by Gaillard Hunt, 254.

3 John F. Kennedy, *Profiles in Courage* (New York: Harper, 1956), 7.

CHAPTER TWENTY-ONE: WRITING THE FUTURE

1 Thomas Jefferson to James Madison, Sept. 6, 1789, *Papers* 15: 392–97. http://press-pubs.uchicago.edu/founders/documents/v1ch2s23.html.

2 Lynne Cheney, *James Madison: A Life Reconsidered* (New York: Viking, 2014), 207.

3 Douglas French, "Principle and Interest: Thomas Jefferson and the Problem of Debt," Foundation for Economic Freedom, Oct. 1, 1996. http://fee.org/freeman/detail/principle-interest-thomas-jefferson-and-the-problem-of-debt.

4 John Patrick Diggins. *Ronald Reagan: Fate, Freedom, and the Making of History* (New York: W. W. Norton, 2007), 183.

5 Max Farrand, *The Records of the Federal Convention of 1787*, vol. III, 33, 1911. George Mason to George Mason Jr., June 1, 1787.

6 *The Life and Selected Writings of Thomas Jefferson* (New York: Modern Library, 1998), 615. Letter to Samuel Kercheval, July 12, 1816.

CHAPTER TWENTY-TWO: A BIPARTISAN ANSWER

1 David J. Hill, "Larry Page: With a Healthy Disregard for the Impossible, People Can Do Almost Anything," *Computing Singularity*, May 27, 2012, http://singularityhub.com/2012/05/27/larry-page-with-a-healthy-disregard-for-the-impossible-people-can-do-almost-anything/.

CHAPTER TWENTY-THREE: ELECTORAL AND CAMPAIGN REFORM

1 Liz Kennedy, "Protecting the Freedom to Vote: The Voter Empowerment Act of 2012," Demos, May 17, 2012, http://www.demos.org/publication/protecting-freedom-vote-voter-empowerment-act-2012.

2 P. J. Huffstutter, "Officials Face Election Day Stumper, with Possible Payoff Online," *Seattle Times*, originally published Oct. 31, 2006, http://seattletimes.com/html/nationworld/2003332210_tuesday31.html.

3 "Election Day Registration," *Canvass* (NCSL elections newsletter), http://www.ncsl.org/research/elections-and-campaigns/same-day-registration.aspx.

CHAPTER TWENTY-FOUR: THE MONEY PROBLEM

1 Nicholas Confessore, "Koch Brothers' Budget of $889 Million for 2016 Is on Par with Both Parties' Spending," *New York Times*, Jan. 27, 2015, http://www.nytimes.com/2015/01/27/us/politics/kochs-plan-to-spend-900-million-on-2016-campaign.html.

2 David Horsey, "Christian Grey and the Koch Brothers Share a Similar Desire for Dominance," *Los Angeles Times*, Feb. 13, 2015, http://www.latimes.com/opinion/topoftheticket/la-na-tt-christian-grey-and-koch-20150213-story.html.

3 Ian Vandewalker, "Outside Spending in Senate Races Since Citizens United," Brennan Center for Justice at New York University School of Law, 2015, https://www.brennancenter.org/sites/default/files/analysis/Outside%20Spending%20Since%20Citizens%20United.pdf.

4 Jill Lepore, "The Crooked and the Dead," *New Yorker*, Aug. 25, 2014, http://www.newyorker.com/magazine/2014/08/25/crooked-dead.

5 Francis Fukuyama, "America in Decay: The Sources of Political Dysfunction," *Foreign Affairs*, Sept./Oct. 2014, http://www.foreignaffairs.com/articles/141729/francis-fukuyama/america-in-decay.

6 Ibid.

CHAPTER TWENTY-FIVE: CONGRESSIONAL REFORM

1 George Packer, "Threats to Homeland Security," *New Yorker*, Feb. 25, 2015, http://www.newyorker.com/news/daily-comment/threats-homeland-security.

2 Christopher M. Davis, "The Amending Process in the Senate," *Congressional Research Service*, March 15, 2013, http://www.senate.gov/CRSReports/crs-publish.cfm?pid=%26°2%3C4RLO8%0A.

3 Jason Grumet, *City of Rivals: Restoring the Glorious Mess of American Democracy* (Guilford, CT: Lyons Press, 2014), 59.

CHAPTER TWENTY-SIX: A CALL TO SERVICE

1 Robert Kagan, *The World America Made* (New York: Vintage, 2012), 25.

2 "Governing in a Polarized America: A Bipartisan Blueprint to Strengthen Our Democracy," Bipartisan Policy Center (BPC) Commission on Political Reform, June 24, 2014, 75–76.

3 Ibid., 71.

4 "The Case for National Service," Servicenation.org, http://www .servicenation.org/the_case_for_national_service.

5 Holly Yan, "Obama, Maybe It's Time for Mandatory Voting," CNN. com, March 9, 2015, http://www.cnn.com/2015/03/19/politics/obama-mandatory-voting/index.html.

6 Alexandra Pannoni, "Foster Civil Discourse in High School Classes," *U.S. News & World Report*, Jan. 26, 2015, http://www.usnews.com/ education/blogs/high-school-notes/2015/01/26/foster-civil-discourse-in-high-school-civics-classes.

7 Hunter Schwarz, "North Dakota Is Second State to Require High School Students to Pass a Civics Test to Graduate," *Washington Post*, Feb. 2, 2015, http://www.washingtonpost.com/blogs/govbeat/wp/2015/ 02/02/north-dakota-is-second-state-to-require-high-school-students-to-pass-a-civics-test-to-graduate/.

8 "Governing in a Polarized America: A Bipartisan Blueprint to Strengthen Our Democracy," Bipartisan Policy Center (BPC) Commission on Political Reform, June 24, 2014, 17.

9 Ibid., 84.

CONCLUSION

1 Winston Churchill, *The Grand Alliance* (New York: Houghton Mifflin, 1970), 540.

2 Alexis de Tocqueville, *Democracy in America*, ed. J.P. Mayer, translated by George Lawrence (New York: Harper and Row, 1966, 1988), 627.

3 Adapted from "The Serenity Prayer" by Reinhold Niebuhr.

4 Excerpt from "The Young Dead Soldiers Do Not Speak" by Archibald MacLeish (published anonymously), Library of Congress, http://www .loc.gov/teachers/lyrical/poems/docs/young_trans.pdf.

5 *One Bright Shining Moment: The Forgotten Summer of George McGovern*, First Run Features 2005, directed by Stephen Vittoria.

6 Barack Obama interview with David Remnick, *New Yorker*, Feb. 23, 2015, http://www.newyorker.com/magazine/2015/02/23/2005-2015.

Index

Abourezk, Jim, 125
action, 2, 5, 23, 105, 124, 139–140, 191,
    211–215, 220
Adams, John, 16, 25, 30, 67, 96, 99, 157,
    180–181, 183, 244
Adams, John Quincy, 46
adversarial system, 1
Affordable Care Act, 93, 213, 236–237
Afghanistan, 144, 164
airplanes, 84, 87, 89, 234
Akaka, Danny, 134
Alexander, Lamar, 95
amendments, to bills, 40, 202, 237–242
American culture, 57
American formula, 257–258
American public
    See also public opinion
    divisions within, 42
    lack of faith in government of, 115–116
American Revolution, 57, 61, 179–180
American values, 250–251
AmeriCorps VISTA, 253
anger, 31, 115–116, 197
anthrax attack, 4, 173–175
Apotheosis of Washington, The (Brumidi), 37
Aristotle, 179
Armey, Dick, 87
Ashcroft, John, 80
astroturfing, 188
Axelrod, David, 118, 149, 226

baby boomers, 254
Baker, Howard, 35–36, 106–110, 123, 213
Baker, James, 71

Baker, Peter, 143, 152
Baker, Richard A., 187, 208
Bash, Dana, 91
Bassett, Isaac, 36
Bayh, Birch, 103
Beeman, Richard, 182
Benton, Thomas Hart, 46
Berle, Adolf, 113
Beschloss, Michael, 55, 182–183, 185
Biden, Joe, 60
Bill of Rights, 12, 180, 208
bills
    amendments to, 40, 202, 237–242
    holds on, 70, 237–240
    knowledge of, 236–237
Bipartisan Policy Center (BPC), 213–216,
    234, 243–244
bipartisanship, 4, 28, 95–96, 213–216
Bishop, Bill, 58, 59
Boehner, John, 142, 149
Botton, Alain de, 184
Boxer, Barbara, 95–96
Boyd, Malcolm, 259–260
BPC Commission on Political Reform,
    214–216
Bradley, Bill, 28
Breaux, John, 31, 41, 58, 87, 89
Broderick, David C., 47
Brooks, David, 30, 57, 119
Brooks, Preston, 47
Brownstein, Ron, 44, 55
Brumidi, Constantino, 37
bullying, 123, 127
Burke, Edmund, 187

Burns, James MacGregor, 16, 111, 113, 116, 118, 126
Burr, Aaron, 47
Bush, George H. W., 166
Bush, George W., 20–21, 48–49, 75, 120, 143, 152, 157, 166
    Congress and, 21
    presidential style of, 163–165
    tax cuts, 172–173
Bush, Jeb, 154
Byrd, Robert C., 46, 103, 126, 132, 134, 136, 193–196, 239

cabinet, 151–152
Calhoun, John C., 63, 103, 108, 166
campaign contributions, 19–20, 32, 225–232
campaign reform, 222–232
Capitol, 37–38
Card, Andy, 165
Caro, Robert, 39, 129
Carter, Jimmy, 157, 159
Chafee, John, 137
checks and balances, 1, 10, 21
chemistry, 3, 4, 17, 28, 44, 50, 65–73, 148–149
    among leadership, 114–115
    roadblocks to, 83–89
Cheney, Dick, 152, 164, 176
Chestnut, Jacob, 37
Church, Frank, 103
Churchill, Winston, 182, 210, 257
citizenship, 243–244
Citizens United case, 225–229, 231
civic participation, 243–255
civics courses, 251
civility, 46–47
civil service, 252
Civil War, 18, 36, 66, 181
Clay, Henry, 36, 63, 66, 92, 103, 108, 181
Clinton, Bill, 157, 165
    compromises by, 67
    Congress and, 21, 150
    impeachment of, 4, 52–53, 94, 115, 129–137
    personality of, 161–163
    welfare reform under, 20
Clinton, Hillary, 153–155
cloture votes, 190, 238
Club for Growth, 42
Coates, Dan, 212
Cold War, 144

collective action, 23, 140
colleges, 252–253
Colmer, Bill, 122
committees, 76–77, 235–236
communication
    instantaneous, 59–60
    between leaders, 3–4, 68–70
    need for, 3–4, 10
    with opposing party, 93
    between president and Congress, 144
competitive spirit, 9, 17
Comprehensive Immigration Reform Act, 188–192
compromise, 3, 17, 28, 66–68, 73, 91–93, 212
confirmation bias, 59
conflict, 4, 10, 55
Congress
    See also House of Representatives; Senate
    113th, 2
    committees, 76–77, 235–236
    disapproval of, 2
    divided, 30
    dysfunction in, 2, 44, 142–143
    foreign policy and, 139–145
    gridlock in, 39, 201–202, 242
    inertia in, 1–2, 39, 211–212, 234–235
    majority in, 201–202
    moderates in, 41–43
    Obama and, 148–150, 153
    personal relationships in, 65–73, 83–89
    public opinion of, 115–117
    ratification of, 11
    schedule of, 86–89, 234–235
    tension between president and, 20–22, 141–144
congressional leadership, 21–22, 234
congressional reform, 233–242
Conservative Political Action Committee (CPAC), 53–54
Constitution, 2–3, 9–10, 39, 183, 207, 257
Constitutional Convention, 11, 12, 83, 180, 202–203
Coons, Chris, 212
courage, 3, 4, 182–185, 193, 198–199, 201, 260
Craig, Larry, 80
crisis, 143, 167–172, 182–183
CSPAN, 54, 94
cultural diversity, 1, 257–258
culture, 57, 114
Cuomo, Mario, 148

Currie, Betty, 133
cybersecurity, 210–212

Dalrymple, Jack, 251
Daschle, Tom
    on 9/11, 168–170, 171
    anthrax crisis and, 173–174
    background of, 124–127
    on campaign finance, 227–228
    on chemistry, 49–50
    on Clinton impeachment, 131–132
    on education, 248
    as leader, 126–127, 186
Davis, Jefferson, 36, 107
Dayen, David, 28
Dean, Howard, 53
debates, 94, 95, 108–109, 202–203
Declaration of Independence, 111, 180
defensive governing, 202–204
democracy, 38, 183–184
    opposition parties and, 16
    pillars of, 249
    representative, 12–13
Democratic-Republican Party, 16
demonization, of opposition, 93
Department of Homeland Security, 177, 211,
    233
DeWine, Mike, 89
Dickinson, John, 180
Dionne, E. J., 23
Dirksen, Everett, 104, 107, 160
diversity, 1, 13–14, 23–24, 257–258
Dodd, Chris, 36, 126
Dole, Bob, 35, 46, 123, 213
Douglas, Helen Gahagan, 159–160
dual tracking, 239
Dunkelman, Marc J., 33, 60, 92–93
duty, 257–260

education, 247–248, 251–253
Election Day, 118, 221
elections
    of 1986, 28
    of 2000, 75, 78–79
    of 2008, 113, 147–148
    of 2014, 31, 32, 117, 155
    of 2016, 153–154, 155
    bipartisanship during, 28
    moving on after, 45–46
    permanent campaign and, 25–34, 39, 118
    in UK, 223–224
    voter turnout for, 31–32, 218, 220–222

electoral reform, 217–224
electorate, siloed, 57–59
electronic voting, 222
Ellis, Joseph J., 11–12, 15, 18, 67, 72–73, 97,
    179, 180–181
Emancipation Proclamation, 181
energy efficiency, 43
Europe, 145
executive orders, 141, 149–150, 191
experience, 91–93

factions, 14–16, 18
"Farewell Address" (Washington), 15, 35
fear, 201–204
The Federalist Papers, 12, 14, 38, 136
    No. 10, 13
Federalists, 14, 16, 180
Feinstein, Diane, 189
filibusters, 66, 190, 237–240, 241
"filling the tree," 241–242
filter bubble, 58
First Continental Congress, 10–11,
    83, 180
five-day workweek, 234–235
501(c)(3) organizations, 19
flip-flopping, 203
Foley, Tom, 204
Foote, Henry S., 46
foreign policy, 139–145
foresight, 183
Founding Fathers, 9–16, 18, 66–67, 72–73,
    179–183
Frank, Barney, 116, 183
Franklin, Benjamin, vii, 25, 67
freedom, 250–251
Freeman, Joann, 47
Friedman, Thomas L., 257
Frist, Bill, 27–28, 49, 241
Fukuyama, Francis, 230, 232
fundraising, time spent on, 29, 230
future, 207–212, 259–260

Gang of Eight, 175–176
Gephardt, Dick, 164
Germany, 145
Gibson, John, 37
Gingrich, Newt, 47–48, 204
Glickman, Dan, 215
Goethe, Johann Wolfgang von, 243
Goodwin, Doris Kearns, 47, 55–56, 120
Gorton, Slade, 133, 220
governing, vs. campaigning, 92

government
    aversion to, 244–245
    challenging, 22–23
    crisis in, 2
    dysfunction in, 17–18
    public faith in, 115–116
    role of, 14–15
    size of, 14–15
    student, 252
Graham, Lindsey, 144, 189
Gramm, Phil, 76, 133, 135
Great Senate Deadlock of 1881, 75
Green, Theodore F., 101
Gregg, Judd, 81
gridlock, 39, 201–202, 242
Gutmann, Amy, 28

Hamilton, Alexander, 14–15, 16, 47,
    135–136, 187
Hanna, Marcus, 47
Hart, Gary, 46
Hastert, Dennis, 164, 171
Henry, Patrick, 61
heroes, 92, 112, 160, 182, 252
higher education, 247–248, 252–253
holds, 237–240
Hollings, Ernest "Fritz," 54
Holt, Rush, 183
House of Representatives
    Clinton impeachment and, 134–135
    responsiveness of, 38
Huckaby, Jerry, 89
hyper-partisanship, 10

immigration reform, 43, 188–192
impeachment trial, of Clinton, 4, 52–53, 94,
    115, 129–137
inclusion, 104, 119, 127
incumbents, reelection of, 116, 224
individualism, 23
information sharing, 126–127, 177–178
information technology, 56, 57, 59
Inhofe, Jim, 96
insiders, 85–86
inspiration, 112–113
institutions, 116, 137, 188, 208, 222, 243
integrity, 66, 203
intelligence communities, 175–178
interest groups, 230, 232
Internet, 49, 56, 57, 60–61, 86
Iowa Caucus, 218–219
Iraq, 144, 203

Iraq War, 178
Isaacson, Walter, 92
ISIS, 144

Jackson, Andrew, 201
Jay Treaty, 15, 187
Jefferson, Thomas, 2–3, 7, 13, 15, 16, 25, 26,
    30, 67, 96–97, 157, 207–209
Jefferson's Manual, 46
Jeffords, Jim, 79–81
Jobs, Steve, 87–88
Johnson, Andrew, 133
Johnson, Lyndon, 39, 101–104, 150,
    159–160, 161

Kagan, Robert, 140, 243
Kemp, Jack, 28
Kempthorne, Dick, 215
Kennedy, John F., 29, 36, 44, 65, 67, 68, 81,
    104, 124, 165–166, 203–204
Kennedy, Ted, 65, 94, 135, 189, 199
Kerry, John, 151, 198, 203
Keynes, John Maynard, 203
Kissinger, Henry, 151
Knowland, William F., 36
Koch, Charles, 226
Koch, David, 226
Kosovo, 145
Kyl, Jon, 189, 212

Landrieu, Mary, 85
Lane, Eric, 9, 12, 67
leaders
    chemistry of, 114–115
    as conciliators, 106–110
    Daschle on, 125–126
    as facilitators, 103–106
    focus of, 117–118
    foresight of, 183
    future, 245–246
    Lott on, 122–123
    majority leaders, 39–40
    minority leaders, 40
    vs. power holders, 118
    public opinion and, 185–191
    qualities of, 184–186
    strengths of, 101–102
    young, 209–210
leadership, 3, 4, 99
    communication between, 68–70
    congressional, 21–22, 234
    in crisis, 112

of Daschle, 126–127
inspirational, 112–113
of Lott, 123–124, 186
need for effective, 45, 111–120
leadership PACs, 231
Leader's Lecture Series, 102–107
League of Nations, 139, 142
legislators
experienced, 91–93
transience of, 84–89
voting by, 186–187
Leibovich, Mark, 199
Lewinsky, Monica, 133
Lieberman, Joe, 132, 133, 136, 220
Limbaugh, Rush, 190
Lincoln, Abraham, 16, 120, 151–152,
181–182, 185
Lincoln, Blanche, 41
Livingston, Bob, 88
lobbyists, 148
Lott, Trent, 17, 21
on 9/11, 167–168, 170
anthrax crisis and, 174–175
background of, 121–124
on campaign finance, 228–229
on Clinton impeachment, 129–131
on education, 247–248
on immigration reform, 188–192
as leader, 123–124, 186
stepping down as leader by, 48–50

Mack, Connie, 69
MacLeish, Archibald, 258–259
Madison, James, 2–3, 10, 12–16, 18, 25, 38,
39, 59, 67, 97, 180, 183, 202, 207
majority leaders, 39–40
Mandelbaum, Michael, 257
Manifest Destiny, 179
Mann, Thomas E., 32
Mansfield, Mike, 102, 103–106, 123
Marshall, Humphrey, 187
Mason, George, 135, 208
Matthews, Chris, 71, 72, 101
McCain, John, 45, 144, 193, 196–199, 230,
237
McCain-Feingold bill, 229–230
McConnell, Mitch, 21, 39, 40, 149, 226, 242,
247
McCullough, David, 37, 183
McGovern, George, 103, 121, 125, 198
McGroarty, John Steven, 185
media, 5, 51–61, 94

melting pot, 257–258
midterm elections
of 1986, 28
of 2014, 31, 32, 117, 155
Miller, Aaron David, 52, 112, 113, 120, 167
Miller, Zell, 41
minority, amendments by, 237–240
minority leaders, 40
Mitchell, George, 92, 126, 213, 239
mob rule, 13
moderates, 41–43
Mondale, Walter, 121
money, in campaigns, 19–20, 225–232
Monticello, 25
Moran, Jim, 51
Mount Vernon, 25, 245
Moynihan, Daniel Patrick, 59
Myhrvold, Nathan, 112

NAFTA, 150
National Democratic Institute, 96, 227
National Primary Day, 218
national security, 140, 144–145, 176–178
national service program, 246–247
negative campaigning, 30–32
Nelson, Ben, 41
Netanyahu, Benjamin, 142
New Hampshire, 218–219
new media, 56, 57, 60–61
newspapers, 30, 51, 59
New York Times, 59
Nickles, Don, 76, 123, 168, 195
9/11, 4, 167–172, 210
Nixon, Richard, 95, 104, 130, 151, 157, 199
No Child Left Behind, 78, 81, 94

Obama, Barack, 260
2008 campaign of, 113
Congress and, 21, 22, 153
executive orders by, 141, 149–150, 191
immigration reform and, 191
isolation of, 21
national security and, 144–145
presidency of, 147–153, 157
press and, 52
relationship with Congress, 148–150, 153
on voting, 249
Observer Effect, 52
obstruction, 92
Old Senate Chamber, 102–103, 134
O'Neill, Tip, 20, 47–48, 71–72, 101, 161
opposing opinions, 58–59

opposition parties, 16, 18, 93
optimism, 11, 118, 143, 209
Oreskes, Michael, 9, 12, 67
Ornstein, Norman J., 32

Packer, George, 43, 233
Packwood, Bob, 28
Page, Larry, 215
partisan issues, 42
partisanship, 1–3, 10, 12, 18–19, 42,
    96–97
partisan warriors, 17, 49, 123
party system, 10–16, 18, 97
Patriot Act, 175–176
patriotism, 22–23, 172, 182
Paul, Rand, 144
Peace Corps, 253
permanent campaign, 25–34, 39, 118
personal attacks, 46–48, 56–57
personal relationships, 65–73, 83–89,
    161–163
persuasion, 71
polarization, 30, 33, 44, 92, 214, 244
political advisors, 30
political campaigns
    financing of, 19–20, 225–232
    negative, 30–32
    permanent nature of, 25–34, 39, 118
    positive, 33
    reform of, 222–232
political climate, 33
political culture, 114
political duels, 47
political elections. *See* elections
political parties
    creation of, 18
    divisions among, 15–16, 18
    extremists in, 42
    primary system and, 217–220
    purpose of, 18–19
    tension between, 17–24, 96–97
    weaknesses of, 19–20
politicians
    media and, 51–61
    professional, 25–29
    residency of, 85
politics
    dysfunction in, 34, 44
    as personal, 45
    as profession, 25–29
    polling places, 221–222
    positive campaigning, 33

Powell, Colin, 152, 176
power
    balance of global, 139–140
    misuse of, 119
    of president, 141–143, 158–160
Pownall, Thomas, 139
pragmatism, 118–119
presidency, 157–160
president
    See also specific presidents
    cabinet and, 151–152
    closing off of, 20–21, 150–151
    foreign policy and, 141
    moments of crisis and, 112, 182–183
    office of the, 157–160
    power of, 141–143, 158–160
    tension between Congress and, 20–22,
        141–144
press, 51–61
preventive action, 211–212
primaries, 5, 31, 42, 217–220
progress, 208–209, 258
public opinion, 2, 22–23, 115–117, 185–187
public service, 243–255
Putin, Vladimir, 140

Reagan, Ronald, 20, 25, 28, 66, 71–72, 101,
    113, 160–161, 191
Rees-Mogg, William, 111
regular order, 45
Rehnquist, William, 135, 136
Reid, Harry, 21, 22, 39, 60, 77, 80, 189, 196,
    241
relationships, 65–73, 83–89, 161–163
religious freedom, 180
representative democracy, 12–13
representatives. *See* legislators
Republican Party, 20, 154–155, 201–202
responsibility, 249–250
restrictive views, 60
Rice, Condoleezza, 152
risk, 258
Roberts, Pat, 77, 85
Robinson, Joe, 36
Rockefeller, Nelson, 22
rolling holds, 240
Rome, 13
Roosevelt, Franklin D., 30, 51, 120,
    152, 233
Roosevelt, Teddy, 19, 47, 55–56, 184–186
Rostenkowski, Dan, 28
Rough Riders, 185

Rouse, Pete, 148, 173
Rove, Karl, 20, 48, 165
Rubio, Marco, 154
rule changes, 215
Rumsfeld, Donald, 152, 178
Rusk, Dean, 4
Russell, Richard, 160
Russert, Tim, 54
Russia, 140

sacrifice, 258–259
Santorum, Rick, 133
Schumer, Charles, 95
Second Continental Congress, 83
Senate
  of 2001, 3–4
  50-50, 75–81
  deadlock in, 75–81
  desks, 35–36
  dining room, 87–88
  filibusters, 66, 190, 237–240
  gridlock in, 39
  history of the, 35–39, 194
  moderates in, 41–43
  narrow majority in, 39–40
  nature of the, 38–39, 41, 46–47, 119,
    194–195
  permanent campaign and, 33–34
  Republican takeover of, 20
  violent incidents in, 46–47
Senate Chamber, 36–37, 43, 102–103, 134
Senate Conservatives Fund, 42
senators
  See also legislators
  election of, 187
ServiceNation, 246
Seventeenth Amendment, 187
Shapiro, Ira, 33–34
Shriver, Sargent, 160
Simpson, Alan, 123
Simpson-Mazzoli Act, 28, 191
Sisco, Gary, 102
slip-ups, 53–54
Snowe, Olympia, 41, 44, 215
social interactions, 87–88
social media, 56, 59–61
soft money, 230
South Carolina, 218–219
South Korea, 142
Soviet Union, 144
Spanish-American War, 185
Specter, Arlen, 137

Stewart, David O., 11, 135
student debt, 247
student government, 252
Sumner, Charles, 47
Sunday talk shows, 54–55
sunshine laws, 95
super PACs, 19, 226, 229, 230, 231

Tauzin, Billy, 89
tax cuts, 78, 172–173
technology, 210–211
texting, 59–60
Thatcher, Margaret, 223
third parties, 19
third-person references, 46
Thompson, Dennis, 28
Thune, John, 85
Thurmond, Strom, 48, 53
Tocqueville, Alexis de, 23, 205, 244, 258
transient culture, 84–89
transnational forces, 140, 144
transparency, 94–97
treaties, 141
Trent Lott Leadership Institute, 248
two-party system, 19, 65

Udall, Mark, 144
unanimous consent, 237–240
United Kingdom, elections in, 223–224
United States
  diversity in, 1, 13, 23–24, 257–258
  foreign policy of, 139–145
  greatness of, 23–24
universities, 252–253
U.S. Congress. *See* Congress
U.S. government. *See* government

Vietnam War, 142
vision, 3, 4, 205, 207–212
Vitter, David, 96
volunteering, 253–254
voters
  angry, 31
  opinions of, 185–191
  polarization and, 33
voter turnout, 31–32, 218, 220–221, 249

Wade, Benjamin, 133
Walker, Scott, 219
Wall Street Journal, 59
Warner, John, 239
War on Terror, 175–177

war powers, 141, 143
warrantless wiretaps, 175–177
Washington, D.C., 5
  antipathy toward, 85–86, 87, 235
  culture of, 147
  time spent in, 84, 234–235
Washington, George, 15, 18, 25–26, 35, 37, 38, 157, 183, 245
Watergate scandal, 95
Webster, Daniel, 36, 103, 196
wedge issues, 42

Wells, Susan, 102
Whitehouse, Sheldon, 212
Wilson, Woodrow, 139
World War II, 112, 182, 257
Wright, Jim, 204

"The Young Dead Soldiers Do Not Speak"
  (MacLeish), 258–259
youth, 209–210, 245–250, 252–253

Zelizer, Julian E., 35

A Note on the Authors

Trent Lott served in the U.S. House of Representatives and Senate representing the state of Mississippi for thirty-five years. During his sixteen years in the House he served on the Rules Committee and as Republican whip for eight years. As a senator, he was majority whip and majority leader. He is currently Senior Counsel at Squire Patton Boggs, where he co-chairs the public policy practice. He is the author of *Herding Cats*.

Former U.S. Senator and Democratic Majority Leader Tom Daschle co-founded the Bipartisan Policy Center and serves as chair of the Center for American Progress and vice chair of the National Democratic Institute. He is the founder and CEO of The Daschle Group, which advises clients on a broad array of economic, policy, and political issues. His books include *Like No Other Time*; *Critical*; *Getting It Done*; and *The U.S. Senate: Fundamentals of American Government*.

Jon Sternfeld is a writer and editor. He lives in New York with his wife and two children.